Natural Burial

This book unravels the many different experiences, meanings and realities of natural burial. Twenty years after the first natural burial ground opened, there is an opportunity to reflect on how a concept for a very different approach to caring for our dead has become a reality: new providers, new landscapes and a hybrid of new and traditional rituals. In this short time the Natural Burial Movement has flourished. In the UK there are more than 200 sites, and the concept has travelled to North America, Holland, Australia, New Zealand and Japan.

This survey of natural burials draws on interviews with those involved in the natural burial process – including burial ground managers, celebrants, priests, bereaved family, funeral directors – providing a variety of viewpoints on the concept as a philosophy and landscape practice. Site surveys, design plans and case studies illustrate the challenges involved in creating a natural burial site, and a key longitudinal case study of a single site investigates the evolving nature of the practice.

Natural Burial is the first book on this subject to bring together all the groups involved in the practice, explaining the facts behind this type of burial and exploring a topic which is attracting significant media interest and an upsurge of sites internationally.

Andy Clayden is a Senior Lecturer and Landscape Architect in the Department of Landscape, Sheffield University. His research focuses on the temporal and dynamic nature of landscape, which has had a major influence on his design teaching and how people experience and engage with the natural burial and cemetery landscape.

Trish Green is a Research Fellow at the University of Hull. Her main academic interests lie in the relational aspects of life course transitions, ageing and gendered subjectivities, and the emotional meanings of time, space and place. She has conducted research and co-authored several articles on natural burial.

Jenny Hockey trained as an anthropologist and is Emeritus Professor of Sociology at Sheffield University. Widely published in *Death Studies*, she was founding president of the Association for the Study of Death and Society and remains a member of the editorial board of *Mortality*, the European Journal of Death Studies.

Mark Powell trained in social anthropology at the Queen's University, Belfast. His research focuses on the relationship between social identity, cultural belonging and environments. Based at the School of Civil Engineering and Geosciences, Newcastle University, he works across disciplines to investigate the social and cultural dimensions of hard infrastructural environments.

Natural Burial

Landscape, practice and experience

Andy Clayden, Trish Green, Jenny Hockey and Mark Powell

Routledge
Taylor & Francis Group

LONDON AND NEW YORK

First published 2015
by Routledge
2 Park Square, Milton Park, Abingdon, Oxon OX14 4RN

and by Routledge
711 Third Avenue, New York, NY 10017

Routledge is an imprint of the Taylor & Francis Group, an informa business

© 2015 Andy Clayden, Trish Green, Jenny Hockey and Mark Powell

The right of Andy Clayden, Trish Green, Jenny Hockey and Mark Powell
to be identified as authors of this work has been asserted by them in accordance with
sections 77 and 78 of the Copyright, Designs and Patents Act 1988.

Every effort has been made to contact and acknowledge copyright owners. If any material
has been included without permission, the publishers offer their apologies. The publishers
would be pleased to have any errors or omissions brought to their attention so that
corrections may be published at a later printing.

All rights reserved. No part of this book may be reprinted or reproduced or utilised in any
form or by any electronic, mechanical, or other means, now known or hereafter invented,
including photocopying and recording, or in any information storage or retrieval system,
without permission in writing from the publishers.

Trademark notice: Product or corporate names may be trademarks or registered
trademarks, and are used only for identification and explanation without intent to
infringe.

British Library Cataloguing in Publication Data
A catalogue record for this book is available from the British Library

Library of Congress Cataloging in Publication Data
Clayden, Andy.
Natural burial : landscape, practice and experience / Andy Clayden, Trish Green,
Jenny Hockey and Mark Powell.
pages cm
Includes bibliographical references and index.

1. Burial–Great Britain. 2. Funeral rites and ceremonies–Great Britain. 3. Landscape
design–Great Britain. I. Title.
GT3243.C56 2014
393'.1–dc23
2013047923

ISBN: 978-0-415-63168-6 (hbk)
ISBN: 978-0-415-63169-3 (pbk)
ISBN: 978-1-315-77169-4 (ebk)

Typeset in Sabon by
Servis Filmsetting Ltd, Stockport, Cheshire

Contents

Figures

Acknowledgements

We would like to thank the following people:

The Economic and Social Research Council for funding the research: Back to Nature: The cultural, social and emotional implications of natural burial (2007–2010) (Award: RES 062-23-0448). The project advisory board: Rosie Inman-Cook, Douglas Davies, Anna Jorgensen, Leonie Kelleher, John Mallatratt, Sue Nadin, Ken West, Mike Jarvis and Julie Rugg. Diane Palmer for her assistance in preparing the GIS plans. Paul Buck, Department of Landscape, University of Sheffield, for his assistance in developing the project website design and upkeep. Amanda Baxter for her help with proofreading. Our families for their patience and understanding. We would also like to thank our publishers and especially Louise Fox for her support and working with us on this project.

Finally, but most importantly, enormous thanks are due to Ken West for his pioneering work and his sustained commitment to his original vision; Al Blake, East Meon; Eira and Ifor Humphries, Abermule; John Mallatratt, Ulley; Sue Nadin, Wisewood; and all of our research participants, without whom this book would not have been possible.

1

Introduction

The four authors of this book have worked together on natural burial since 2007. Andy Clayden, a landscape architect engaged in teaching, research and practice, has been somewhat outnumbered by the anthropologists and sociologists in the team he has led: Trish Green, Jenny Hockey and Mark Powell. The diversity of our backgrounds has made for some challenging discussions within which all four of us have revisited our assumptions about the character of the world – and learned an awful lot from one another. While 'nature' and 'the natural' had previously been self-evident categories for Andy, as a landscape architect, for the social scientists accustomed mainly to text-based work among small populations, the materially grounded qualities of landscape design, as well as the scope of geographic information system (GIS) surveys, represented new terrain. Our joint work therefore utilises concepts and methods we developed while working together in an interdisciplinary fashion.

As this chapter describes, the team's distinctive mix of approaches is reflected in the account of burying naturally that we provide. Here is an opportunity to enter and re-enter the natural burial ground from the perspective of: someone choosing and paying for their own gravesite; the members of a funeral party; bereaved people whose friend or relative is interred there; a site owner or manager; someone who labours there, perhaps digging graves or cutting back vegetation; and a priest or officiant, a funeral director, or simply a member of the local community. What intrigues us about natural burial, as both site and practice, is its mix of tradition and innovation, its openness to diverse and sometimes conflicting interpretations. As such it is truly a 'contested site'. Questions our research have uncovered include: what is 'nature' and the 'natural'? Should a burial site be 'sacred' and can a farmer's field acquire this status? Is burial 'in perpetuity' a human right? And might death become forgotten if quietly folded away into the landscape? Natural burial, then, not only resonates with many traditional views of landscape and nature, from high art to ploughing, but also *challenges* some established mortuary practices.

Chapter 2 describes natural burial's recent history in some detail. Here we set the scene by explaining what we understand by natural burial – as a concept, a site and a practice – and how it has developed in the UK over the last 20 years. With Andy Clayden's long-standing interest in cemetery design,[1] creating spaces for a different approach to burial gave us an important starting point. Here we cite Carlisle municipal cemetery – described more fully in Chapter 2 – where the manager and registrar, Ken West, encountered two single women with concerns about the legacy of traditional burial.[2] Without descendents to tend their graves, they wanted a simple plot to contain their bodies, without the paraphernalia of headstone, curtilage and hothoused flowers. They also had concerns about the natural environment, wanting their remains to disappear into a nourished landscape. When combined with Ken West's career history, these imperatives proved fertile. Although trained in a more environmentally sensitive approach to landscape maintenance in the 1960s, for Ken cemetery management had become a chemical-based containment of nature by the 1980s, one that left him feeling disillusioned. In 1993, as a result, part of Carlisle municipal cemetery was set aside as a 'natural burial ground' where trees alone marked the graves. As we explain, this single-site development occurred at a time when a broader range of environmental concerns were capturing the public's imagination and indeed government and policy agendas (see, for example, HC91-1, 2000–01[3]).

Over 200 other natural burial grounds materialised in the next two decades – and we recorded their profiles in a GIS survey.[4] Despite this proliferation, however, natural burial has yet to take over from established disposal practices, such as whole-body burial in a churchyard, municipal or private cemetery, or cremation followed by the disposal of ashes either at the crematorium or in a site of survivors' choosing. While national figures for burying naturally are not recorded, we have been able to estimate that by 2007 the practice accounted for approximately 1 per cent of the total number of burials and cremations (see Chapter 2). One of our first research questions therefore concerned public awareness of natural burial. Even its name was confusing: green burial, woodland burial, natural burial? To find out more about public perceptions we invited people to participate in one of three focus groups following a minibus trip to an undisclosed location: a natural burial ground local to Sheffield.[5] For ethical reasons we informed them we were visiting some kind of burial ground before they boarded the bus. This meant that everyone who came on the trip – as they all did – were entering the natural burial landscape without the recent benefit of Google or a chat with a neighbour. We wanted to know how people for whom death was not pressing would understand that landscape. Their responses were mixed, particularly the diversity of their understandings of what was 'natural'. Striking among these early findings was evidence that (a) some participants were heartily relieved to find a burial space where the Church could not 'breathe down your neck' and (b) the distribution of ephemeral memorabilia across the burial field struck some as 'tatty', a scattering of 'bling' uncontained by grave curtilages.

Our sample was small, albeit representative of women and men, plus a spectrum of ages. And they were visiting one particular natural burial ground. As Andy Clayden already knew, it was not typical because there is no typical natural burial ground. Visiting another 20 sites throughout the UK was therefore our next priority: from farmers' fields to dedicated space in municipal cemeteries to large-scale commercial ventures (see Chapter 3).[6] Interviews with owners or managers were coupled with tours of the sites that included taking photographs and subsequently making drawings. Yielding a considerable body of data, site visits revealed the diversity of owners' and managers' previous experiences, motivations, design strategies, degrees of involvement with families and local communities and levels of environmental concern. Some had sought out suitable land; some already owned it. Some were burying into established woodland and meadows; others were concerned to generate and sustain new environments.

The variety of orientations towards establishing a site was compounded by the diversity of mortuary and memorialising practices owners and managers supported, discouraged or refused. But asking them about their aspirations and their regulations did not necessarily reveal what happened *in practice*, nor its longer-term cultural, social and emotional implications for immediately bereaved people and the local community or for the practices of clergy, humanist and alternative officiants, and funeral directors. To understand more about their embodied experiences, we chose four sites which represented some of the broad divisions that we knew were out there: a municipal cemetery with a dedicated natural burial area; a field set aside on a farm; a burial ground within a sustainability centre and a site established by a funeral director in a field purchased for this purpose. Extensive, semi-structured interviews with whoever owned, managed and worked at the site were combined with similar work among people who had preregistered for a grave, had buried someone at the site or had been involved with the site in a professional capacity and, more briefly, with whoever lived locally to the site. Having people talk to us in this way evoked memory and reflection, storytelling, emotional disclosure and humour. But while we visited people at home – and were often shown photographs and other memory objects related to the dead – the physical and social world of the natural burial ground itself remained more distant than we wanted. We therefore used participant observation, traditional to anthropological research, and helped dig graves, clear vegetation and give support at funerals at two of the four sites chosen (see Chapter 5).

As you read on, therefore, you will find very different points of entry into the topic – and indeed into the natural burial ground. Depending upon the research method used to gather particular data, the 'voice' you hear within the book shifts, from the whole team's authorial firstperson *plural* to the first person *singular* of Andy Clayden's longitudinal observational study. In the latter case, the perspective of a single team member is the vehicle through which the life of the natural burial ground has been explored through repeated visits and photographic surveys over a period that is now in its fifth year (see Chapter 8). Counter to the myth that natural burial is a cheap option espoused by an alternative fringe of hippies and tree-huggers, our research testifies to the diversity of people who have chosen or become involved in this practice. Not only those who provide and manage the sites, but also those who bury or work there, share a variety of belief systems and values – from orthodox Christianity to Druidism – and they include policemen, market gardeners, bikers, artists, soldiers, professional photographers and businessmen.

Digging deeper

What this chapter has described so far is the gathering of information in limited public circulation. Even if someone has buried a relative or friend at a natural burial site, their experience is likely to be highly context-specific. So our data provide a broad outline of sites offering natural burial throughout the UK,[7] along with insights into the lived experience of burying naturally and its aftermath. This does not, however, explain how natural burial came to develop when it did. What made it 'catch on'? What is its appeal? And what might its contribution be to a future where disposal of the dead represents a national problem

(HC91-1, 2000–01[8]), with concern at government level about dwindling burial space; political and public reticence over grave reuse; and costly measures required to manage the environmental dangers of cremation?

Here our mix of disciplinary backgrounds provides the foundation for responding to questions of this kind; expertise relating to land management and the designed environment plus the theoretical and methodological resources of two disciplines that contribute much to our understanding of human societies and cultures. Natural burial is a collective practice where individuals draw on existing repertoires of belief and practice, acting upon them – or not – within social contexts where people and their physical environments come together. While social policy, business studies and the psychology of bereavement may give us part of the story, what we offer here is an understanding of human experience within that much bigger setting of its history, its landscapes and an ultimately shared social encounter with human mortality. How do particular environments shape what happens after a life has ended? And does burying into such landscapes inevitably change them? To address these questions, we drew on a proliferating Death Studies literature to find out whether what we were hearing about and observing was:

1 . . . a creative resistance to modernist disposal and memorialisation?

Many authors have argued that death has been sequestered – or removed – to hospitals, residential homes, funeral parlours and cemeteries.[9] This means that individuals can feel distanced from relatives and friends who are dying or are recently dead, with little experience or expertise to contribute to their care or remembrance. Natural burial, by contrast, has been aligned with the Natural Death Movement[10] and DIY funerals[11] where people close to the deceased somehow take charge of their body, perhaps dressing it, decorating their coffin and providing transportation to a ceremony at which they themselves officiate.

2 . . . an aspect of the re-enchantment of death?

In contrast with the rational principles underlying institutional care of people who are dying or dead, a raft of new practices have humanised some aspects of death and dying by giving more space to the imagination and to emotional experience: the Hospice Movement that provides palliative rather than curative care for dying people, partly by involving relatives and friends;[12] the Natural Death Centre that promotes openness about death and dying;[13] the new legitimacy of informal wayside[14] and burial ground memorialisation,[15] and related practices from digital memorials[16] to private ritualisation at a domestic or personally meaningful site where ashes are disposed of.[17] This materialisation of memory[18] helps create 'continuing bonds'[19] between the living and the dead, a practice which may signify a resurgence of nineteenth-century Romanticism.[20]

3 . . . a form of symbolic and environmental regeneration?

Davies argued that natural burial may provide 'an authentic basis for understanding both life and death for those for whom either "heaven" or "memory" is an unbelievable or inadequate means of making sense of life and of death'.[21] Does the growth of natural burial grounds since 1993 herald a new collective sense of 'ecological immortality', he asks, as the un-embalmed body returns to the earth. This perspective reflects Carlisle municipal cemetery's former manager, Ken West's, staunch commitment to environmentally sensitive burial. But does this orientation inform people's choice of disposal option or pervade the natural burial providers' sector? We wanted to know whether a 'natural' mortuary landscape is valued as 'wilderness' or deplored as 'wildness' in order to address questions of aesthetics and memorialisation policies, as well as access problems in less manicured burial grounds.

4 . . . an erasure or indicator of identity?

Traditionally, a marked grave leaves indicators of religious, professional and familial identity. Yet some natural burial landscapes bear little overt evidence of who is buried where. Are we somehow eradicating local and national historical records? Or does natural burial allow someone's identity to be more faithfully expressed, when compared with a religious framing that meant little to them? Is a lifetime's gardening or hillwalking evoked in this choice of burial location? Are political or spiritual values manifested in an option which minimises environmental damage, resonates with nature-based religious beliefs and creates few hierarchical distinctions?

These possibilities demand an exploration of the wider historical context within which Ken West and the two single women had their conversation. Below we consider what took place before the early 1990s, which saw a long intertwining of traditional, collective practices with a newer ethos of personal choice and ideological heterogeneity.[22] We ask how this pervades the development of particular death care professions and the changing rituals and practices accompanying the disposal of the body. In particular, we attend to the relationship between human remains and ideas about nature and the (cultivation of) landscape. We then review theoretical resources that might enhance our understanding of death-related experience as an embodied, materially grounded process.

The fate of the body

Churchyards throughout the UK contain the bony remnants, or charnel, from many more bodies than their headstones might suggest.[23] Those unmarked deaths may well have occurred without the services of wise women, cunning men or local layers-out, never mind qualified medical professionals and undertakers. Nonetheless, burial in consecrated ground was important and in that sense the Church – whether Anglican or Roman Catholic – accommodated bodily remains and took responsibility for the passage of souls to everlasting life.[24] The question as to who is in charge of the body and/or soul at the point of death and thereafter provides an important anchor in charting the wavering fate of the dead body. Discussing these issues in relation to death, dying and bereavement, Walter traces an initial shift from the traditional authority of the Church to the modern era of professionals such as doctors and funeral directors, and then to a neo-modern era where individual choice is promoted, with advice and support deriving from informal sources.[25] Yet, as Walter points out, these eras are not discrete; rather, in the neo-modern or postmodern era, death care providers are likely to offer the 'consumer' a mix of innovative and selectively reconfigured traditional deathways.[26] This is exemplified in the post-cremation disposal of ashes, an independent ritual practice which 'may frequently be informed by the recollection, or awareness, of practices surrounding whole body burial';[27] these include sustaining bodily integrity, creating a bounded site of disposal, and visiting and maintaining the 'grave'. In the comparatively unregulated environment of the UK, however, *where* we choose to dispose of ashes and indeed the whole body has, until recently, been largely the choice of the individual. Yet in this liberal environment, individuals nonetheless appear to balance their scope for freedom with an ongoing commitment to traditional practices.[28]

This neo-modern juxtaposition of traditional and more innovative practices is also characteristic of natural burial. Control of the body, for example, is legislated for; an unexpected death gives the coroner 'a right to possession of the body for the purposes of the inquiry. The coroner also determines when the body may be disposed of . . . the bereaved have been divested of the body of someone who, to varying degrees, they once "possessed".'[29] Similarly, as Howarth notes, 'the modern funeral director's power hinges on *possession* of the body'.[30] Yet, if we examine the history of undertaking, we find that this role is relatively recent and, as our data show, is yielding to consumer demand for greater access to the body, from its care through to its transportation to the burial site (see Chapters 6 and 7). Known as funeral directors only from the 1940s, in the 1920s and 1930s rural undertakers in East Kent were part-time, combining death care with carpentry, building and timberwork.[31] Since bodies remained at home after death, the allocation of mortuary space was less necessary – and difficult to incorporate into what was essentially a builder's yard. However, undertakers contributed significantly to domestic ritual, providing carpets, candlesticks, pall-cloth, coffin trestles and coffin for the 'lying in' – and black boards for the windows. Up to the Second World War, coffins were often 'walked' to the funeral and subsequently to the burial ground, sometimes with the use of a hand bier. Horse-drawn or motorised transport was introduced sporadically, though care of the horse could be burdensome. The example of East Kent demonstrates a wider historical trend as populations grew, causing delays in the provision of funerals which made care of the body at home less feasible. The cremation rate also increased from 3.84 per cent of all disposals in 1939 to nearly 25 per cent by 1955,[32] rendering carefully crafted coffins less necessary and placing more emphasis on the transportation of the body to what was likely to be the more distant location of the crematorium. From 1940, then, funeral directors were setting themselves up as single-purpose businesses and seeking a professional status equal to that of doctors or the clergy; for example, through quasi-medical practices such as embalming,[33] the acquisition of motor-powered hearses and a role as 'intermediary between the bereaved and the organizations that furnish the mode of disposal'.[34] As stated in the *Manual of Funeral Directing*, they became: 'technical advisor, agent, contractor, master of ceremonies and custodian of the dead'.[35] To whom these professionals then *transfer* the body is, however, an important question,[36] and, to address this stage in the process, we need to look back, ultimately towards the nineteenth century.

Prior to the Second Vatican Council (1962–1965), for example, the unbaptised children of thousands of Roman Catholic families had to be buried in unconsecrated ground, barred from salvation and condemned to limbo.[37] Deciding who could and could not be buried in a churchyard – and their degree of closeness to the protection yielded by the church building – has thus for long been an indicator of that institution's centrality in determining the fate of the body and soul. By 1993, however, when the first natural burial ground was set up in Carlisle, the Church's relationship with death had changed very considerably. Indeed, by the middle of the nineteenth century the Anglican Church had already lost considerable ground to the State.[38] Industrialisation and urbanisation during the late eighteenth and early nineteenth centuries, when London's population doubled from 985,000 in 1801 to almost two million in 1841, brought massive overcrowding in city churchyards.[39] The stacking of coffins and the protrusion of bones through the earth made such churchyards the source of many worries: whole-body resurrection remained the hope of the faithful, yet the Church was clearly failing to protect the remains of the body; the miasmas or foul-smelling emanations from decaying bodies threatened to spread the epidemics that had already accelerated the death rate; the development of professional medicine, partly through the dissection of the body, fuelled a market for fresh corpses that was fed by grave robbers. Though the smell of decay emanating from the 'stinking rich' and particularly the saintly, who were buried within the church itself, had been seen as a *beneficial* 'odour of sanctity' prior to the mid nineteenth century,[40] the rotting poor were deemed a danger to the living. Consecration was seen as a protection against these difficulties, yet the Church was clearly failing to protect; St Martin-in-the-Fields accommodated up to 70,000 bodies in a 200-foot-square churchyard,[41] a 'squalid and insecure' form of burial for the working and lower classes.[42]

While dissenters and others who had broken away from the established Church set up independent burial grounds – or cemeteries, such as Bunhill Fields in London – as early as 1665, it was the joint stock companies' recognition of a market for unconsecrated burial grounds outside the evil-smelling metropolitan centre in the second quarter of the nineteenth century that paved the way for the Burial Acts in 1850 and 1852. These prohibited burial within London's city boundaries, an arrangement that by 1853 was extended to the rest of England and Wales and subsequently Scotland. By 1894 the Local Government Act had made local authorities responsible for setting up cemeteries.[43] Nonetheless, cemeteries were not universally welcomed in the first half of the nineteenth century: *The Quarterly Review* of 1844 stated that 'most people's idea of a Cemetery is a something associated with great Egyptian lodges and little shabby flower-beds, joint-stock companies and *immortelles*, dissent, infidelity, and speculation, the irreverences of Abney Park, or the fripperies and frigidities of Père la Chaise'.[44] Yet, as Morley stresses, the Church failed to contribute to this changing mortuary landscape, seeking to retain the income from burial fees; when Kensal Green Cemetery was established, the local minister of the Church was £200 a year worse off.[45] However, the greater cost to the established Church was the loss of custody over both the dead and the ritual that attended their demise. For example, its rejection of cremation as a hygienic response to overburdened burial grounds during the nineteenth century – at a time when 'a free-thinking attitude ... blossomed', has been interpreted as a recognition that traditional religious views no longer held sway.[46] Change, controversy and conflict have therefore characterised many of the changes in where and how the dead are laid to rest. Curl's account of the architecture and planning of the nineteenth-century cemetery laments its rejection after the First World War, when it was seen as an example of 'the dark romantic gloom of Victoriana'.[47] This sentiment was echoed by many of our research participants for whom established mortuary practices still bore the corseted pomp of Victorian death.

Important to the economic success of nineteenth-century cemeteries had been the public's freedom to 'erect whatever sort of monument it pleased',[48] and, in the early twentieth century, questions of choice and control were again key to the mortuary landscapes created after the First World War. Bourke discusses the war's implications for the aesthetics of mortuary environments, showing how civilian awareness of its carnage – when any ceremonial burial was a matter of luck – combined with the legacy of unmanaged bodily decay in urban church-yards.[49] Out of the dirt, smell and chaos of those deaths, she argues, came a desire for the clean, spare lines of Modernism, epitomised in the cemeteries established for the war dead. The complexities of this process are, however, evident in Winter's counterargument that: 'A complex traditional vocabulary of mourning, derived from classical, romantic or religious forms, flourished, largely because it helped mediate bereavement.'[50] What Bourke highlights is a profound tension between the State – which had conscripted the men whose bodies they then refused to repatriate – and bereaved families on whose behalf the parliamentarian Sir James Remnant noted: 'the right which is inalienable to every man, the right to do as he likes with his own dead. ... The dead are certainly not the property of the State or of any particular regiment; the dead belong to their own relatives.'[51] On the one hand, the Imperial War Graves Commission favoured a modernist aesthetic which downplayed hierarchical distinctions, arguing that every dead soldier's sacrifice was equal. Yet many bereaved families still wanted 'the romantic myths of traditional British funeral practices'.[52] What needs to be remembered, therefore, is that apparently radical changes within the mortuary landscape can reflect continuities as much as innovations. Relevant here is the long-standing relationship between nature, mourning and death. While natural burial grounds from the 1990s onwards eschewed the elaborate masonry of Victorian cemeteries for woodlands and meadows, as innovative burial spaces, they nonetheless reflected a longer-standing liaison between mourners and the natural world.

Following ethnographic work at the City of London Cemetery, Francis *et al.* describe its changing relationship with nature, from its establishment in 1853 through to the beginning of the twenty-first century.[53] The pervasive influence of cemetery designer John Claudius Loudon is evident in the prioritising of well-drained soil, existing vegetation and orientation to wind and sun, features common to garden planning.[54] Established following an Act of Parliament to accommodate the city's dead, it combined rational principles – straight driveways giving hearses efficient grave access, with curving peripheral pathways that lent a more rural atmosphere. Indeed John Simon, the city's medical officer for health, advocated an environment of 'trees and turf and shrubs, of bends and undulations', 'artificial devices' that, he said, would break up an otherwise uniform view of ranked headstones that risked 'vulgarising' death.[55] Implemented by landscape designer and gardener William Davidson, the final design reflected three landscape traditions: an eighteenth-century park or villa; nature orchestrated to reflect a human aesthetic; and a country garden. Davidson's approach embodied Victorian values that associated physical and moral well-being with exposure to fresh air and nature. In 1843, Loudon described churchyards and cemeteries as 'scenes not only calculated to improve the morals and the taste, and by their botanical riches to cultivate the intellect, but they serve as historical records'.[56] These values reflect a Romantic tradition that understood nature as an appropriate environment for expressing the depth of one's grief and, therefore, the closeness of bonds within the middle-class Victorian family.[57] Returning from southern Europe, the Romantic poet Shelley envisioned cemeteries set 'among ruins, covered in winter with violets and daisies. It might make one in love with death, to think that one should be buried in so sweet a place'.[58] This view persisted in modified form in the City of London Cemetery's 1929 brochure, which described the absence of yew and other trees of mourning, stressing instead the presence of flowers and deciduous trees 'whose perpetual renewal is a refutation of human grief'.[59] As whole-body burial began to be complemented by cremation – a practice that accounted for nearly 25 per cent of all disposals by the mid 1950s[60] – a crematorium and garden of remembrance were added to the City of London's mortuary landscape. Here, the planting of roses – with names evocative of mourning such as 'Remembrance', 'Loving Memory' and 'Peace' reiterated a rural aesthetic and sustained the individuality of the deceased via an attached memorial name plaque.[61]

Relevant here is also the lawn section established in this cemetery, its uniform memorials and grid layout maximising the efficient use of land and mechanised gardening equipment. Within the bigger picture of UK cemeteries, the siting of crematoria in their grounds during the first half of the twentieth century in order to reduce both the costliness of the land needed and the 'strangeness' of this new method of disposal also contributed significantly to the growth of lawn sections. As Rugg explains:

> the practice of cremation took the corpse from a traditional milieu (the cemetery), and introduced a highly technical intervention that again defined its practitioners as specialists. The lawn cemetery, admittedly on a less effective scale, aimed to effect a similar transition, in looking to remove the corpse from a family-controlled environment into one in which scientific principles and regulations were dominant.[62]

Thus, the distaste for the decomposing body which had emerged during the late nineteenth century can be linked not only with the rise of cremation, but also the minimising of grave markers and the loss of curtilage in the lawn cemetery, both of which made the body's presence less evident within that landscape.[63]

During this period many cemeteries had expanded in an unmanaged fashion, with peripheral zones that once evoked the countryside subsequently assuming the qualities of suburbs, sprawling out from some urban centre.[64] The lawn cemetery is, however, a managed landscape that resonates with stage models of grief which emphasise control, closure and recovery,[65] a framework subsequently challenged by a new legitimation of 'continuing bonds' with the dead from the mid 1990s onwards.[66] Lawn cemeteries also reflect cemetery management's development as a specialist profession, a trend with environmental implications, as Ken West argues;[67] 'by the postwar period there was a concern to apply scientific principles to the task of "lawnscaping", for example, the use of chemicals such as maleic hydrazide to retard the growth of grass'.[68] Of particular significance too, was the rising cremation rate.

Issues later encountered by natural burial ground owners and managers were already evident in the lawn sections of cemeteries such as in the City of London. Common graves, initially included within the lawn section, were barred in the 1960s as numbers decreased – and in response to the 'congestion' of 'ugly' vases and jam jars with which poorer families marked such graves. Nonetheless, people buying a private grave – without curtilage – feared the possibility of walking across it. A potential purchaser said: 'No one walked on him while he was alive.'[69] Minimising the presence of the dead also brought memorialising problems that cemetery management sought to remedy with small border gardens in front of headstones. 'Mourners seized the opportunity',[70] digging up the cemetery's shrubs to plant their own rose bushes. While the Victorian cemetery had been a haven for communal mourning, the lawn grave was a private, family site within a professionally managed environment.[71]

Back to nature?

In 1975 Curl said of nineteenth-century cemeteries that 'It is tragic that in an age when so much lip service is paid to conservation, the cemeteries are not appreciated as they should be.'[72] Describing the 'anticlimax' of a cremation service, he decried it as 'a comment on our society, where death is played down'.[73] With reference to the *place* of cremation – crematoria – Grainger describes them as 'essentially ambiguous and evasive buildings' which challenge the architect in their requirement to provide a functional *and* symbolic environment.[74] That said, the potential of their immediate setting as garden sites offering consolation and indeed hope of regeneration in an afterlife was recognised by cremationists, architects and landscape architects. The creation of Gardens of Remembrance and Gardens of Rest in the 1920s resonated with a rise in the popularity of gardening, at its peak when the UK's first crematorium opened in Hull in 1901. In particular, a new informality had captured amateur gardeners' imaginations and found echoes in a growth of interest in the English countryside.[75]

Tellingly, Curl identified the *ecological* costs of cremation 30 years before emissions became regulated, and advocated 'bury[ing] in the medieval fashion in shallow graves without coffins and reus[ing] the ground'.[76] Such concerns about human beings' relationship with the natural world are therefore nothing new, leading us to expect unanimity of voices on the topic of natural burial. However, as noted, there are instead a diversity of interpretations and experiences associated with it, as a concept, site and burial practice. We therefore need to consider which theoretical resources best illuminate these varied, intersubjective engagements. As noted, owners, managers and bereaved people may see things differently, as might the professionals and local communities associated with the sites. Our concern, however, is not to simply juxtapose competing readings of the same landscape, possibly with an eye to reconciling disjunctures or conflict. To do justice to what happens to people at the end of life, and to the decisions that they make, we need to go beyond the idea that different interpretations of natural burial are simply the effects of different 'points of view' or, put more theoretically, whichever cognitive lenses or filters are trained upon a shared landscape.

In 1973, the anthropologist Clifford Geertz described 'man' as 'an animal suspended in webs of significance he himself has spun'.[77] Whether such 'webs' were seen as interior to the individual or residing in shared environments such as households or villages, they were understood as the modus operandi without which 'man's behaviour would be virtually ungovernable, a mere chaos of pointless acts and exploding emotions, his experience virtually shapeless'.[78] This idea pervaded twentieth-century social anthropology, resonating with an awareness that people in small-scale societies with similar environments often classify aspects of their everyday lives differently.

While different peoples – or indeed people – may not 'see' the same things, the assumption that they are each applying their own cognitive schema presupposes a *separation* between human beings and the world they live in. In that our focus is the *merger* of human remains with their surrounding world, Ingold's work on the perception of the environment has been compelling.[79] He critiques precisely the idea that we classify different parts of our world according to a cognitive need for order and predictability. Instead, drawing on the ecological psychology of Gibson and the philosophy of Heidegger, Ingold recruits the phenomenological approach developed by Merleau-Ponty to argue, with him, that 'since the living body is primordially and irrevocably stitched into the fabric of the world, our perception of the world is no more and no less, than the world's perception of itself'.[80] This approach has shown us that different interpretations of natural burial emerge out of people's embodied *experience* – as the chapters ahead demonstrate. Initially Ingold called this a 'dwelling perspective' which takes 'the human condition to be that of a being immersed from the start, like other creatures, in an active, practical and perceptual engagement with constituents of the dwelt-in world'.[81] So, whether our focus is a farmer who turns a field over to burial ground and distributes graves in a rigg-and-furrow pattern (see Chapter 4), someone digging one of these graves, or indeed a family engaging with a deceased member whose body was buried there, each individual, Ingold would argue, is operating *within* an inhabited or dwelt-in setting. How they understand that setting is therefore shaped by an embodied experience of dwelling.

This is, however, a dynamic environment: vegetation is unlikely to be restrained by chemicals or intensive mowing and pruning; annually the land absorbs more bodies; and a wider society's attitude towards natural burial remains open to innovation. Following his work on lines – whether made by the writing or weaving hand, or by dancing or wayfaring feet,[82] Ingold quite literally 'moved on' from his notion of a dwelling perspective.[83] In place of 'dwelling', he offers the term 'inhabiting' to define a perspective that prioritises mobility, or creating a path, rather than enclosure within a dwelling house or forest glade. This, he argues, is key to human *being*. Chapter 8 examines the temporalities of natural burial, and it is precisely the dynamism of living, dying and decaying within a world of growth and change that engages us here.

Hallowed ground?

The term 'hallowed' has two meanings, both of which relate to the natural burial ground. While it can mean holy or sanctified, hallowed also connotes reverence or respect. In that most natural burial grounds are unconsecrated, the main exception being the Anglican Arbory Trust's site at Barton Glebe in Cambridgeshire,[84] how might they provide an atmosphere of respect – or become 'protected from activities deemed "disrespectful"'?[85] They may possess few of the permanent markers of human culture which have traditionally lent burial grounds a 'sacred' status and provided containment for the human body: for example, durable coffins, gravestones, a boundary wall and dedicated buildings.[86] In their absence, how do those whose paths intersect within the natural burial ground not only apprehend its purpose, but also engage with loss, grief and the decay of the body. In their anthropology of absence, Bille *et al.* question the privileging of *presence* within material culture studies, arguing for a view of absences as 'cultural, physical and social phenomena that powerfully influence people's conceptualizations of themselves and the world they engage with'. These authors advocate a focus on 'the mutual interdependence in people's lives of the materially present and the materially absent', one which recognises the 'local, complex and not necessarily consistent' processes through which the properties of absence and presence gain significance.[87]

This brings us to questions of identity. As Chapter 3 explores, the identities of those who *provide for* the practice of natural burial, whether through creating and managing sites, offering care of the body or assisting in the creation of ritual, are no longer self-evident. While the Church, the local authority and the funeral director have for long represented the institutions that take charge of the body – as described above – natural burial is also the outcome of initiatives undertaken by charitable trusts, private companies or indeed individual landowners and farmers. In that identity can be seen as the self in interaction with the other,[88] and is therefore both personal and social, the kinds of *relationships* that pertain between a farmer who has established a natural burial ground on their land and local funeral directors, for example, or a funeral director who owns a site and the families and friends of people buried there, have an important bearing on how that site is managed and how bereaved people may experience it. As is evident within our data, a bond between provider and user was not uncommon. Rather than the bureaucratised connection between a local authority and its bereaved population, personal relationships were not uncommon, certainly at sites belonging to farmers, charitable trusts and landowners, and an ethic of care might extend well beyond the period immediately after the death and committal.

This sense of belonging has associated implications for the identities of deceased and bereaved people, as Chapter 6 describes. One of the questions we set out to answer was whether the absence of a traditional material culture of death served to erase the identity of the deceased, or, as Davies and Rumble suggest, whether natural burial can be seen as 'a practice [that] increases the assonance between lifestyle and death-style and, in that sense in giving an individual a greater sense of integrity of identity than would be afforded in a form of funeral that compromised a person's lifestyle'.[89] Importantly, though – and here Ingold's argument that meaning-making emerges through 'inhabiting' is relevant[90] – identity needs to be understood as a lived process rather than the affixing of symbols to the mortuary landscape, in particular on headstones. Thus the changing relationship that pertains between the living and the dead emerges via materially grounded practices – or their absence. Chapter 6 therefore gives insights into the kinds of possibilities and choices that both natural burial grounds and their owners and managers enable. For example, some managers support families and friends who wish to take charge of the body of the deceased and care for it during the period between death and interment; some facilitate new temporalities of disposal such as horse-drawn processing to the gravesite or an open-ended period of time for the committal.

In that a key dimension of natural burial is the space in which it occurs, and the place-making practices that unfold within it, the intersecting parameter of time needs to be borne in mind as well. Social science perspectives on time have highlighted the difference between linear and cyclical time,[91] between sociocultural/collective and individualised phenomenological time;[92] treated time as the 'embodied practices by which people do time'[93] and as a multiplicity that social theory has neglected.[94] In the natural burial ground, people are exposed to a whole variety of temporalities. Thus the funeral cortège is likely to be an informal grouping of mourners who process through the landscape, sometimes for up to 20 minutes, following a coffin. Their embodied social engagement with one another, often the friends and relatives who together make up the life course of the deceased, complements their engagement with the body in its coffin which slowly moves ahead of them towards the grave. Both bereaved people and officiants valued this more fluid and extensive approach to the time and space of a funeral, a resource that allowed for more creative engagement with funeral ritual itself – and something which providers take pride in making available to users. Olney natural burial ground, for example, offers a personalised, handwritten promise of 'a peaceful relaxed atmosphere where there are no time constraints placed upon you' on its website's homepage.[95] Along with this less constrained time of engagement with the deceased, both before and during burial, visits to the site bring engagement with the cyclical time of seasonal growth and decay and its relationship with the time of year that the death and burial took place. Over time the rawness of a recently dug grave may be replaced by new growth, plantings, a shrub or a tree; and over time an empty burial field may become mature woodland. Can we therefore argue that burying naturally allows the linearity of modern, collective Western time to be transcended through exposure to the cyclical time of the natural world and the 'fresh start' of new growth at the gravesite? Or, does a lack of mortuary items and the potential bareness of the grave confirm the finite nature of a lifetime and so encumber passage and contain passing? Are seasonal periods of decay, when trees are bare and grasses die back, experienced as finitude or transition – and how might their sensuous or affective qualities be compounded by an absence of curtilage and memorials that potentially contain and retain the individuality of the deceased?

What these questions require is a different approach to the notions of both death ritual and mourning. In particular, traditional anthropological models of ritual emphasised its time-bound structures, even if submission to ritual practices engendered an altered sense of time.[96] Subsequent theorists, such as Turner[97] and Seremetakis,[98] called for a more fluid interpretation of ritual practices. Seremetakis offered the concept of ritualisation to encompass not just the often hierarchical deployment of officiants and mourners within the constrained time zone of 'the funeral', but also more informal ritualised processes such as what Rugg calls 'pilgrimages' to the burial site for 'tending or viewing a particular grave'.[99] How the site of the dead body and the previous domestic environment intersect is also a feature of Seremetakis'[100] concept of ritualisation. Again, as Davies and Rumble[101] argue, assonance between death-style and lifestyle is important here. Moreover, as Clayden and Dixon demonstrated,[102] plantings at the natural burial ground may well replicate those in the private garden and indeed bear symbolic resonances understood only by immediate family and close friends.

Though ritualisation might seem to describe a process of *mourning*, that is a set of behaviours that we can differentiate from the emotions that characterise grief,[103] the two are inevitably intermeshed. Durkheim,[104] for example, argued that it is through participating in collective ritual that we come to feel emotionally stirred, as opposed to a view of ritual as a necessary framework for containing otherwise disruptive feelings. In the period immediately after the publication of Klass *et al.*'s 'Continuing bonds'[105] and Walter's 'A new model of grief',[106] a new legitimacy was afforded to embodied, materially grounded relationships between the living and dead. In other words, while bereaved people everywhere and throughout history have not infrequently retained a connection with someone they were close to in life, during the second half of the twentieth century in particular, westerners were encouraged to undertake 'grief work'[107] in order to achieve 'closure' and reinvest emotionally in *new* relationships and identities. Natural burial gained in popularity during precisely the period when the notion of 'continuing bonds' was in ascendancy. Yet the memorialising practices through which bereaved people often sustained the identities of the dead and their relationships with them were not always easily incorporated within the natural burial ground; the proliferation of elaborate informal memorialising at the site of the grave was at odds with an emphasis on minimalising the ecological footprint of a burial, whether it took the form of grave gardening or the accumulation of personalised photographs, ornaments, toys and other memorabilia. This was a time when the relative anonymity of ash scattering at the crematorium, not infrequently in the absence of bereaved family and friends, was being challenged. Whereas only one in ten sets of ashes were removed from a crematorium by family or friends in 1970, by 2004 over 56 per cent of all cremated remains were being removed for disposal elsewhere.[108] The sites to which they were relocated included parks, football grounds and parts of the natural landscape that bore significant memories of the deceased person; the Peak and Lake Districts, Loch Lomond and the Yorkshire Moors might all evoke family holidays, walking tours or a honeymoon. Private places such as the home, the bedroom, the lounge and the wardrobe also became sites of more temporary storage, perhaps pending a final decision or their mingling with the ashes of a surviving partner or parent.[109]

Thus, while ashes might sometimes be 'released' into wind or water, when the relationship between the deceased and bereaved individuals had been particularly close, or the death was in some way very traumatic, the place-making affordances of ashes were more in evidence. This leads us back to the natural burial ground where the space allocated to the corpse is less likely to bear material evidence of their presence or identity. In some cases this can lead to tension between management and bereaved people, the latter's planting and memorialising activities contravening the ethos and sometimes the regulations of the site. Similarly, these activities can create divisions among bereaved people themselves, some of whom may have deliberately chosen natural burial for its lack of grave markings and who therefore find laminated cards and ornamental fairies inconsistent with the 'nature' they sought to embrace. Chapter 4 takes us into environments of this kind and explores precisely how owners', managers' and bereaved people's alternative mortuary landscapes are generated and experienced. In the case of one family, for example, the invisibility of a site's burials allowed them to focus without distraction on the spot where their mother was interred, the entire burial ground becoming 'mum's field'. What we argue here is that this diversity of 'views' of the natural burial landscape reflect a longer historical trajectory, one within which different relationships with the landscape have shaped the way it is perceived. Thus, in their perspectival or panoramic orientation towards the land, a wealthy seventeenth- and eighteenth-century class perpetuated an Enlightenment view which separated human beings from 'nature', generating a monocular vision. They can be contrasted with those who worked directly upon the land, who belonged to it rather than owned it and so experienced it via binocular vision. As our data show, for some of those who choose to bury naturally, the 'view' is a decisive feature. For them, the landscape is a monocular vista. However, when returning to the site in the months that follow a death, they may engage more directly with the grave and its potential for plantings, a 'binocular vision, movement and knowledge gained from coordinated use of the senses in carrying out various tasks' (see Chapters 5 and 8).[110]

This book therefore demands that we give particular attention to the concepts of 'nature' and 'landscape' in order to consider precisely how they might enable particular experiences of human transience. As Chapter 8 makes clear, the very notion of 'landscape' has an extensive, politicised history, one evidenced in tension between the desire for an interment that offers a panoramic view and the less distanced experience of a landscape that permits activity and intervention. How ecological considerations figure within individuals' choices of natural burial remains an important question, and our data demonstrate the very varied ways in which different people understand the relationship between the dead body, the earth and the vegetation that grows in it.

2

The inception and development of natural burial in the UK

The previous chapter provided an exploration of the period before 'natural burial' existed and addressed the historical processes underpinning a range of different approaches to the management of the dead body, its disposal and the memorialisation of the deceased. What we learn from a historical perspective is the persistence of certain beliefs, values and practices along with the repeated introduction of new approaches and the tensions which these either resolve or stimulate. This material provides an important backdrop for our account of why and how Ken West, when head of Carlisle Bereavement Services, took the bold steps to provide a radically different burial alternative, which he later described as *'woodland burial'* (see also Chapter 1). Ken's long experience of working in cemeteries, which he discussed with us during our interview with him, provides a fascinating window into the management of cemetery landscapes and how this began to shape his early ideas of revitalising the cemetery in order to strengthen its ecological conservation value and at the same time develop an affordable and sustainable burial service. Having established the very first woodland burial ground in May 1993, through a process of working with the public, bereaved people and other interested parties, he has continued to define and redefine natural burial as both a landscape and a practice.[1]

The chapter explores in some detail the development of natural burial in the UK over the last 20 years. It has evolved and continues to develop at a remarkable pace as new and alternative providers have sought to reinterpret natural burial for themselves. Here we draw on data from our geographical information system (GIS) developed over the course of our research; these highlight shifts within the Natural Burial Movement in terms of distribution, ownership and design interpretation; for example, the early dominance of the local authority sector and a noticeable recent decline in the growth of small-scale independent providers as changes to the planning process now require a much greater initial investment, rendering natural burial a less attractive commercial proposition. The chapter is therefore intended to set the scene and context for the chapters that follow, where our research becomes more narrowly focused on a representative sample of burial grounds identified within our GIS.

From environmental conservation to natural burial

By the time Ken West was appointed as Manager and Registrar at Carlisle Bereavement Services in 1983 he already had over 20 years' experience of working in cemeteries.[2] This experience would significantly influence how he went on to manage the cemeteries at Carlisle and the woodland burial site he created there. In our interview with Ken he recalled how, while working in Shrewsbury in the 1960s, he had witnessed and participated in the changing maintenance of the cemetery landscape that would have far-reaching consequences for their future as havens for wildlife: '*The burial market has been running down for decades, because we'd all decided from the ... forties ... fifties ... and sixties cremation was the only way forward ... everybody got into efficient grounds management, and efficient grounds management was mowing.*' He described how, during this time, part of the old cemetery at Shrewsbury was still cut by scythe and how it was rich in wildflowers with '*clouds of butterflies*' in summer. Ken's work at that time included being part of the chemical spraying team: '*we sprayed that old cemetery, took out all the wildflowers ... the insects and butterflies disappeared, all the voles disappeared and the place is now as dead as a dodo*'.

Ken's experience would later inform the grounds management plan he developed at Carlisle Cemetery, which focused on environmental conservation and came long before he had considered woodland burial. Ken was required by the council to make savings to his annual budget. Through observation of the absence of wreaths or cut flowers on particular graves throughout the year, but especially

Figure 2.1 *Conservation area at Carlisle cemetery, where grass cutting has been reduced from 16 cuts to 1 cut per year. The mown edge and wooden sign help to inform visitors how this area is being actively managed for owl conservation (September 2012).*

at Christmas and Easter, he concluded that small pockets of graves were no longer visited. In these areas he reduced the mowing regime from 16 cuts to 1 cut per year – a 75 per cent saving on his annual maintenance costs. He described the emerging landscape as *'astounding . . . the most beautiful meadows you ever saw'*, including *'pig nut, black nap weed, oxeye daises and orchids'*. Each year the diversity of species increased, and over time the conservation area was gradually extended to ten hectares. The cemetery landscape changed dramatically to include a much wilder habitat where Victorian monuments and headstones were partially obscured in spring and summer by tall grasses and wildflowers. A survey of old cemeteries by Julie Dunk and Julie Rugg in the early 1990s revealed the reluctance of cemetery managers at this time to implement a similar approach, concerned that the public would interpret it as neglect.[3] Anticipating this concern, Ken produced leaflets and posted on notice boards to explain the environmental benefits of a reduction in mowing. Guided walks of the cemetery led by Ken and his staff were also an opportunity to explain these changes and, most importantly, gauge public reaction. Ken recalled the positive responses they received during these events and how some of the participants even requested: *'Can we be buried in the conservation?'*.

It was, however, a chance conversation with two elderly women from Dumfries that crystallised Ken's thoughts about how nature, conservation and burial might be integrated in a more purposeful way. His expertise had been recognised by a local Bereavement Services officer,[4] who had advised the women to contact Ken for advice as they were considering being buried in their own garden. They told Ken that not only did they dislike the formality of the cemetery but also that, because they had no family, their graves would not be cared for and would soon look neglected. He asked: *'[if I could provide] some form of tree burial, like a nature reserve . . . would that be better?'* It was an idea to which they responded positively. Ken realised *'there was a gap in the market'*.

Ken told us that by 1990 he had *'extended his thinking to create an innovative woodland burial scheme'* and later that year submitted a feasibility study to the council, which was approved. It would be another three years, however, before resources were made available. During this time Ken continued to develop and promote his ideas, which he presented in 1992 at a national conference attended by members of the burial and cremation authorities.[5] His woodland burial ground finally opened in May 1993 and was established on reserved burial land adjacent to the cemetery that the council had previously rented to a farmer to graze his livestock. From the outset, Ken was clear about his priority for the environment. He planned to establish a native oak woodland, with locally sourced trees planted on each grave. He said, *'we're now going to be prescriptive . . . if you want to go in the woodland burial, the environment comes first . . . you cannot have a memorial on the grave. If you are not comfortable with that you must choose another option.'*

Ken later adapted the design to include a stone sheepfold that was built next to the woodland. The sheepfold had both a practical and aesthetic function. It provided a sheltered place to sit where memorial plaques and floral tributes could be displayed, while ensuring there was no visual intrusion on the emerging oak woodland. By encouraging bereaved people to memorialise away from the grave, Ken also hoped to minimise any infringement on the woodland habitat and so protect vulnerable flora and fauna. As we go on to

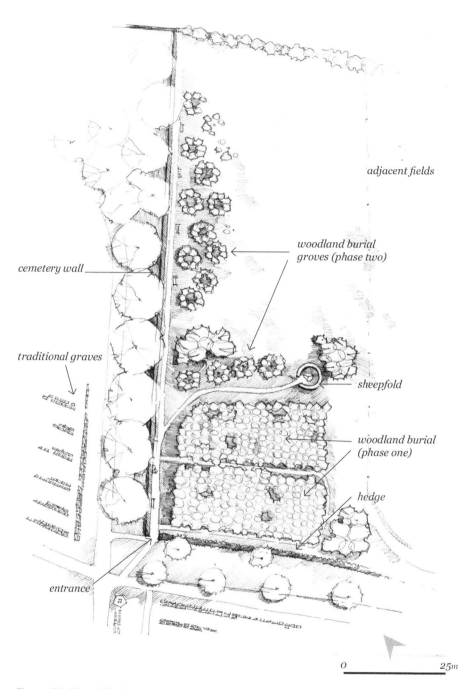

Figure 2.2 *Plan of Carlisle woodland burial area showing its relationship to the existing cemetery outside the cemetery wall and hedge. The plan also shows the more recent development of woodland groves, a very different approach from the first phase, where burials were arranged in a more conventional grid.*

Figure 2.3 *The entrance to the woodland burial area shows the contrast between the more formal mown cemetery and woodland section that lies beyond the Victorian brick wall and hedge (September 2012).*

discuss in Chapter 4, the expectation that bereaved people would commit to a collective memorial landscape in which individual graves might no longer be easily identified or accessible has led to significant challenges for many natural burial providers, who have subsequently adapted their design and management to meet this unanticipated need to memorialise at the grave. At Carlisle this has been achieved in the first phase of woodland development partly through the introduction of the sheepfold but also as the emerging woodland has become more dense and impregnable. The introduction of the sheepfold has also been important in reinforcing the identity of the woodland burial area as distinct from the adjacent Victorian cemetery. It is also reference to the wider vernacular Cumbrian landscape, where stone sheepfolds are a unique feature of upland farming; and it thereby helps to create a coherent panoramic, monocular view of the landscape and nature,[6] one that in addition discourages the binocular view which might emerge if people were able to carry out planting and other activities at the site of the grave they visit (see Chapter 1).

While the concept of being buried within native oak woodland at Carlisle was new, there was already a long-established tradition of woodland cemeteries in northern Europe. These were first developed in Germany at the beginning of the twentieth century in response to the impoverished appearance of many municipal cemeteries.[7] Waldfriedhof Cemetery in Munich, designed by the architect Hans Grässel in 1907, is believed to be the first, although the South Cemetery in Stockholm, by architects Gunnar Asplund and Sigurd Lewerentz, is perhaps the most famous of this type.[8] Ken was aware of the Scandinavian woodland cemeteries and conscious that some people might not understand

Figure 2.4 *A stone sheepfold, set apart from the woodland and accessed by an informal path, creates a sheltered seating space where memorial plaques and floral tributes can be displayed without intruding on the woodland. This image also shows the contrast between the more densely planted first woodland phase on the right and the second phase of woodland groves where burials are arranged in a circle around a wooden marker (September 2012).*

how the woodland he was proposing would be different: '*We knew about the [woodland] cemeteries in Scandinavia, we'd seen the slides . . . but there's never been the grounds management of the same sort.*' As Ken was well aware, in the German and Scandinavian sites, each grave is memorialised and the woodland understorey is more intensively managed through regular cutting to maintain access to each grave.

The presence of large, imposing mature trees is a common characteristic of many of the UK's Victorian and Edwardian cemeteries. Their arrangement is, however, frequently park-like in character and includes the careful selection of specimen trees and shrubs, often chosen for their symbolic qualities, including 'weeping and fastigiated trees, yews and dark-foliaged evergreens',[9] positioned along avenues and arranged to frame buildings and selected views. There are, however, more contemporary examples that predate Carlisle and express a very different approach to the deliberate selection and arrangement of trees and are also driven by a strong environmental agenda. Although not originally conceived as a cemetery when it was opened in 1971, Oakley Wood Crematorium in Warwickshire is set within established woodland of 'oak, pine and silver birch'.[10] The local authority has tried to preserve the woodland character by restricting memorialisation of interred ashes to a selected area and prohibiting the introduction of ornamental trees and shrubs. Interestingly, in 2010, the authority responded to the unique woodland setting of the crematorium to include a natural burial option where whole-body burials are now incorporated within the existing woodland.

Figure 2.5 *Waldfriedhof Woodland Cemetery in Munich, Germany. Designed by Architect Hans Grässel (1907). The graves are located within the woodland, which is more intensively managed to maintain access to individual graves (June 2013).*

There have been other precursors to Ken West's activities at Carlisle that also challenged conventional approaches to cemetery design. The proposed design for a new cemetery for the Parish of Saddleworth near Oldham, for example, included a burial ground free of memorials and enclosed by native woodland shelterbelts. In 1984 Saddleworth Parish Council commissioned landscape architect Robert Camlin to design a new cemetery on land that overlooked Saddleworth village.[11] Taking its inspiration from the vernacular landscape, the design for the burial ground included a series of wildflower meadows free from memorials that would be used for burial, enclosed by native woodland shelterbelts and drystone walls. The intention was to preserve the integrity of the meadows by locating the headstones in the surrounding woodland edge. This would simplify and reduce the need for regular grass cutting and retain the meadows as informal recreation spaces for parishioners and hillwalkers, now and in the future.

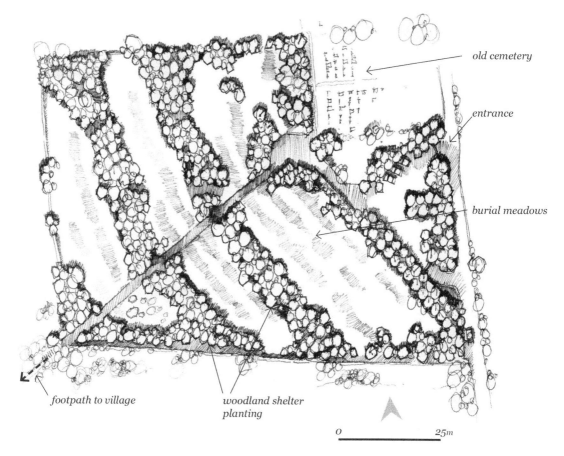

old cemetery

entrance

burial meadows

footpath to village

woodland shelter
planting

0   25m

Figure 2.6 *The design for a new cemetery at Saddleworth, near Oldham, by landscape Architect Robert Camlin (1986) included burial meadows where the intention was that these would remain clear of memorials, which would be placed along the woodland edge.*

For reasons that remain unclear, when the cemetery opened in 1986 this aspect of the design was not realised. Memorial headstones have been placed on each grave and the grass is regularly cut, thereby diminishing its potential habitat value and increasing the costs of maintenance. The original proposal shared many similarities with what was to be developed at Carlisle, and, for whatever reason, the subsequent change in approach towards memorialisation was an early indication of the challenges that many natural burial providers would later face.

From 1993 onwards, Ken's focus on the environment defined the landscape of woodland burial as one free of memorials. However, the underpinnings of this definition did not include consideration of the treatment of the body and its containment. As he acknowledged during our interview, *'when we first started we didn't know anything about cardboard coffins'* and *'we allowed embalming and chipboard coffins'*. As the potential for these processes and materials to harm the environment became more widely understood they represented an anathema for those committed to the idea of an environmentally sensitive burial. Woodland burial thus began to take on a broader definition that intimately connected the environment both above and below ground. When willow, bamboo and recycled cardboard coffins later became available, Ken continued to innovate by searching for more affordable and sustainable alternatives. Using unbleached woollen offcuts from a local mill, he developed a burial shroud that he later supplied to the public. While in the context of our recent burial culture these developments might appear innovative, as Ken noted, '*Under the Burial in Woollen Acts (1666–80) . . . we always used to bury people in woollen shrouds.*' Even in the late nineteenth century Dr Francis Seymour Hayden, 'an outspoken opponent of cremationists', was advocating the use of wicker and papier-mâché coffins to promote decomposition and to enable grave reuse.[12] Data from one of our interviews with a funeral director, which we return to in Chapter 7 also highlighted the 'natural' qualities of the traditional funerals.

> This is natural burial as you get, died at home, stayed at home, coffin was made here, English Oak, English Elm, Pitch Pine, okay, that's what was made, horse-drawn hearse up to the house, body remained in the house, the service was held in the house. Right, coffin was then taken by horse drawn to the, to the cemetery, to Firpool Cemetery, which is our closest cemetery, buried in the ground. Now that, that is as natural burial as you're going to get, and that's about the most traditional funeral you're going to get. So actually, this is where, everyone is, oh I love these modern green funerals, and actually it isn't. The most, the most green is probably the most traditional.
>
> (Paul Masters)

Woodland burial as practice

The data above describe how woodland burial emerged as a *place*, but there is also the question of what it means as a practice. In his interview with us, Ken recalled how he was frequently asked: '*How do I do a woodland funeral?*' He had not anticipated the question but welcomed it as a sign that the public were beginning to define woodland burial in response to the new opportunities it presented them with. He was contacted by members of the Bahrain faith who wanted to discuss how they might use the burial ground. They told him: '*It's important that we go out in . . . the most humble way possible, we mustn't spend an awful lot of money . . . going into the woodland with a cardboard coffin is perfect for us.*' They also asked: '*We could do our own funerals? . . . could we bring the coffin up in a van . . . and handle it ourselves and do it?*'. Ken welcomed their request: '*It gave the indication to people that DIY funerals took place in woodland burial . . . that was good because people felt empowered . . . there is no set way because it's new and that was what people liked.*' The funeral, as much as the landscape, therefore began to define woodland burial as users felt inspired to be actively engaged in the process of burying their dead. The burial ground thus began to be perceived as an opportunity to return to old customs, develop new rituals and participate in ways not possible within the time and logistical constraints of the crematorium. As a result, it is very much an example of 'neo-modern' death, as described by Walter[13] (see Chapter 1).

Throughout the early 1990s there were other significant developments that would bring a different perspective and momentum to the Natural Burial

Movement and also redefine woodland burial. In 1991 psychotherapists Nicholas Alberry, Josephine Speyer and Kristian Heal co-founded the Natural Death Centre (NDC), a charity that campaigned for social change in the care of the dying and dead. In response to the death of his father, Nicholas Alberry identified 'the need for a natural death movement to parallel the natural child-birth movement and to spread the tenets of good hospice care to those dying of all causes'.[14]

The NDC was and continues to be an important advocate for natural burial. Aware of the developments at Carlisle, the NDC was keen to promote DIY funerals where families could be supported by alternative death care providers and celebrants. In 1994 the NDC launched the Association of Natural Burial Grounds (ANBG) with the intention of ensuring 'that every locality should have its own natural burial ground'.[15] In doing so they redefined and renamed what had been widely accepted as woodland burial 'to embrace new schemes being introduced that created natural habitats other than woodland'.[16] Replacing 'woodland' with 'natural' also enabled the NDC to broaden the definition to reflect a stronger social dimension while also rejecting the 'unnatural' process of embalming.

This was also the year that *Green Burial: The DIY Guide to Law and Practice* by John Bradfield was published.[17] This book was significant in its promotion of the therapeutic benefits of DIY funerals, but, perhaps more importantly, it provided advice to landowners regarding the law related to burial on private land. The new independent providers added yet another dimension to the definition of natural burial in that it was no longer confined to the municipal cemetery but quickly expanded to include land owned by farmers, funeral directors, charitable trusts and private companies. In the space of just two years, woodland burial had evolved from a single burial ground into a national 'natural burial' movement, with its own association and multiple sites managed by local authorities and independent providers.

Ken West continued to play an active role in shaping the development of natural burial, one that went beyond his pioneering work at Carlisle. In 1993 he was elected President of the Institute of Burial and Cremation Administration (IBCA) and in his presidential address to the national conference, hosted in Carlisle in 1994, he introduced his idea of a Charter for the Bereaved.[18] Administered by the IBCA (later to be renamed the Institute of Cemetery and Crematorium Managers (ICCM)), it was first implemented in 1996 and presented a set of minimum rights, standards and targets that UK burial and cremation providers who adopted the Charter would adhere to. While ground-breaking in many other respects, within the context of natural burial it was significant in establishing a target that included a 'natural option, such as wood-land burial'.[19] As we discuss in Chapter 3, this would have a major impact in promoting natural burial, especially within the local authority sector.

In response to his concerns about the environmental performance of a number of sites he had visited, in 2000 Ken went on to develop the first and only UK ecological classification scheme for natural burial. This set out a framework of environmental standards that could be applied to determine if a site could be classified as 'natural burial'.[20] The scheme was submitted to the NDC but was not implemented as there were concerns that it would exclude, as Ken perceived it, '*some of the commercially successful members [who] were regularly mowing grass and planting non-native trees*'.[21] The standards also set a minimum size of two hectares that would also exclude many local authority sites. Aware of the impact this might have, he went on to develop a burial ground sustainability index that '*would consider the five fundamental factors of mowing, memorials, coffins, embalming and management*'.[22] Each burial ground could be scored against the index, thereby allowing comparison between providers. While this approach offers a simple and transparent method of providing consumers with an environmental profile for each burial ground, there is little evidence that individual providers are either aware of this index or have chosen to evaluate and publicise the score for their burial ground.

Before we go on to explore how natural burial has evolved over the last 20 years, we need to state that there are still no agreed national standards for natural burial or legislation that requires the monitoring of sites. In 2009 the Ministry of Justice issued guidance to natural burial ground operators which included environmental considerations but did not set any explicit requirements or standards.[23] While the ANBG requires its members to comply with its code of conduct, they only own or manage approximately 20 per cent of all UK natural burial sites.[24] In addition, while this code makes reference to conserving the environment, prohibiting embalmed bodies and promoting the use of biodegradable coffins and shrouds, it is unclear how this is to be monitored or enforced. We should also note that while our evolving definition has focused on the landscape, the absence of memorialisation and ecologically sound body preparation that discourages the use of embalming fluids, most natural burial sites also accept the interment of ashes. While for many this would appear to be in opposition to the environmental objectives of natural burial,[25] some of these risks are being addressed through European legislation to improve the efficiency and emissions of cremation.

The UK and its emerging natural burial landscape

Having explained how natural burial came to be launched and its implications for the environment both below and above ground, we now consider the distribution of sites across the UK and the diversity they represent. One of the key aims of our research was to develop clear baseline data for the existing natural burial provision throughout the UK. We wanted to establish where each site was located and when it opened, who owned it, how natural burial was being interpreted (for example, was it meadow or woodland), the size of the burial ground and finally demand. These data would enable us to identify any emerging trends across the UK in terms of the provision and interpretation of natural burial. This collection of data would also enable us to find out whether the concept that Ken West developed at Carlisle (the planting of a native tree on each grave) continued to prevail or if natural burial was being reinterpreted as providers adapted to the challenges and opportunities burying naturally presented. The maps we present here are extracted from the GIS we developed throughout the course of our research and present a UK-wide picture of natural burial up until the project came to its conclusion towards the end of 2010. The maps record the distribution and ownership of burial sites and their different design interpretations.

In gathering our data we were assisted by the ANBG, who provided access to their list of natural burial sites. This information was supplemented by telephone interviews with each burial ground provider and reviews of their website information. The interviews were also an opportunity to identify other burial grounds that providers were aware of that were not yet included in our database. As the research project progressed, we provided public access to our record of sites, including a map that showed the location of each site,[26] via the project website. New providers were invited to contact the research team to register their burial ground. At the end of the research project these data were presented at the first UK conference on natural burial in 2010 that was hosted at the Department of Landscape, University of Sheffield and jointly coordinated with the NDC.[27]

Distribution of UK natural burial sites

Figure 2.7 records the location of the 207 natural burial grounds we had identified by September 2010. The map also identifies a further 35 sites which were either in the process of obtaining planning consent (24) or were proposed (11). Perhaps not surprisingly, the map reveals a correlation with the more densely populated areas in the north of England, Midlands and south east. In the more remote rural and upland areas, the absence of natural burial sites might suggest that the existing burial provision adequately meets current demand. These communities are typically more settled and exhibit a stronger family attachment to the existing cemeteries and church burial grounds.

The map also reveals a concentration of burial grounds along the south coast of England that includes less densely populated areas. Our interviews with providers in Devon, Cornwall, Hampshire and the Isle of Wight suggest two possible explanations. The south coast has a large retirement population and many of these people no longer live near to their families or traditional places of burial. Natural burial provides an alternative that does not anticipate the grave being regularly visited and maintained and reflects the motivation of the two women who originally contacted Ken to discuss burial in their garden. Providers also spoke of families who did not live locally but who had a strong attachment to the area that had been forged over many years during family holidays. For some families this attachment might have had more emotional significance and be more enduring than their connection to where the family had lived. These burial grounds therefore provide an opportunity to sustain a connection with a place and landscape that is rich in memories.

Distribution of sites by ownership and design interpretation

Figure 2.8 shows the distribution of sites by ownership. As noted earlier, one of the defining characteristics of the Natural Burial Movement has been the introduction of independent burial providers which, in addition to local authorities and the Church, we have categorised as: private companies, farmers, landowner/partnership, funeral directors, and charitable trusts. We differentiated 'private companies' from 'funeral directors' and 'farmers' where land had been purchased or leased expressly for the purpose of providing natural burial or where it was the principal commercial activity. Landowner/partnership arrangements are relatively few in number but are distinct in that they reveal a more recent

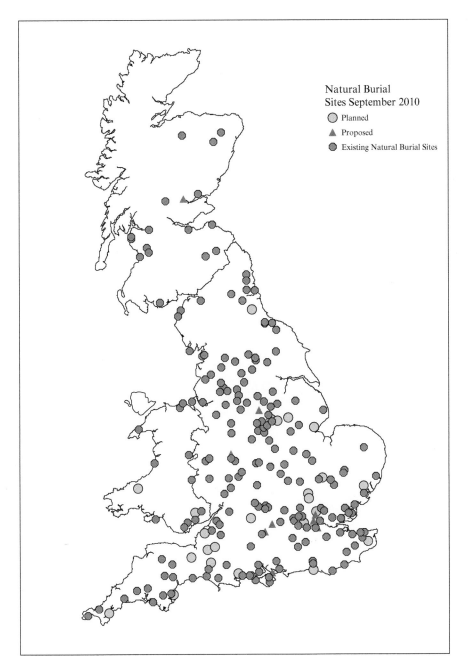

Figure 2.7 *The location of all UK natural burial sites in September 2010, including those that were in the planning process and sites that had been proposed but not yet submitted for planning approval.*

trend in natural burial where a company with expertise in this area collaborates with a landowner.

Figure 2.9 shows the distribution by design interpretation. Each burial ground was assigned to one of the following groupings: mature woodland; newly planted woodland; woodland through burial; meadowland through

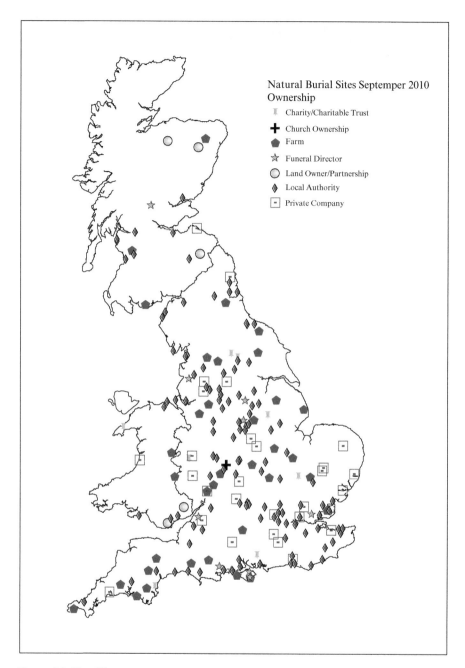

Figure 2.8 *The different ownership of natural burial sites and their distribution across the UK.*

burial; woodland and meadowland through burial; and orchard. Each group describes the habitat that the burial ground owner seeks to preserve or create and, with the exception of 'newly planted woodland' and 'woodland through burial', are self-explanatory. These last two approaches focus on the establishment of new woodland but in the case of 'newly planted woodland' this

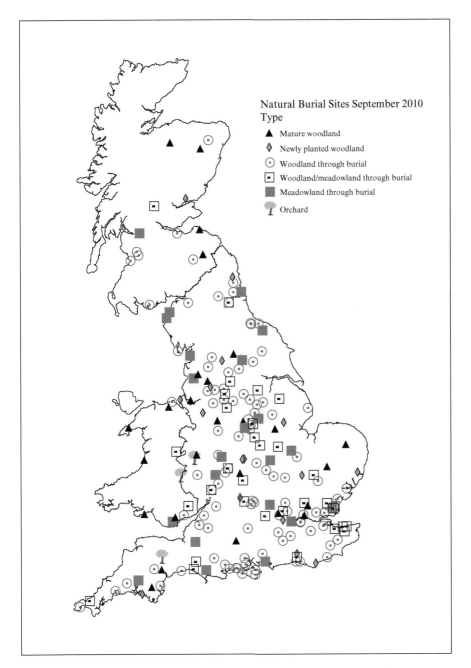

Figure 2.9 *The different design interpretations of natural burial sites and how these are distributed across the UK.*

is independent of burial. The tree planting happens before burial and graves are accommodated within the emerging woodland glades or between trees. At 'woodland through burial' sites the trees are planted after the burial, either on or near to the grave. While each of these categories broadly captures the differences between natural burial provisions, they cannot hope to reflect the nuances

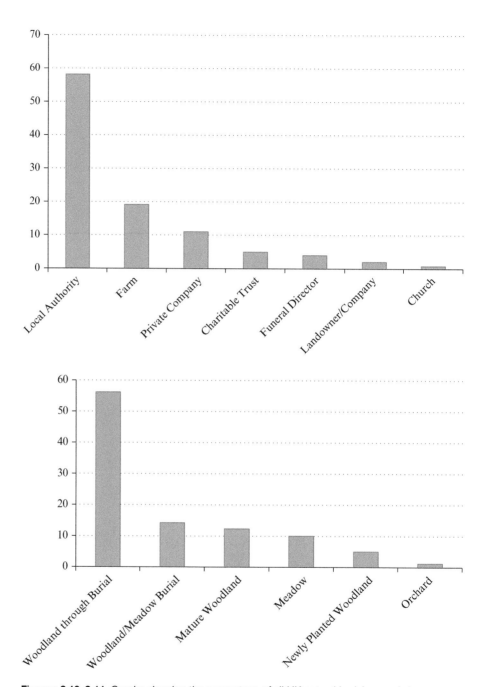

Figures 2.10–2.11 *Graphs showing the percentage of all UK natural burial grounds by ownership and type. Local-authority-managed sites account for more than half of all UK natural burial grounds, where the most common design interpretation is the planting of a tree on each grave.*

of interpretation that exist between each of the sites, which we explore in more detail in Chapter 4.

When viewed together the maps reveal a broad correlation between the ownership of burial grounds and type of natural burial. Local authority sites account for more than 50 per cent of all UK natural burial grounds and are typically located in the more densely populated cities and conurbations in a corridor that extends from the large industrial cities in the north-west of England and Midlands through to London in the south-east.

The distribution of local authority sites also shows a close fit with those sites that we have identified as 'woodland through burial' and which also account for more than 50 per cent of all UK natural burial grounds. As we discuss in Chapter 3, the preference of local authorities to implement this interpretation of natural burial relates to their early adoption and the unique constraints within which they operate.

Looking beyond the local authority sites, the distribution of burial grounds and design types becomes more dispersed and diverse as the provision extends into more remote areas. Notably, there is an increase in the proportion of independent providers. Each of these sites is a new burial ground that is not restricted to the location of established cemeteries and is consequently free from the constraints that these place on space, design and management practices. These new providers seem instead to be responding to a landscape of open fields, woodland and hedgerows, engaging at an early stage with the affordances of such settings.[28] The map reflects this opportunity and reveals a relationship between independent sites and natural burial grounds that are characterised by mature woodland, meadows, newly planted woodland and orchards.

Emerging trends in ownership and design interpretation 1993–2010

In summary, our data in 2010 revealed a complex national picture characterised by a diversity of providers and design interpretations. These distribution maps do not, however, convey how this new burial landscape has been arrived at or where natural burial might now be heading. To explore how the picture has evolved we need to analyse our database going back to 1993. The accompanying graphs present data for the number of burial grounds by ownership and type at five-year intervals between 1993 and 2007 and a three-year interval from 2008 to 2010, when our research concluded.

In the first five years, 53 natural burial sites were established, of which more than 80 per cent (43) were developed by local authorities that allocated space for natural burial within their existing municipal cemeteries. As we discuss in Chapter 3, local authorities were well placed to respond quickly to the opportunity of providing natural burial. Staff working in Bereavement Services would have been aware of the developments at Carlisle through their professional affiliations and conferences, and, most importantly, they had access to land that had planning consent for burial.

The speed at which independent providers were able to move to offer natural burial is also noteworthy. While the numbers are small – fewer than three sites each per group of farmers, private companies, charities and funeral

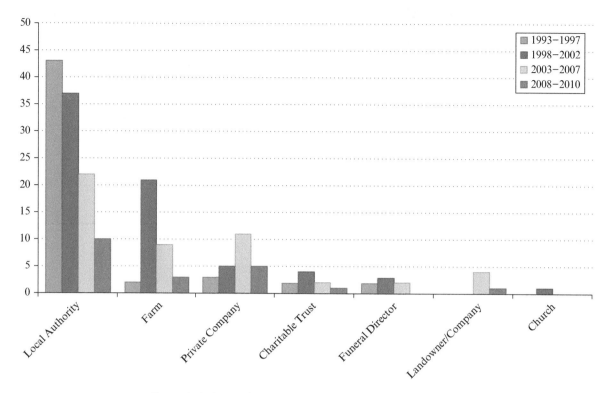

Figure 2.12 *Graph showing the total number and ownership of natural burial grounds in five-year intervals from 1993 to 2007 and a three-year interval from 2008 to 2010, when our research concluded.*

directors – these groups were able to secure planning consent to establish their own burial sites.

In this early phase, 'woodland through burial', where typically trees were planted on each new grave, was by far the most common design interpretation accounting for more than 80 per cent of all sites. This figure echoes the dominance of local authority provision and a willingness on the part of these providers to apply, in broad terms, the concept developed at Carlisle. However, it would be erroneous to suggest that all innovation was coming from the independent sector; although charitable trusts had experimented with mature woodland and orchard burial, a small number of local authorities had also introduced meadows and newly planted woodland.

Between 1998 and 2002 natural burial experienced its most rapid period of expansion, with the establishment of 71 new burial grounds. Local authorities continued to be the most dominant group, although their overall share dropped by 30 per cent to just over half of all new sites. Of the independent providers, burial grounds located on farms showed the most significant growth, increasing to 30 per cent of all new sites. The farming community may not have had the same access as local authority employees to information about the developments that were taking place in natural burial, but they had instead been alerted to the possibilities of natural burial through media coverage specifically targeted at those working in rural communities. In the late 1990s the BBC's TV programme *Countryfile* broadcast an interview with a farmer who had opened

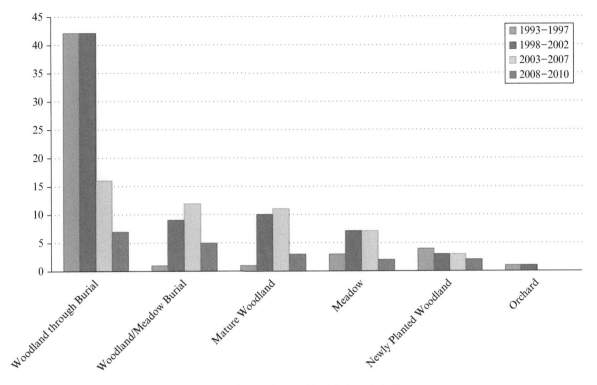

Figure 2.13 *Graph showing the total number and type of natural burial grounds in five-year intervals from 1993 to 2007 and a three-year interval from 2008 to 2010, when our research concluded.*

a natural burial ground on his land. Several of the farmers we interviewed described this as the catalyst for their decision to provide natural burial.

Throughout this period of growth, 'woodland through burial' continued to be the most common interpretation of natural burial, but its popularity among providers diminished. The main areas of growth were in 'mature woodland', where graves are arranged between established trees; 'woodland and meadow', where typically new woodland planting defines the burial meadows but is not used for burial; and 'meadow burial', where the objective is to improve the species diversity of existing grassland. 'Mature woodland' demonstrated the most significant growth and was employed by farmers, private companies, charitable trusts and local authorities. Closer scrutiny of our data does, however, highlight the approximate nature of these groupings when the size of the burial ground is taken into consideration. For example, sites that we have categorised as 'mature woodland' and which are managed by a local authority are typically small, often less than 0.5 hectares. They are an opportunistic response to providing a natural burial option, exploiting areas within the cemetery that have established trees and burial space. Allerton Cemetery in Liverpool, for example, developed its natural burial provision in an existing area of shelterbelt tree planting that subdivided the cemetery into two sections. The 'mature woodland' sites in the independent sector are all significantly larger, ranging from 2 to 20 hectares, and incorporate a greater diversity of woodland habitats that include open glades, woodland edge, coppiced woodland and mature stands of trees.

Between 2003 and 2007 the number of new sites declined from 71 to 49 in comparison with the previous five-year period. Local authorities were still the largest single provider, but their overall contribution dropped below 50 per cent. The proportion of sites located on farms also declined alongside an increase in private companies which, in this period, accounted for over 20 per cent of new natural burial grounds. An alternative model of natural burial provision also emerged; the collaboration of landowner and private company with expertise in natural burial. For example, Usk Castle Chase, one of our research sites, is jointly managed with Native Woodlands Ltd, who in 2013 managed eight sites across the UK.[29] This approach combines knowledge of the existing landscape with experience of and expertise in how to plan and deliver natural burial.

The time frame between 2003 and 2007 evidenced a continuation of the trends in natural burial established in the preceding period. There was a further decline in the proportion of 'woodland through burial' sites and an increase in the number of 'woodland/meadow' and 'mature woodland' burial grounds. If we look at the 11 new mature woodland sites established in this period, 9 of these were developed by independent providers of which 8 were private companies or landowner/company partnerships. All of the independent sites were large in scale, ranging across 2–14 hectares. This trend of increasing numbers of independent providers and much larger sites was also mirrored for the 'woodland/meadow' type burial grounds.

In the three-year period from 2008 to 2010, when we concluded our research, there was a further decline in the number of new natural burial sites, with fewer than seven burial grounds opening each year, a 50 per cent reduction when compared to the late 1990s and early 2000s. While this period is illustrative of three as opposed to five years, the trends are broadly similar. Local authorities account for approximately 50 per cent of all sites, farms show a small decline and there is an increase in the number of sites managed by private companies. The size of burial grounds and design interpretations also broadly reflect the trend up to that point, with an increase in larger sites developed by independent providers and a growing proportion of woodland/meadow burial grounds.

In the 17 years that elapsed since natural burial was first introduced, then, there have been significant developments in the provision of natural burial in terms of site ownership, design interpretation and the scale and complexity of burial grounds. While local authorities continue to supply the largest number of sites, it is the independent providers and specifically private companies that are currently in ascendency. The number of sites developed by charitable trusts, funeral directors and the Church are small, but they remain an important feature of the UK natural burial picture where there is frequently much higher demand than many local authority sites can account for. What is perhaps most surprising, given the initial enthusiasm, is the decline in the number of farm sites.

Since all new burial grounds must obtain planning permission before there can be a change of use to the land, the decline in farm sites could reflect changes to the planning process that have made it more demanding and costly to submit a planning application.[30] For example, in 2002 the Environment Agency (EA), a statutory consultee to the planning process, issued guidance to local planning authorities on 'Assessing the Groundwater Pollution of Cemetery Developments' that was subsequently revised and is now in its third edition.[31] This publication was based on research commissioned by the EA and published in 2002 – R&D Technical Report P223.[32] The guidance introduced a three-tiered approach to assessing the risk of pollution from burial. The tier 1 survey is essentially desk-based and aims to identify the vulnerability of groundwater to contamination, including boreholes, wells and springs.

It is likely that all new natural burial sites, depending on where they are located and their relationship to the water catchment and source water pro-tection zones, will need to complete a tier 2 survey as a minimum. This is considerably more onerous and costly and includes the excavation of trial pits, boreholes and quarterly sampling for at least a year before consent may be considered. Where a planning application is approved, there might also be con-ditions attached to the consent that require ongoing site monitoring. In addition to these costs there will be additional expense in commissioning consultants to conduct ecological field surveys and archaeological reports. For many providers, especially owners of small farms where the demand for burial is unknown, the economic return on the initial investment might be too uncertain and therefore too risky to warrant investment.

The data we have presented in this chapter therefore reveal a recent trend towards much larger independent sites where there is a greater potential eco-nomic return on the initial investment of establishing the burial ground, sites which might also include new buildings to accommodate staff and funerals. It could be suggested that this has happened as a consequence of the changes to the planning process. Related to the increasing scale of independent burial grounds, we have also observed a trend towards more complex interpretations of natural burial. These much larger sites often encompass a range of existing habitats that no longer fit comfortably into the design groupings we devised when we began our research. Burial ground developers have informed us that they are attracted to these more mature settings because they immediately convey to consumers a clear impression of an established nature rather than one reliant on the planting of trees or wildflowers following a burial that will only develop across time. This suggests that an ecologically driven commitment to creating a sustainable future environment is not the dominant motivation among consumers. Rather, the prospect of a 'beautiful place', already in existence, has proved attractive to bereaved people and indeed pre-purchasers.

The larger scale of recent independent sites also allows providers to offer a *choice* of different burial settings and prices. For example, GreenAcres Woodland Burials in Epping Forest, which opened in 2008, is 20 hectares in size and includes areas of mature oak woodland, coppiced sweet chestnut and hazel and open glades. Its ongoing management often requires woodland clearance and new tree planting to improve the species mix and habitat diversity. Several of the newer sites such as this one therefore straddle the different categories we originally devised, as they combine mature and new woodland planting with open burial glades.

2010 onwards

Comparison of our data with the list of sites maintained by the ANBG reveals that by March 2013 natural burial provision had increased by an additional 40 sites, thereby extending the total provision in the UK to 247 sites.[33] These new burial grounds echo the trend up to 2010, with ownership evenly divided between local authorities and independent providers.

We were unable to contact each of these new sites directly or amend our GIS to include their data, but we were able to confirm their details against the information on their websites. The breadth and quality of the information varied significantly between sites but, taken as a whole, the most noticeable difference was between the independent providers and the local authorities. The independent providers typically included a site history, design, a gallery of images, regulations and prices on their websites, whereas the local authority websites were generally very sparse in this respect and rarely went beyond identifying those cemeteries where an area had been allocated for natural burial.

Without contacting each site directly, it was not possible to determine the design interpretation or the ownership of independent sites within our groupings. What was striking, however, was that only a quarter of the new sites were members of the ANBG and that this fraction did not include any of the new local authority providers. This might suggest that, as natural burial has become more mainstream, providers no longer require the support or publicity that the ANBG provide. Local authority providers might also believe that, given their situation of having established cemeteries that offer different burial and cremation options, they are better serviced by the organisations to which they are already affiliated. The ICCM, for example, which provides support and training to local authority employees has developed its own 'Natural Burial Charter', which specifically aims to address the provision of 'natural burial within the "local authority context"'.[34] The Charter looks to reposition natural burial so that there is less of a focus on the site and greater emphasis on the treatment of the body and how each burial and grave can contribute towards a more sustainable future. Many of the larger independent sites are also members of the ICCM.

International context of natural burial

While not the focus of our research, there has also been considerable international interest in the UK Natural Burial Movement, reflected in the growing number of countries now providing natural burial in some form, including Australia, Germany, Japan, the Netherlands, New Zealand and North America. Here we identify a number of important developments that illustrate how the concept is continuing to evolve and be redefined in response to the different cultural, legal and environmental contexts each country represents.

The US was one of the first countries outside Britain to develop a natural burial alternative. Ramsey Creek Preserve, South Carolina opened in 1998 and is believed to be the first green burial site in the US.[35] Like many early providers of natural burial in the US, Ramsey Creek was focused on habitat preservation or, as it has become more widely known, 'conservation burial'. The conservation burial sites were critical of how natural burial had been interpreted in the UK on the grounds of their limited ecological contribution: 'most of the projects in the UK are so small – often less than 5 acres – or are located so haphazardly they fail to achieve even modest conservation goals'.[36] In North America there is an acute awareness of the damage that non-native species can have on native habitats and ecosystems. While these concerns are also applicable to the UK, there is considerable debate over how native and non-native species are defined as well as their potential to deliver environmental benefits.[37]

The Natural Burial Movement has grown at a rapid pace in North America and the Green Burial Council (GBC), an independent organisation that promotes natural burial, has identified over 300 approved funeral and cemetery providers.[38] In 2011 the GBC introduced an ecological rating for burial grounds that is similar to the ecological classification that Ken West proposed to the NDC ten years earlier. Sites are assessed against a range of environmental objectives and assigned one of three categories: hybrid burial grounds; natural burial grounds; and conservation burial grounds. The most demanding assessment is reserved for 'conservation burial grounds', which is set above 'natural burial' and must include a partnership with a recognised conservation organisation that guarantees long-term stewardship of the land.

In Germany there are much stricter laws than in the UK, and burial is only permitted in a cemetery.[39] In 2001 the Friedwald Company gained approval to open the first new woodland cemetery at Reinhardwald near Hesse. Unlike Germany's established woodland cemeteries, these new sites only permit the burial of cremated remains.

This interpretation of natural burial has developed rapidly throughout Germany, and, at the time of writing, there are in excess of 100 similar woodland sites that are managed by two companies, Friedwald and Ruheforst.[40] While this interpretation presents a new alternative within the German context, when compared with the UK, where people have for many years routinely strewn ashes in public and national parks and nature reserves, this development might not be viewed as either alternative or new, nor indeed ecological given that they accept cremated remains.

In the Netherlands the burial laws are more relaxed than Germany, and, while considerably fewer in number, there are sites that permit natural burial and the interment of ashes.[41] A report to explore the potential long-term legacy of natural burial in the Dutch landscape was commissioned by the Netherlands Architecture Fund and produced by Vollmers and Partners in 2011. It suggests a much more ambitious and coherent approach to natural burial provision on a national scale.[42] Designs that respond to different local contexts within a national framework provide an opportunity for natural burial to contribute to sustainable objectives that extend far beyond a site-specific approach, such as increasing green infrastructure and improving public access to recreation space.

Demand for natural burial in the UK

There are no national records maintained for the number of burials or interments of ashes at natural burial sites in the UK. In contrast, the Cremation Society has detailed accounts that chart the development of cremation in Britain from 1885, when the first cremation took place at Woking Crematorium.[43] This record is an extremely valuable resource that allows a clear picture to be presented of the changing demand for cremation at both a national and regional scale when set against annual mortality figures.[44]

In 2009 we wrote to each of the 20 natural burial sites we had surveyed with a request for their annual burial figures for the period 2002–2008. Ten sites responded, all of which were in England. These included three local authorities, two charitable trusts, three farms and two private companies. While we recognise that this is only a small sample, in the absence of any other data it does provide at least some indication of demand and how this might vary between providers.

Our data suggest that the public response to natural burial was more positive than it was for cremation when that was first introduced. Woking Crematorium performed only three cremations in its first year in 1885. In contrast, there were seven natural burials at Carlisle in 1994, its first full year of opening. By 1905, 20 years after the first cremation at Woking, there were 13 crematoria in the UK that in total had completed 569 cremations, 0.1 per cent of the total number of deaths in that year.[45] The aggregate data for just ten natural burial sites in 2007, 14 years after Carlisle opened, was 641 interments that included 404 burials and 237 interments of cremated remains. If we take the average number of burials (not including cremated remains) for each of our ownership groupings and multiply this figure by the number of sites in the corresponding group for England and Wales, the total figure represents approximately 1 per cent of all burials in England and Wales in 2007. Cremation only reached this threshold in England and Wales in 1932, almost half a century after its introduction.[46]

Caution should be taken in reading too much into our figure for natural burial; as noted, it relies on a small sample that also excludes the contribution that is being made by other providers not represented in the response, sites managed by funeral directors and landowner/company partnerships. However, while there are some discrepancies in calculating the total number of natural burial sites (at the time of writing, ANBG have this at over 260 and a recent article published in the *ICCM Journal* records 274 sites[47]), it is interesting to note that the provision is now close to or exceeds the total number of UK crematoria, which was 266 in 2012.[48]

Figure 2.14 shows the breakdown of natural burial and ash interments and the combined figures for this six-year period. In this relatively short time frame the total number of natural burials more than doubled. This increase in demand should be understood in the broader context of mortality rates which fell between 1994 and 2008: there was a 9.8 per cent reduction in the total number of deaths – a fall of nearly 50,000. Thus, although the total number of burials has declined, natural burials have continued to increase.

What is also striking about Figure 2.14 is the proportion of interments of cremated remains in natural burial sites, which accounts for approximately one-third of all interments. This has taken place in the context of an increase in the proportion of dispersals via cremation: from 71.8 per cent to 75 per cent during the time period in question.[49]

We had not anticipated this given the environmental arguments that have been made against cremation.[50] What is noticeable in our data is that the proportion of ash interments at private company sites was twice that of burial. From a purely commercial perspective it makes little financial sense to exclude ashes when 75 per cent of all bodies are cremated. Ashes plots or the scattering of ashes is also a more affordable option and enables managers, especially in mature woodland sites, to use areas that might not otherwise be suitable for burial. Perhaps conscious of the potential contradictions that natural burial may raise for some consumers, providers at these sites are cautious to promote natural burial as an environmentally responsible alternative to cremation,

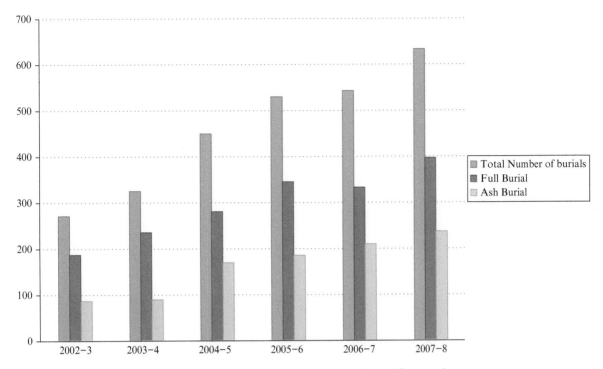

Figure 2.14 *Burial data from ten natural burial sites shows an increase in demand for natural burial and a growing proportion of ash interments.*

instead focusing on the landscape and how this is managed to create habitat and a sustainable resource.

Figure 2.15 shows the average burial numbers (not including ashes) for each of the different providers from 2002–2003 to 2007–2008. What is apparent is the significantly higher number of interments in the private company and charitable trust sites when compared with local authorities and farms. This finding is certainly supported by the data from our interviews at other burial sites. As we have already identified from our database, private company and charitable trust sites are invariably much larger burial grounds that offer a range of different burial settings and facilities and are usually permanently staffed. In terms of the sites that we are reporting on here, with the exception of one private company, all were already established sites in 2002, the date from which we requested burial figures. These same sites also recorded similar trends in the numbers of pre-purchased graves. The decline in private company interments for 2007–2008 was explained by one of the managers, who said this was in response to a significant price increase imposed to control demand for increasingly scarce grave space.

Two of the three local authorities' natural burial sites are small and set within the existing cemetery. Burial rates have slowly increased, but remain fewer than 20 per year and occasionally drop below 10. The remaining site is Carlisle and, as we have already indicated, this is a much larger and more established burial space. The burial records show that demand slowly increased up until 2000 and for the last ten years has been consistently in the mid to high 30s

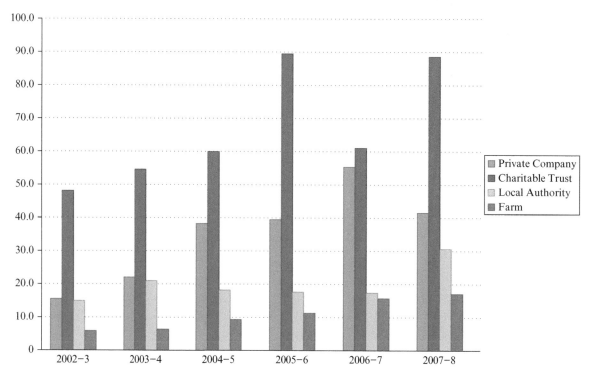

Figure 2.15 *Graph showing the average number of burials at ten English natural burial sites 2002–2007.*

Note: *Farm data for 2002 is based on one site, while, for other years, the data is based on three sites.*

and occasionally mid 40s per year. Ashes are also accepted and the proportion of these varies at 10–20 per cent of natural burials from year to year.

Two of the three farm sites included in this data opened in 2003 and therefore do not contribute to the 2002 records. They are all relatively small sites located in rural communities. Two of these sites consistently have 8–14 burials per year. The third site shows a gradual increase in burials and exceeded 20 in 2006. These sites are typical of this group in that they offer no additional services or provision to host a funeral.

Summary

The data presented in this chapter raise a number of questions. For example, has natural burial – which began as a response to addressing the challenges of increasing cemetery maintenance costs, environmental degradation and a request from the public for a more simple and less costly alternative – become an additional consumer option and business opportunity? To what extent do those who choose and provide this option embrace its ecological ideals? Is the beautiful landscape simply a more appealing environment than the crematorium or municipal cemetery and its more conventional material culture of death?

Certainly we can see from our GIS data how quickly the concept developed by Ken West has travelled and been reinterpreted as new providers develop alternative ideas of what it means to bury naturally. Nationally, demand is still small, but at a local level it can be very significant, especially at some of the larger independent sites where the number of burials has increased year on year.

In the following chapters we show the diversity of motivations for natural burial among providers and users, both pre-purchasers and bereaved people, as well as death care professionals. As the design and production of these landscapes continues to evolve – and to offer greater choice and service – the complex, dynamic and negotiated processes, which together constitute 'natural burial, as concept, burial site and practice', become more available for analysis.

3

The landscape of natural burial and motivations of providers

Having established the broader UK picture of natural burial in Chapter 2, we now move into the landscape of natural burial as we explore how it is being interpreted on the ground and developed through practice. This next phase of our research included visiting 20 natural burial grounds in England and Wales and interviewing owners and managers. The sites were selected from our database and included the breadth of different types of ownership and approaches to the design and management that we had identified. At the time of our research, this sample represented approximately 10 per cent of all UK natural burial grounds. It also included established sites that had been operating for a number of years and burial grounds that had opened more recently. They would provide an opportunity to investigate how practice was shaping the natural burial landscape and how new providers were learning from the experience of others. By visiting and photographing these sites we also wanted to understand how bereaved people were engaging with landscape and what influence they had on the appearance and management of the burial ground. In addition, as Chapter 6 discusses, we wanted to understand how the burial ground landscape shaped their experience of loss.

From the 20 sites we visited, four were chosen to be the focus of more detailed research. They included: a local authority woodland burial ground set within an established municipal cemetery; a farm where the burial meadow is managed by a husband and wife; an independent funeral director who owns a small woodland burial ground; and a charitable trust that among its environmental and educational activities also manages its own mature woodland burial ground. At each of these sites we interviewed: bereaved people, clergy and celebrants, funeral directors, gravediggers and, where appropriate, people who lived near the site. The data from each of these four burial grounds provide the main focus for discussion in this and each of the chapters that follow.

The chapter is divided into two sections. We begin by providing a description and illustrations of each of the four burial grounds so the reader has a context in which to locate the discussions that follow in this and subsequent chapters. The chapter then considers what motivated each of these providers to open a natural burial site; here we also draw on data from our wider sample of 20 burial grounds.

Setting the scene: introduction to the four research sites

Site one: Woodland Burial Ground, Wisewood Cemetery, Sheffield, South Yorkshire

Wisewood Cemetery was opened in 1934 and is managed by Sheffield City Council Bereavement Services. It is a comparatively large cemetery of eight hectares (16 acres) and is located on the north-west edge of the city, in the Loxley valley. The cemetery is accessed from the main road through a gated entrance, which includes a single-storey red-brick lodge. From the entrance a tree-lined avenue leads down into the cemetery, which takes the form of a large rectangular south-facing space, surrounded by open fields and overlooking a wooded

access road

traditional graves

adjacent fields

tarmac path

woodland burial

cemetery boundary

adjacent fields

0 _____ 25m

Figure 3.1 *Wisewood Woodland Burial Ground, Wisewood Cemetery, Sheffield.*

Figure 3.2 *View looking towards the Woodland Burial section and wooded valley beyond, across an area of traditional graves (Wisewood, November 2013).*

valley. The cemetery is formally set out with a large circular tarmac drive that provides the principal access for vehicles and combines with a narrower rectangular grid of roads. Together these define the burial sections. The character of the cemetery is essentially an open lawned landscape, visually dominated by headstones and occasionally interspersed with mature trees. A large informal hedge that includes mature trees and a fence to keep out livestock defines the perimeter of the cemetery. In 1996 a woodland burial area was opened at the edge of the cemetery in a burial section that had not yet been used.

The woodland burial ground, which we subsequently refer to as Wisewood, is located in the south-west corner of the cemetery. It is approximately half a hectare (one acre) in size, a rectangular plot that is defined by the tarmac access roads that enclose it. At the entrance there is a wooden sign, 'Wisewood Woodland Burial Ground', which is set against an informal cluster of semi-mature trees and shrubs. By 2010 there had been approximately 150 burials, of which about 30 per cent were interments of cremated remains. When the woodland section first opened, there was very little demand; but in the past ten years this has gradually increased and there are now 8–15 burials per year.

The character of the woodland burial ground changes significantly throughout the year and is noticeably different to the adjacent burial sections where traditional headstones and kerb sets predominate. In winter, the grass in the woodland burial ground is short and the graves, which are formally set out on a grid, are far more visible. Each one is planted with a native tree and there is also a stone plaque, laid flat on the grave and inscribed with the name of the deceased. The memorial trees are mostly small, each one secured by a tall wooden stake. Species include: rowan, white beam, ash, alder and silver birch. In summer, when the trees are in leaf and the grass has grown to waist height, the burial ground takes on a very different identity. Individual graves are less visible and the emerging woodland becomes more evident and distinct from the rest of the cemetery. There is, however, evidence of individual graves where bereaved people have resisted seasonal change and 'a return to nature'. On these graves the grass is kept short by regular cutting; there may also be bedding plants in summer, with slate or bark chippings used to suppress the grass and ornaments and plastic and cut flowers added (see Figure 3.3).

Figure 3.3 *A neat lawn has been maintained around the grave and a small wooden home-made bench has been placed beside it (Wisewood, June 2009).*

Site two: Green Lane Burial Field and Nature Reserve, Abermule, Montgomery, Mid Wales

Green Lane Burial Field was opened in 2003 on a farm near the village of Abermule in Mid Wales. From here on we refer to this burial ground as Abermule. The farm, which is predominantly managed for cattle and sheep, is owned by Ifor and Eira Humphreys. The burial ground is approximately half a hectare (one acre) in size and is part of a much larger 4.5 hectare (11 acre) field which includes steeply wooded slopes of oak, ash, cherry, rowan, hazel and gorse. When our research concluded in 2010, there had been approximately 110 burials, of which less than 10 per cent were cremated remains. Burial numbers have continued to increase year on year from one burial in 2003 to approximately 30 burials in 2011.

Access is via a narrow lane that also services the farm directly opposite the burial ground (see Figure 3.4). At the entrance a large wooden gate and sign mark a drive that leads down the hillside to a small parking area at the foot of the burial field. To the left of the drive a steep bank is partially covered in gorse and an avenue of young trees; to the right the land falls away sharply to

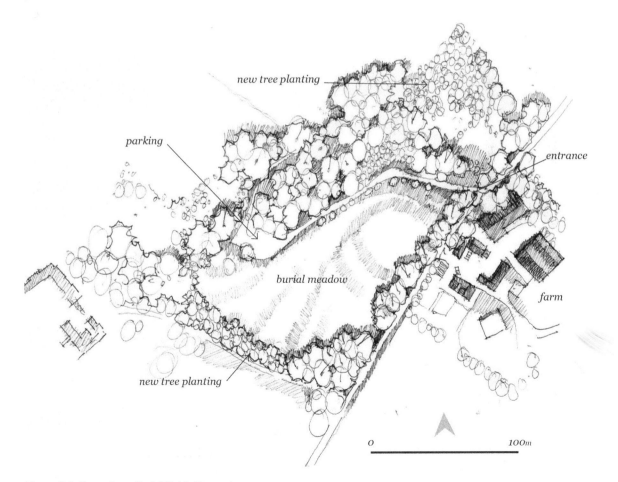

Figure 3.4 *Green Lane Burial Field, Abermule.*

Figure 3.5 *Looking out from the top of the field, near to the lane that separates the burial ground from the farm, the only evidence of any graves is the occasional cluster of daffodils (Abermule, April 2008).*

woodland, allowing open views across the valley. The burial field itself rises gently at first and then begins to climb away from the parking area, where there is a picnic table and a track that leads down into the woodland nature reserve. Mature trees partly contain the burial field with a hedge running alongside the road at the top of the field and so forming its skyline. On the far side of the burial ground a large and imposing detached house is partially screened by trees and a belt of new woodland planted by Ifor and Eira with the support of a woodland grant. Standing at the top of the field there are excellent views across the Severn valley to the surrounding hills – something bereaved people commented on in their interviews. At the time of our first visit in spring there had been approximately 50 burials, but there was almost no evidence of any of these graves, apart from the occasional cluster of daffodils. Closer inspection did, however, reveal small round stones that had been painted with the grave number and pushed into the turf. Without prior knowledge of their existence they would remain unnoticed. Around the perimeter of the burial field some of the newly planted trees have a large oak peg at their base, onto which a memorial plaque has been fixed. There is also the occasional memorial bench placed within this woodland edge.

Site three: South Yorkshire Woodland Burial Ground, Ulley, Rotherham, South Yorkshire

The South Yorkshire Woodland Burial Ground was opened in 1995 in farmland between the cities of Sheffield and Rotherham. It is owned by Peace Funerals, an independent funeral directors business with premises in Sheffield. From here on we refer to this site as Ulley – the name of the nearby village. The burial ground

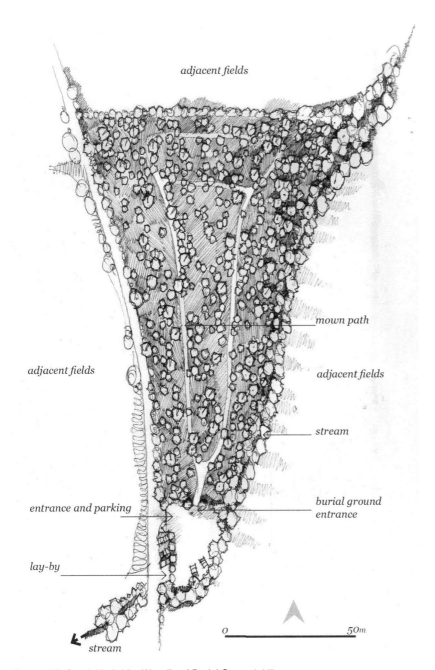

adjacent fields

adjacent fields

adjacent fields

mown path

stream

entrance and parking

burial ground
entrance

lay-by

stream

0 ————————————— 50m

Figure 3.6 *South Yorkshire Woodland Burial Ground, Ulley.*

is 1.2 hectares (3 acres) in size. When our research project concluded in 2010 there had been approximately 450 burials, of which a third were interments of cremated remains. In recent years the number of burials has gradually increased to an average of 50 each year.

Access to the burial ground is from a narrow lane that connects the villages of Ulley and Aston cum Aughton (see Figure 3.6). At the site entrance there is

Figure 3.7 *At the entrance to the burial ground there is a large sign and a car park which has recently been landscaped to increase the available parking (Ulley, November 2011).*

a car park and a large sign bearing the name of the burial ground and contact details for Peace Funerals (see Figure 3.7). From here, the visitor walks between two yew trees that mark the entrance to the burial ground, and from there a mown path makes a large loop through the woodland (see Figure 3.8). In 2010, in response to the need for more parking, Peace Funerals had the entrance area re-landscaped, which has increased the parking provision and opened up the view into the burial ground from the road.

In some respects Ulley is very similar to Wisewood in that most graves are marked with a tree and a stone plaque and there is similar evidence of personal memorialisation in the form of cards and small items placed on graves or attached to the memorial trees. Fields also surround this site, and, like Wisewood, its appearance and character changes with the passing seasons – which we explore in more detail in our longitudinal study of this site in Chapter 8. Beyond these similarities, however, Ulley is quite different in that it is not contained within a traditional cemetery with its familiar context of buildings, roads and gravestones, set out in a formal grid. The space allocated for woodland burial at Ulley is also much larger and appears more coherent and established as it blends with its rural surroundings. Many of the trees are much larger and more widely dispersed across the site; some of the older oaks, ash and willows are over 10 metres high, with broad canopies. Ulley has also had approximately four times as many burials, and in consequence its woodland has a much greater impact, than at Wisewood. In some areas the trees have begun to merge with one another, their summer canopies combining to enclose spaces and create smaller, private 'rooms' within the burial ground. Indeed, the character of the woodland

Figure 3.8 *The entrance to the burial ground from the car park is defined by two yew trees (Ulley, December 2010).*

itself is very different. While Wisewood has a mixture of familiar native trees, Ulley adds many different ornamental varieties that one might see in the local park or a neighbour's garden to this mix:[1] a monkey puzzle, a Christmas tree, different varieties of fruit tree and many dwarf weeping willows. The mown path also encourages the visitor to walk within this burial ground, and the site feels more enclosed with its mature hedge and earth bank and a small stream flowing along the eastern edge. Importantly, the layout of graves themselves also appears less formal than Wisewood, with new and old graves appearing side by side.

Site four: South Downs Natural Burial Site, the Sustainability Centre, East Meon, Petersfield, Hampshire

The South Downs Natural Burial Site was opened in 2001 and is managed by staff at the Sustainability Centre, a charity owned by the Earthworks Trust, which was established in 1995. The Sustainability Centre is located in the South Downs National Park and near to the village of East Meon. From here on we refer to this burial ground as East Meon. The land originally belonged to the Ministry of Defence (MoD) and was the home of the Royal Navy's Communication Branch and Special Communications Unit, HMS *Mercury*. In 1993 the MoD closed the site, which was then taken on by Hampshire County Council who developed part of it as an education centre. In 1995 the ownership and management was transferred to the Earthworks Trust, an independent charity who provide environmental training courses and activities for school

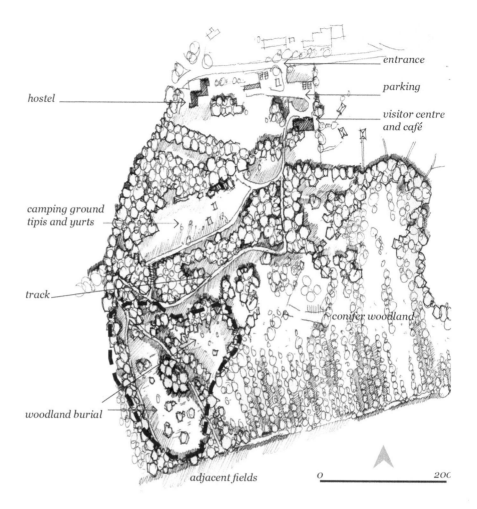

hostel

entrance

parking

visitor centre
and café

camping ground
tipis and yurts

track

conifer woodland

woodland burial

adjacent fields

0   200

Figure 3.9 *South Downs Natural Burial Site, East Meon.*

groups and adults. The site covers a total area of 22 hectares (55 acres) and
is predominantly conifer woodland, some native broadleaf trees and natural
chalk downland. Within this area there are a number of buildings that originally
belonged to the MoD and, at the time of our study, were used by the Trust as a
visitor centre and hostel for school groups and adults attending courses at the
centre or for visitors to the area. Approximately 2.4 hectares in size (6 acres),
the burial ground is set within the woodland. When our research concluded in
2010 there had been approximately 700 burials, of which a small percentage
(less than 5 per cent) were interments of cremated remains. Unlike many of the
sites we have visited, where the initial public response was muted, demand grew
quickly at East Meon and in recent years has exceeded 100 burials per year.

At the entrance to the Sustainability Centre there is a car park and visitor
centre, which is a large, single-storey brick building. The Centre has a lively
and informal atmosphere and includes a reception, offices, café, meeting rooms
and display boards highlighting the various activities of the Trust. From there,

Figure 3.10 *Walking down to the burial ground, visitors pass the camping field with its collection of timber-frame buildings, tipis and yurts (East Meon, July 2008).*

it is approximately a ten-minute walk to the burial ground along a track that is wide enough to accommodate a four-wheel drive vehicle. The track passes beneath mature broadleaf woodland before opening out into a large open field that includes tipis, yurts and a cluster of traditional timber-frame buildings in various stages of completion (see Figure 3.10). This is the centre's camping ground and event space. From here the track narrows and steepens as it descends into denser woodland planting of conifers and some deciduous and native evergreen trees. A small wooden sign, '*South Downs Natural Burial Site*', set to one side of the path, is the first indication that the visitor is entering a burial ground. This site feels far more enclosed and sheltered than Wisewood, Ulley or Abermule. Only to the south do the trees and landform give way to views across the adjacent fields and South Downs. On either side of the track a series of open glades includes new tree planting set among more established deciduous trees (see Figure 3.11). Within each of these glades, neat earth mounds show both the location and orientation of each grave; and, although there are new trees planted between the graves, no stone or wooden plaques stand to mark the graves. While there is evidence of memorialisation, it is different from that which we have seen at the other burial grounds and is almost entirely made from objects gathered within the burial ground and adjacent woodland, including: sticks, leaves, flowers, fir cones and lumps of white chalk. On some graves these have been arranged to form a name, a small cairn or a crucifix. While there is very little evidence of any planting or 'gardening' of graves , some have been cleared of the encroaching woodland plants. Closer inspection also reveals occasional personal items such as pieces of glass and crystal placed on the grave,

Figure 3.11 *Areas of forest plantation have been cleared and, between the graves, native broadleaf trees have been planted (East Meon, April 2008).*

or suspended on a makeshift frame of small branches above it. Within the burial ground there is also a grove of mature yew trees, which creates a very different and distinctive character from that of the rest of the site. In the deep shade of these trees and clear of any woodland plants, the mounds of each grave are more visible and prominent.

What is the motivation to open a natural burial ground?

As we have already observed, one of the most significant features of the Natural Burial Movement in the UK has been the introduction of a disparate group of new providers, many of whom had little or no previous experience of managing a burial ground, caring for the dead or working with bereaved people. What is so appealing about 'natural burial' that would motivate someone to make a commitment that may well extend beyond their own lifetime and therefore be passed on to those who inherit or purchase the land, a commitment that fundamentally changes the owner's relationship with the land, how it is managed and who has rights of access? The private landowner or farmer, for example, who may be accustomed to having little contact with the general public, fundamentally changes this relationship by opening a burial ground and inviting the dead and bereaved people into and onto their land.[2]

In the following sections, we explore the motivations of each of the following groups of providers: local authorities, farmers, funeral directors, charitable trusts, independent landowners and private companies. Our discussion includes the four main research sites that we have introduced and also uses data gathered from our interviews with burial ground managers from other sites. We should, however, note it was not always possible to speak with those who had been responsible, at the outset, for developing the natural burial ground since some had retired or moved on. While providers who had taken over this responsibility were typically familiar with how their site had initially been developed, one manager at a small private site described the potential vulnerability of burial grounds to a change in staff and ownership. Similarly the character of the burial ground might change significantly when new ownership is in place. When a small private site we visited had been sold for example, the new staff adopted a more relaxed approach to memorialisation that permitted a tree and a headstone and no obvious restrictions on grave marking.

Local authorities

Local authorities own more than 50 per cent of all UK natural burial grounds and were early adopters in providing this burial alternative. They were able to respond quickly to providing this new burial alternative for a number of reasons. First, local authority staff with responsibility for managing cemeteries were alert to the developments that were taking place at Carlisle through their professional associations, journals and conferences. For example, in the interviews with bereavement staff at Ribble Valley Borough Council, which manages Waddington Road Cemetery in Clitheroe, staff said the motivation for opening a woodland burial section in 1995 came from attending a conference that was hosted by the Institute of Burial and Cremation Administration (IBCA).[3] Following the conference they submitted a proposal to their department committee, which approved opening a small woodland section on a trial basis. While demand has been modest it has slowly increased, and in 2000 the woodland section was extended. It is interesting to note that the initial approval was on a trial basis only, which perhaps suggests a different mindset between some local authority providers and independently managed natural burial sites. For local authorities the land is already committed for burial, irrespective of what type of burial this might be. If the demand for natural burial does not materialise, it is relatively simple to limit the area of the natural burial section and return to more traditional practices. For the private landowner, farmer or charitable trust, the decision to open a new burial ground has far greater consequences in terms of restricting how the land will be used in the future and who may access it. For example, where next of kin have also pre-purchased a grave, the legal obligation to maintain the burial ground may extend many decades into the future.

Second, and as we have discussed in Chapter 2, in 1996 the IBCA introduced the Charter for the Bereaved. The Charter was published in response to adverse criticism of modern funeral practices and out of a desire to provide greater clarity about the procedures and services that bereaved people should expect. The Charter also incorporated *Rights*, which Charter members would promise to support, and *Targets* that members would consider developing in the future. While the Charter came after the decision to provide a woodland burial option at Sheffield and Ribble Valley, it was important in that it specifically promoted natural burial, which other local authorities subsequently responded to. The Charter states that: 'Charter members should expand grave choice to enable the bereaved to obtain individuality and some element of choice. The standard should include a minimum of three graves types, e.g. lawn, traditional and a natural option, such as woodland burial.'[4]

Third, local authorities were able to respond quickly because they had land within their existing cemeteries that they could choose to develop as a natural burial alternative. The infrastructure and support services were also in place, and there was no need to obtain planning consent as the land had already been approved for burial. Each of the three local-authority-managed sites that we visited fits with this model of selecting a relatively small area of land, less than half a hectare (one acre), that is discretely located towards the periphery of a larger, established cemetery where land was available. While there are a number of purpose-built, local-authority-managed natural burial sites, which include Lentons Lane in Coventry (see Chapter 4) and High Wood Cemetery in Nottinghamshire, at the time of our study these were rare.

Many local authorities were also acutely aware of their responsibility to develop the service they provide to their community and ratepayers. In the early 1990s the public were becoming increasingly alert to this alternative burial option through the media coverage and activities of the Natural Death Centre. Sheffield Bereavement Services, who manage Wisewood Cemetery, were keen to explore how they might develop the service they provide to the public and employed a customer services officer to research different burial and funeral options. This resulted in two initiatives: a woodland burial ground and an independent funeral option where Bereavement Services would support the family in conducting their own funeral without the assistance of a funeral director. Our interview with the Bereavement Services manager at Sheffield highlighted their concern not to appear out of touch with new developments in burial provision: '*Others were providing woodland burial, so we thought right, you know, not wanting to lose out here or be behind the times we will move on with the woodland site.*'

While the financial benefits of natural burial, in terms of the reduced maintenance costs, were not raised by research participants, it was an important factor in shaping Ken West's original vision of providing an economically sustainable burial service. Most local authorities do not generate sufficient funds from their cemeteries to cover their cemetery maintenance costs but instead rely on income that is generated from cremation to subsidise the maintenance of their cemeteries. Natural burial provides a more cost-effective burial option due to the reduced maintenance costs and also enables authorities to develop areas within their cemeteries that may not have been suitable for traditional burial. For example, at Allerton Cemetery in Liverpool, the local authority designated a strip of mature woodland planting for natural burial. This land was not originally intended for interments but was part of the original structure of planting of the cemetery, helping to subdivide it into different sections. Through natural burial this woodland strip has become an asset that increases burial space and therefore income, while also providing choice for the community.

A number of local authorities have also seized on the opportunity to develop their existing areas of public or unpurchased graves for natural burial. These graves have traditionally been associated with the poor who could not afford a purchased or private grave. Since local authorities do not permit a memorial to be erected on a public grave, this restriction becomes a virtue within a natural burial regime and also enables authorities to generate income from these graves. The absence of any memorialisation has also been seen as an opportunity to provide graves in cemeteries with high conservation value as a result of the coherent quality of their landscape, buildings and memorialisation.[5] Natural burial therefore allows the authority to use this grave space without the concern that a new headstone and memorialisation will disrupt the character of the existing cemetery.

Farmers

Ifor and Eira Humphries own and manage the natural burial ground at Abermule, one of our four study sites. Ifor first became aware of natural burial in 1994 when he heard a radio interview with John Bradfield, who was discussing his recently published book, *Green Burial: the D-I-Y guide to Law and Practice*.[6] Ifor recalled how the idea of a green burial interested him sufficiently to order a copy of the book immediately. On reading it, he was even more impressed by the idea and particularly taken by '*how few rules and regulations there actually are, so that, that appealed to me*'. Ifor said he was not religious and spoke of his dissatisfaction with some of the funerals that he had attended for friends who shared his lack of a faith. The traditional service, he felt, was still caught up in a '*religious package*'. The idea of not being buried in the churchyard or cemetery was also familiar to Ifor, who was aware of other farmers who had been buried on their own land.

Each of the farmers we spoke with said their initial awareness and interest in natural burial was sparked by media coverage. Like Ifor, they recalled catching a programme on the radio or television or reading an article in the papers. Alan Willey, a Northumberland farmer who manages Seven Penny Meadow with his wife and son, jokingly recalled how he had '*been daft enough to watch a programme on* Countryfile' which had featured a farmer who had opened a natural burial ground on his land.[7] The owners of several of the small, independent burial grounds that we visited also mentioned this programme – which is targeted at the rural community and those with an interest in farming and nature – as the initial catalyst that sparked their interest in natural burial. Along with the relative lack of regulations, the potential to diversify farm income was an important motivation for each of the farmers we interviewed. The farms we visited were relatively small – typically less than 150 hectares (300 acres) – and their owners were interested in exploring different ways to generate income from their land.

For almost a decade, due to financial and time constraints, Ifor was not in a position to act on his initial enthusiasm for natural burial. His circumstance changed, however, when he married Eira; and, after the birth of their first child, they were faced with a choice of whether Eira should return to her role as manager of a dress shop in the local town or stay on the farm. The decision to open a burial ground enabled them to identify a role for Eira, who wanted to stay and work on the farm and be with their child and, as Ifor said, '*to use the resources*' that were available to them. They had land and Ifor was confident he had the practical skills and machinery required to manage the burial ground. He also recognised that he did not have Eira's experience of working with the public and what he described as her skills in '*customer relations*'. This is an important point as there is a danger of naïvely assuming that the farmer is an individual male with sole responsibility for initiating, implementing and then managing the burial ground along with the other activities of the farm. This was not our experience. At each of the farms we visited, we observed a collaborative effort that often included other members of the family. The motivation to open a burial ground was therefore typically supported by this wider group and drew on their different experiences and skills. At three of the farms and smallholdings we visited, the women were employed or had been employed in the medical profession, either in nursing or in an administrative capacity. They each recognised that their familiarity with working in hospitals with sick and bereaved people had given them confidence and informed their decision to open a burial ground.

The environmental contribution of the burial ground to the farm and countryside also emerged as a key motivation for farmers. Ifor talked of the tension between commercial farming and conserving and improving habitat and nature. He saw natural burial as an opportunity to reconcile the need to generate income with an environmentally sensitive approach:

> as a farmer we'd all . . . like to be conservationists but equally we need to make money as well, so . . . there's a conflict. . . . By putting these two together, by people giving us money it's, it's cross-subsidising the site as a nature reserve and that's how it's evolving really, the bluebells and snowdrops and primroses, what else, there's all sorts of things there already as part of woodland plants and we've tried to create a hay meadow on the burial area itself which will be interesting to people as well as ourselves.
>
> (Ifor Humphreys, Abermule)

Alan Willey and Martin Chatfield, of Seven Penny Meadow and Crossways natural burial grounds, respectively, had similar motivations. Alan perceived it as an opportunity to restore an area of improved pasture where the land had been fertilised to increase productivity, but, as a consequence, this had reduced the species diversity. His intention was to return it back to a '*sort of old-fashioned meadow*' that would be richer in native species. Martin had aspirations to recreate what he referred to as a '*Devon Wood*' of local native species that he would supply from his own small tree nursery.

Alongside these environmental and economic motivations, there was also evidence of a personal agenda. Like many of our bereaved and focus group participants, farmers such as Martin had found attending a service at a crematorium '*so impersonal*', as he said of his father's funeral. It was this that had motivated him and his wife to take action and open a burial ground, along with the request of a close friend who was terminally ill and who wished to be buried on their land.

Funeral directors

Natural burial grounds that are managed by funeral directors represent a small yet significant number of UK sites. Of the 20 burial grounds that we visited, four of the sites were owned and managed by companies which were also independent funeral directors. It is perhaps not surprising that funeral directors are interested in extending their service, for, although they may not own land or have the farmers' experience and resources to manage the land, they are accustomed to working with bereaved people as well as caring for the dead, and they are also familiar with some of the practicalities of working in cemeteries. Like local authority Bereavement Services, funeral directors share a network of professional associations, journals and annual conferences that alerted them to new developments in the profession. As we also discovered from our interviews with funeral directors, natural burial had become a frequent topic of conversation in both their professional and private lives, as family and friends wanted to find out more about this new burial alternative. While there is, of course, the significant limitation of not owning land, it is surprising that, given their pivotal role in the industry, funeral directors have not made a greater impact as natural burial providers. One important reason for this may be that the industry was initially very concerned about the impact of a low-cost DIY disposal option and the effect this might have on their business. There were also concerns that this was an inappropriate way of disposing of the dead, one that bore associations with the deeply stigmatised pauper burial.

For the established funeral directors we spoke to, however, developing their business by an extension of their services was clearly an important motivation. William Hall, who opened Springwood Woodland Burials on the Isle of Wight in 1995, one of the first privately owned sites in the UK, had alternative motivations and a unique personal circumstance that enabled him to make the transition to burial provider. His family had owned a plant nursery and land that had been used for growing 'pick your own' soft fruits. Access to land, alongside knowledge and skills in horticulture and land management, were instrumental in enabling him to act quickly in developing a burial ground. William also recognised from his experience of being a funeral director on the island that the demographic of the Isle of Wight, which includes a high proportion of elderly people who have retired to the island, meant people were frequently geographically removed from their families and traditional places of burial. Natural burial, with its emphasis on developing a shared memorial landscape, would also release the family from the responsibility of visiting and maintaining the grave.

John Mallatratt, Director of Peace Funerals and owner of the woodland burial ground at Ulley, came to both funeral directing and natural burial later in life while looking for a new challenge, direction and purpose. Dissatisfied with his work in further education and frustrated by his experience of attending the funerals of close family and friends – where he felt on reflection that the family '*should have had more control over what happened, we could have made it a bit more significant for us*' – he was motivated to investigate what he described as an '*alternative funeral director*'. His understanding of 'alternative' was initially informed via the media, which had also raised his awareness of woodland burial. The idea appealed to him and he conducted further research by visiting sites and making contact with the Natural Death Centre (NDC). His wife Mary, who had trained as a nurse and social worker, also supported John's enthusiasm. In 1995 they jointly established Peace Funerals and soon after opened the burial ground at Ulley. From our experience, establishing a burial ground and funeral directing business in parallel is uncommon, but this is perhaps a reflection of the way in which John and Mary developed their understanding of an alternative funeral and burial service through their previous work experience and the fact that they owned neither premises nor land. For them, an important part of providing an alternative funeral service was also centred on providing an alternative burial.

As the Natural Burial Movement continues to evolve, we might expect an increase in the number of sites that are owned by funeral directors. Several of the managers we spoke to considered this as a future possibility. To varying degrees they were already taking on parts of this role by assisting families in collecting and transporting the deceased, contributing to and providing advice on the funeral service and, in a small number of cases, helping the family to prepare the body for burial. Through their contact with the public and bereaved people, they had become aware of an expectation that they should also provide this service.

Burial ground managers also recognised that funeral directors played an important role as gatekeepers when informing the public of the different burial and cremation options that were available. Ray Ward, who jointly owns and manages Herongate Wood burial ground with his daughter and son-in-law, felt compelled to also provide a funeral directing service when demand for their burial ground did not materialise. In developing their proposal for the burial ground, Ray contacted local funeral directors in order to gauge if, in their opinion, there was public interest in natural burial and whether it was a service they would support. Having received an encouraging response from the funeral directors, they decided to proceed with their plans. While reflecting on the service they now provide, Ray told us that part of their success is what he described as 'the continuity of care' that they can provide to bereaved people. This care extends beyond the immediate needs of collecting the deceased, arranging and delivering the funeral, and it can potentially be maintained through an ongoing relationship at the burial ground.

Charitable trusts

The South Downs Natural Burial Site at East Meon is one of approximately half a dozen UK natural burial sites that were managed by a charitable trust at the time of our research. While small in number, they each represent a very distinctive approach to natural burial. Several of these trusts have recognised the potential of providing burial to achieve other objectives that extend beyond the preservation or reinstatement of a particular habitat. By harnessing public demand for natural burial and the income that this can generate, they seek to achieve wider environmental and community goals. The Earth Works Trust, which has overall responsibility for managing the burial ground at East Meon, was established by a group of enthusiasts to promote sustainability and provide environmental education and training. Al Blake, who manages the burial ground and is employed by the Trust, commented that 'the money that comes from the burial site is piled into our educational facilities'. Natural burial therefore enables the Trust to achieve its environmental objective of transforming what was once a conifer plantation into native broadleaf woodland and to use the surplus income to employ staff and help maintain the visitor centre and hostel. Hill Holt Wood in Lincolnshire is another example of a trust that has provided natural burial on a small scale but which, at the time of our study, was seeking to extend into a larger woodland that it had recently acquired.[8] The Trust has set out its objectives on what it describes as economic conservation, or 'Econs', where income generated from the woodland is used to support a range of social enterprises. Similar to the Earth Works Trust, Hill Holt Wood provides environmental courses for schools and training for unemployed people and has also established its own design team that specialises in eco-buildings. The Trust's activities have continued to expand since Nigel and Karen Lowthrop originally purchased Hill Holt Wood in 1995, and it now employs around 30 people.[9] On a much larger scale, the Torbay Coast and Countryside Trust, which was established in 2000, is responsible for managing over 1,750 acres of country parks, nature reserves, woodland, farmland and coastline. In 2006 the Trust developed Cockington Woodland burial site, set within Cockington Country Park, which is managed by the Trust. Once again, income from the burial ground is used to help support the Trust's other activities.

Opening a natural burial ground also proved to be effective in helping to raise public awareness of the Trust's activities and increase membership. Al Blake at East Meon commented that over the years there has been considerable media interest in the burial ground, including national and even international radio and television. As we discovered from our interviews with bereaved people and burial ground managers, it is frequently through the media that people are first made aware of natural burial. One of the managers we interviewed confirmed that the activity on their website dramatically increased whenever there was coverage in the media.

Independent landowners

This group is perhaps the least easily defined for they cannot be categorised by their role as either farmer, funeral director, local authority Bereavement Service or their purpose as a charitable trust. For each of these groups, we have a clearer sense of their identity and therefore where their motivations may lie in providing natural burial. Within the category of 'independent landowner' there is no shared background story, and indeed this comprises a far more heterogeneous assemblage of individuals. What they do share is ownership of land before taking the step of opening a natural burial ground. We interviewed three independent landowners and, while it is difficult generalise from such a small sample, two revealed a journey into natural burial and a motivation that we had not previously encountered. Both were retired when they decided to open a burial ground; and, although it might be expected that starting such a venture in one's later years might raise concerns about the long-term viability of the burial ground, in each case there was an expectation that their descendants would take on this responsibility.

The first independent landowner was a retired self-employed builder who had purchased some land ten years previously in order to prevent any development that might compromise the privacy of his house and garden. After retiring he had experienced a frustrating lack of purpose: '*I retired and there was nothing to do at home.*' His attention had turned to his land, and drawing on his building knowledge he contacted the local planning officer with a view to developing the site for holiday cabins. This was rejected, but in the conversation that followed the planning officer read out a list of changes of use that might be acceptable and which included a cemetery. It was this chance exchange that sparked his development of the burial ground:

I said 'can you read out [speaking with the planning officer] what I can do, on, with this land', because I had nothing to do, you know, so he started going through, well all, what's allowed and this sort of thing and he said 'cemeteries' you see. Oh well he just went past and carried on, not a lot, but, you know, these are the things you could do and I said hang on a bit, go through that again and he said 'cemeteries'; I said 'that's it, I'll make it into a cemetery' and he started laughing.

(Harry Maxwell)

The second landowner, who was also retired and had lived in the same house for over 30 years, wanted to be buried on her own land, which included a small field near the house where she had planted some fruit trees. Through her research to find out if this was possible she contacted the NDC, who confirmed that it was but also encouraged her to think that this might be something she could offer to other people:

So, which is why I started it, was the family joke. I don't want to be, I want to be here in my wooden box, I stood here looking out at the view, I planted a few apple trees for the millennium. . . . And I said 'what a nice place to be buried, I'd love to be buried here' and I followed it on from that, contacting the Natural Death Centre [after seeing a programme on *Countryfile*] . . . they said 'yes, it's quite possible, you can be buried on your own land and include other people; this is how you go about it'.

(Linda Hewson)

With each of these providers, it was evident that the natural burial ground had become an important part of their identity in retirement and given them a new purpose at the heart of a community that they were closely engaged with. None of them referred to income, environment or ecology in our interviews with them, although, like many of our participants, the retired builder was also motivated by his experience of his son's funeral and the difficulties he had encountered in trying to find a suitable burial ground.

Private companies

We distinguish 'private companies' from the other independent providers if land has either been purchased or leased from a landowner expressly for the purpose of providing burial. Our sample of 20 sites included Epping Forest Woodland Burial Park, where we spoke with Nick Taylor who was a director there. At the time of our research Woodland Burial Parks had three natural burial sites: Colney in Norfolk, Epping Forest in Essex and Chiltern in Buckinghamshire. Nick told us about his own experience as an independent funeral director prior to his involvement with Woodland Burial Parks. He expressed his personal frustration at the level of service he had previously been able to offer, given the constraints of cemetery and crematoria provision, and how he was personally motivated by the opportunity to do things differently by taking control of burial provision and so make available a better level of service:

I had thought some 20, 25 years ago, from the background of the poor delivery of the service from crematoriums and cemeteries, that there had to be a better way to do that . . . [speaking about a cemetery he had recently visited] there's a new section of the cemetery where there's memorials, some as little as three years old, that are being laid flat because somebody has deemed them to be unsafe, and it looks terrible.

(Nick Taylor, Epping Forest Burial Park)

Nick also spoke of the company's motivation to see the burial parks as an opportunity to provide a very different and more positive experience for bereaved people, as well as giving children the opportunity to visit the cemetery and learn about the environment:

At Colney we have a day every half term and holiday period for children, we have things like pond dipping, you know, beastie hunts or whatever it is we have, and normally we work closely with the rangers to organise that.

(Nick Taylor, Epping Forest Burial Park)

Since we completed our research, Woodland Burial Parks has changed its name to GreenAcres Woodland Burials and is now a wholly owned subsidary of the Bibby Line Group. In a 2012 article in the *ICCM Journal,* the managing director of GreenAcres outlined the future ambition of the company 'to open two new parks each year between now and 2020' and stated that five new sites were at that time 'progressing through planning'.[10] The future development plans of GreenAcres and the recent involvement of Co-operative Funeralcare, who have taken over the management of three woodland burial sites at Hinton Park, and Poole & Wimborne in Dorset and Mayfields on the Wirral, suggest a new direction for natural provision in the UK. The plans of these companies represent a level of investment in buildings, staff and infrastructure, service provision and development of multiple sites that is on a different scale to all of the other sites we surveyed.

Summary

Our data highlight the different routes through which providers first became aware of natural burial. For those already involved within the death care profession, such as funeral directors and local authority bereavement officers, natural burial was the hot topic of the early 1990s, one that permeated the literature of their professional associations and conferences. For the independent providers, that initial spark of interest often came more by chance: a radio or TV programme, a conversation with a planning officer or an enquiry to the NDC.

There are motivations that cut across our data and include the opportunity that natural burial presented for generating income; for example, by diversifying the revenue on a farm, subsidising the educational or environmental activities of charitable trusts or extending the range of services a funeral director can provide. In each of our groups there were also natural burial providers who described their unsatisfactory or frustrating personal and, in some cases, professional experiences of a funeral at a cemetery or crematorium, which had been an important motivation to do something different, to offer bereaved people a more personal and rewarding experience.

Our data also suggest two different yet overlapping motivations that reflect how the initial focus on the environment, when Ken West opened the first natural burial ground in 1993 (see Chapter 2), developed over time to include a more social or human orientation towards what it means to bury naturally. The four study sites help to illustrate this point. At Abermule and East Meon there was already an attachment to the land and a more explicit connection and knowledge of nature through farming or through the environmental activities of the Trust. At Ulley this connection did not begin to materialise until the land had been purchased; and, while Wisewood was already an established cemetery the focus up to the time of opening the woodland burial ground had been on maintaining and delivering a traditional burial service. These two different orientations – towards ecological and social concerns – are revealed in how burial is accommodated at each of these sites and the extent to which people are permitted to mark and preserve the identity of the grave. At East Meon and Abermule there is very little opportunity for bereaved people to memorialise at the grave, and here the focus is on preserving and enhancing the existing landscape and habitat. At Wisewood and Ulley, where new woodland is being created, the opportunity to choose a tree and a stone plaque and a more permissive approach to tending the grave demonstrate a greater emphasis on the needs of bereaved people. From their experience of managing the burial ground and of contact with bereaved people, each of the providers has chosen to make some adjustments to their practice to accommodate either the social or environmental dimensions of natural burial which were not initially their priority.

In Chapter 2 we unpacked the big picture of natural burial's history and trends, and in this chapter we have taken the reader into a range of quite specific natural burial landscapes, exploring the different motivations of providers. How these motivations were realised in practice and indeed how best we might think about the process of design provides the main focus of the next chapter.

4

Designing and making the natural burial ground

As the previous chapter explained, design can best be understood as an evolving process that is rooted in the 'designer's' previous experience; entangled with their current environment; and oriented towards specific kinds of futures. Design is not, therefore, simply the imposition of a template or cognitive model upon a separate, external world. Following Ingold's arguments for a revisioning of the relationship between human beings and their surrounding world, we can understand design as located, the outcome of a view of the human body as 'primordially and irrevocably stitched into the fabric of the world'.[1] While we have considered how natural burial ground owners' and managers' initial motivations informed their design processes in Chapter 3, it is important to understand the creation of a 'real' physical landscape as part of an evolving continuum of practice. Its prospective goal is a landscape that potentially has huge emotional significance for those who choose to be buried there themselves or who bury a relative or friend there. It is also a landscape wherein owners/managers, to varying degrees, aspire to make an environmental contribution either by preserving or creating new habitats, typically in the form of woodland and/or meadows.

It is therefore important to recognise at the outset that each and every natural burial ground is a designed landscape, even though many providers do not recognise their design contribution.[2] They are responsible for having a vision that will shape what the burial ground looks like, for the habitat they seek to create or preserve and for managing its emerging identity. The cemetery or burial ground is unlike almost any other designed public space, including municipal parks and gardens. It is a landscape that changes incrementally with each new burial; a process that may continue for many decades. It is also the product of a collaborative effort between those who manage the burial ground and those who work in it, including maintenance staff and gravediggers. This collaboration also extends to the bereaved community, whose membership will grow with each new burial. Members of this community may have a strong emotional attachment to the landscape and also feel a sense of ownership and duty of care for the grave of their relative or friend. How these different relationships evolve and are negotiated will have an important impact on shaping these landscapes. Once we take these factors into account, we begin to recognise in the evolution of a natural burial ground a dwelling or inhabiting perspective, as espoused by Ingold.[3] What he draws attention to is the meshing of the sentient human being with environments that are 'always becoming'. Albeit in rather overwrought style, Ingold summarises this argument in the following sentence: 'Bathed in light, submerged in sound and rapt in feeling, the sentient body, at once both perceiver and producer, traces the paths of the world's becoming in the very course of contributing to its ongoing renewal.'[4]

Media coverage of natural burial has often focused on a single sound bite that references a cardboard coffin, a farmer's field and a tree. However, such reporting typically fails to capture the complexity and tremendous diversity of natural burial grounds or the richness of ideas and thinking that have contributed to making these new burial landscapes. Media coverage also fails to convey how the Natural Burial Movement has evolved. Each landscape is in a continuous process of change as it matures and as initial ideas are revisited and adapted in response to a growing understanding of the challenges and opportunities of providing natural burial. As we illustrate in this chapter and also in Chapter 8, which focuses on our longitudinal study of the woodland burial ground at Ulley, many of the sites that were opened in the mid 1990s are well into their second decade and have evolved and matured. Where there may once have been an open field or corner of a municipal cemetery, there is now new woodland and a canopy that reaches above visitors' heads and in summer blocks out the sky and surrounding landscape. Natural burial is therefore no longer an idea in waiting but now exists as meadows or woodland, in various stages of maturity. While natural burial may still be a minority choice nationally (see Chapter 2), it represents an important and increasingly familiar and accessible burial alternative for many communities.

In the discussion that follows, there is insufficient space to capture all of the nuances of design that exist across the spectrum of natural burial sites in the UK. As already argued, each site is the product of a complex set of circumstances and interactions: the landscape prior to it becoming a natural burial ground, the knowledge, skills and vision of the provider and the community who engages with it. In order to appreciate this complexity we briefly return to consider the land that has been chosen, which is not a blank canvas but has its own unique *genius loci*, or pervading atmosphere, that providers are responding to as their vision of natural burial develops. In terms used by Gibson in his account of human perception, we might speak about its affordances, the possibilities it offers.[5] Thus the landscape might suggest and inform the habitat that providers seek to create and how it will interact with the surrounding context, views and topography. For the independent provider (farmer, landowner, charitable trust, etc.), whose land may be situated away from the city, the surrounding landscape is an immediate asset that already conveys a sense of being 'in nature'. In contrast, local authority providers typically respond to a very different situation where natural burial is likely to be embedded within a cemetery landscape that exerts its own formality, order and identity.

Four key themes cut across these two very different situations in which independent providers and providers of new and established natural burial grounds find themselves. Our discussion begins below ground with the burial plan and the challenge of finding the grave in nature – that is, in a site where the traditional marker of a headstone is absent. We then move on to explore different approaches towards designing and managing nature and how these are realised. We will argue that those who have participated in the Natural Burial

Movement have contributed to a highly creative evolutionary process as they have become more familiar with the challenges of burying naturally.

Our focus then shifts to memorialising the dead. In our interviews with providers, they consistently commented on the tension between their own vision for the burial ground and the desire of bereaved people to memorialise the dead through grave-tending practices. Here we explore different design strategies that attempt to reconcile this potential conflict. Finally, we examine the extent to which the burial ground has been designed to service the needs of bereaved people. Here we have witnessed a shift, especially among the larger independent providers, to extend the service they offer by constructing buildings on-site that provide space for burial ground staff, a funeral service and a reception or wake. What we reveal is how the buildings and other structures within the burial ground have also been designed, to varying degrees, to reinforce the 'natural' and possibly 'rural' credentials of the burial ground through the design, choice of materials and methods of construction.

Finding the grave in nature

Traditional cemeteries in the UK (and elsewhere) have a clear and immutable logic that underpins the organisation and layout of the burial ground: the burial plan. This provides an efficient system for locating each grave and maximising the number of burial spaces within the cemetery. The burial plan subdivides the cemetery into sections, which are defined by access roads and pathways, and is often displayed at the entrance to a cemetery to assist visitors in finding a grave.[6] Sections may vary in size and form but, for convenience, are frequently rectilinear so that space can be used efficiently when subdivided into a grid of individual graves. Through this process, each grave can be allocated a unique reference number that is recorded in the burial register along with the details of each burial interment. In the cemetery there is a virtue in this order that preserves the identity of the grave both above and below ground, enabling those working and visiting the cemetery to find each grave. The natural burial ground manager is also required by law to maintain a record of each burial and its precise location although, as our research highlighted to us, their priorities are quite different. Their motivation is to create a landscape where nature can flourish and where individual grave identities will ultimately be transformed into a collective memorial. They must achieve this while also creating a framework that should not be visually obtrusive or detract from the natural setting but will enable them, if required, to return to the precise location of each burial in a changing landscape devoid of any permanent headstones or memorials.

In responding to this challenge, natural burial providers have adopted different strategies that, we suggest, reflect their relationship to the land and the different contexts in which they operate. An interesting characteristic of the Natural Burial Movement is that this experience and knowledge is no longer confined to those who are familiar with working in the traditional cemetery. Indeed, local authority natural burial sites, which invariably form a small part of a much larger and established cemetery, typically struggle to break free from the constraints of the existing cemetery landscape and working practices that may have been established decades previously. For example, at Wisewood Woodland Burial Ground, the formal layout of the cemetery has had a major influence on

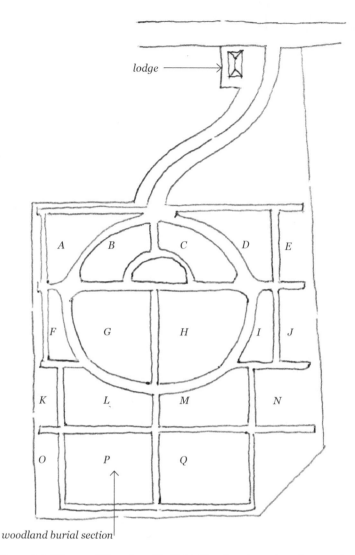

lodge

woodland burial section

Figure 4.1 *Wisewood Cemetery, Sheffield. The plan shows how the cemetery is organised into a series of sections that are alphabetically labelled. This arrangement enables graves to be efficiently arranged and located.*

the form and appearance of the burial ground. The natural burial site is confined to a rectangular section at the periphery of the cemetery that is defined by the access roads that enclose it. Creating a wild and natural landscape within the context of a highly ordered and managed cemetery is therefore a significant challenge. At Carlisle Cemetery, Ken West broke free from some of these constraints by selecting an area of land already approved for burial that was located just beyond the Victorian brick wall and hedge that enclosed the cemetery (see Chapter 2). The wall and hedge provide a visual and physical barrier that separates the cemetery from the woodland burial ground. Instead of looking towards the cemetery with its neatly mown edges and uniform rows of headstones, the burial ground has a strong visual connection with the surrounding fields, an aesthetic that enables visitors to immerse themselves in nature and to imagine the future of the woodland area. From within the traditional cemetery the wall and mature hedge serve a different function, that of securing and shielding the landscape from any outside intrusion. Wisewood Cemetery has an equally, if not more impressive, rural setting; but, without this visual separation, it has been more difficult to facilitate a transition into a very different mortuary landscape experience – although data from interviews with bereaved people who used this site suggest they envisage a future where it will merge with the surrounding countryside, albeit not in their own lifetimes. This natural burial ground thus remains oriented towards the cemetery, maintaining an awkward juxtaposition between two very different sets of regulation; one that permits a headstone and kerb sets to enclose the grave, and that is also more tolerant of additional grave marking, and the other where the regulations discourage anything other than a tree and a stone plaque. It should not be surprising, then, that, where these different regulations co-exist, bereaved people find it difficult to comply and managers might also be reluctant to remove grave adornments that are not permitted. Bear Road Cemetery in Brighton, which is managed by the local authority, has met this challenge by establishing a new hedge between the woodland burial section and the rest of the cemetery. The hedge has the dual purpose of providing a visual separation while reinforcing the environmental objectives of the natural burial ground. The hedge also benefits from being a living structure that can be managed in different ways in response to the contrasting burial aesthetics. From within the natural burial ground, there is an opportunity to adopt a more relaxed maintenance regime allowing the hedge to grow more wild, while, in the cemetery, regular cutting will retain a stronger sense of order and formality (see Figures 4.2 and 4.3).

At Wisewood, evidence of the formality of the cemetery to be found in the woodland burial section is further compounded by a memorialisation and planting strategy whereby a tree is planted on each grave. The newly planted trees form neatly aligned rows that correspond with the burial grid. As a consequence, the resulting order and uniformity of the burial site is more reminiscent of a forest plantation rather than a naturally emerging woodland. As we will see in the following section, however, some local authorities have managed to break free from this constraint by developing planting strategies that deliberately work against the burial grid to give the natural burial section a more relaxed and informal woodland character.

Our visits to natural burial grounds designed by established funeral directors also revealed the influence of their owners' experiences of working within a traditional cemetery. On the Isle of Wight, for example, where local funeral director Geoff Leather developed Fernhill Park Burial Ground, the burial ground is part of a much larger landscape where Geoff worked closely with a consultant forester to create new woodland and re-establish old hedgerows. While this landscape will develop into a relaxed and informal parkland, the area allocated for burials reveals a very different design approach that appears to draw heavily on Geoff's experience of a traditional cemetery landscape. Set within the parkland, the burial area forms a neat rectangle of approximately one acre. In contrast to its immediate surroundings, the grass is regularly mown and contained by a gravel path along which wooden benches have been placed. Geoff commented on how he used the paths and a series of fixed markers to

traditional graves

mown paths

woodland burial

dividing hedge

entrances

lawn

cemetery boundary

0   50m

Figure 4.2 *Bear Road Cemetery, Brighton. The woodland burial section occupies an area that was previously set aside for public graves where the remaining space now enables woodland burial. The plan shows a more wild and informal landscape, separated from the more formal area of traditional graves.*

traditional graves   dividing hedge   woodland burial

Figure 4.3 *The section shows the transition between the more formal area of the cemetery and neatly maintained lawns and the wilder, informal landscape of the woodland burial.*

Figure 4.4 *Wisewood Cemetery, Woodland Burial Ground, Sheffield. The underlying order of the burial grid is reflected in the arrangement of memorial trees that echo the order beneath the ground. This image also includes the access road that contains the burial section (January 2008).*

Figure 4.5 *Fernhill Park Burial Ground, Isle of Wight. The burial section retains a formal rectangle contained within a stone chip pathway along which benches are evenly spaced. New woodland planting and less frequently cut grassland is set back from the more formal burial space (March 2008).*

help locate each grave: '*Well, it's just a grid situation . . . there are pegs all down the pathway, every four feet and every eight feet, so what we do, we put a taut line across and grid like that, so we know we're always accurate.*'

From Geoff's perspective, the order he has put in place within the context of a wilder, '*messy*' landscape provides clarity for his staff in terms of locating graves and managing the burial space.

Burial ground managers we interviewed spoke of the different strategies they had adopted that enabled them to preserve an uncluttered view of the landscape and one not visually dominated by memorials, while also establishing an orderly and efficient approach to arranging and locating each grave. At Ulley, for example, owner John Mallatratt had the burial ground resurveyed after approximately 50 burials had taken place so that the precise location of each tree could be located on the digital burial plan. These trees have subsequently been used as fixed points from which to locate new graves. As the number of burials has increased, this function of locating graves has been transposed to trees that were planted after the initial survey. At Green Lane Burial Field, Ifor and Eira do not permit any grave markers other than a small stone that is painted with the grave number and pushed into the ground. The field must be kept clear of any memorials that might damage machinery when the meadow is cut each year and the hay is removed. To locate existing and new graves, Ifor has established fixed markers around the edge of the field that are set back in the adjacent woodland so that they do not intrude on the meadow. From these fixed points, tape measures can be used to locate the corner of each grave. Independent provider and funeral director Ray Ward, whose vision was to create new woodland near Brentwood in Essex, took a 'belt and braces' approach in a landscape where no individual memorial trees would be placed on graves. He said:

> By law you have to know where every person is and how you can find them. I've thrown a grid over the whole thing . . . I have stainless steel post(s) about two foot long, really thick gauge . . . that'll last a thousand years with an alphanumeric code on the top and that's banged into the ground with a collar to keep the grass away.

Each of these approaches seeks to preserve the grid below the ground without impacting on the surface landscape. Other site owners have developed different design strategies which strive to create a more harmonious relationship between the burial plan and the emerging landscape. At Seven Penny Meadow, farmer Alan Willey ploughed his field into traditional rig and furrows. Rig and furrow was a typical feature of upland landscapes and consisted of parallel rows of troughs and mounds that provided better drainage for growing crops. The recreation of this vernacular landscape had both practical and aesthetic advantages for Alan. He commented: '*the rig and furrows are permanent . . . we've got a map and starting at the bottom and we are just working our way up*'. Each rig is assigned a letter and space for two graves. Aesthetically it also evoked a time that preceded modern agricultural practices and the mechanisation of farming, which Alan felt was more in keeping with nature and the wildflower meadow that he and his family hoped to establish. Alan also commented that there were unforeseen benefits to this approach. The

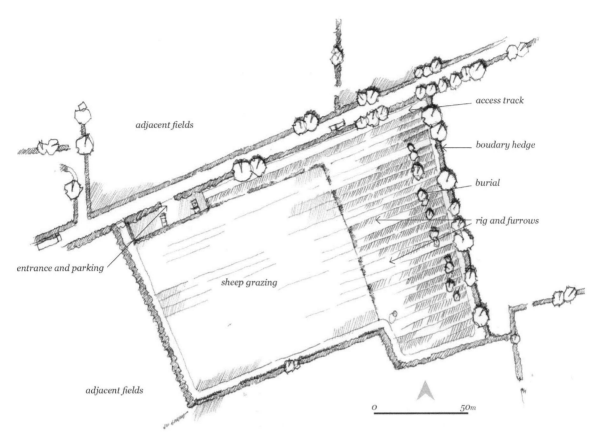

access track

boudary hedge

burial

rig and furrows

adjacent fields

entrance and parking

sheep grazing

adjacent fields

0   50m

Figure 4.6 *Seven Penny Meadow, Medomsley, County Durham. The plan shows the parallel rig and furrows that were ploughed back into the field and are used to inform the location of each grave.*

rigs also helped to shed rain away from a freshly dug grave, prior to burial, and also maintained a drier access pathway and space where mourners could gather. A family returning to the site could find the grave by locating the appropriate rig. Martin Chatfield at Crossways Woodland Burials also recognised the value of establishing structure within the landscape that would help guide visitors returning to a grave. To separate the burial ground from a much larger existing field that he used for grazing sheep, he built traditional Devon hedges that consist of an earth bank planted with hedgerow species. If at some point in the future the burial ground is extended, his intention is to continue with this system of hedges to create smaller recognisable compartments or rooms within the emerging woodland.

GreenAcres Woodland Burials manage four of the largest private natural burial grounds in the UK, including Epping Forest Burial Park, which opened in 2008, and Rainford, Colney and Chiltern Woodland Burial Parks. The sites were selected by GreenAcres because they were already mature woodland, thereby enabling the company to project their interpretation of natural burial consistently. In this woodland context it was not feasible to impose a rigid burial grid without potentially damaging the existing character and habitat

Figure 4.7 *On each of the rigs there is space for two graves set side by side. Seven Penny Meadow, County Durham (January 2008).*

of the landscape. Instead, they chose to work with the woodland by mapping significant trees they felt would provide a memorial focus. Thus, the location of graves responds to the existing landscape; graves are arranged in a circle, six metres from the centre of a tree. Nicolas Taylor, who then managed the site at Epping, described how they maintained a digital plan that was regularly surveyed from fixed points set out in the woodland: '*We also put a small metal rod in the grave so that if the grave disappears altogether we can scan with a metal detector.*' This distinction, between the imposed grid and a map generated by a reading of the positions of existing trees, reflects Ingold's comparison between 'the straight line of modernity [that is] driven by the grand narrative of progressive advance' and the 'line of wayfaring [which is] accomplished through the practices of dwelling and the circuitous movements they entail'[7]. As the data show, in the complex, organically generated environment of the natural burial ground, a grid, whether visible or not, may well be at odds with the intentions of both the providers and the users of a site.

The designs of the burial plans at Ulley, Seven Penny Meadow and Epping Forest share a more relaxed approach to the space they allocate for each burial, which may be less than half the density of many local authority sites. This relaxation is an important contributory factor that has enabled these sites to negotiate the challenge of implementing a system that allows the grave to be found while still realising their vision of nature. Many local authority sites do not have the opportunity to adopt a more flexible approach, partly because they are constrained by the existing cemetery landscape but also because of the pressure on their diminishing burial space.

Figure 4.8 *Individual mature trees are identified within the existing woodland as the memorial focus around which the graves are arranged in a circle. GreenAcres Woodland Burials, Epping Forest, Essex (April 2008).*

Designing for nature

The previous section illustrated how the need for a system for locating each grave and the development of a burial plan seemingly have important implications for the design and aesthetics of the natural burial landscape. Chapter 2 showed the UK distribution of natural burial grounds, their ownership and the different design interpretations. Here, we explore in more detail how providers have set about the task of realising their vision of nature and the natural burial landscape. We begin with sites that focus on creating new woodland, which is by far the most typical interpretation of natural burial. It is also possibly the most challenging because, from the outset, users are required to imagine a landscape that does not yet exist but is dependent on burial and therefore their commitment for it to be realised.

New woodland burial

We can broadly divide the new woodland sites that we have visited into two categories. There are sites that have implemented a tree planting strategy that closely ties the development of the woodland to burial, and which we refer to as 'woodland through burial'. In contrast to this approach, in a smaller number of sites, the establishment of the woodland is managed separately from the process of burial, and this we refer to as 'woodland independent of burial'.

Woodland through burial: sequential, dispersed, grove and scattered models of design

Woodland through burial includes all burial grounds where a memorial tree is placed on (or by) each grave. This was the first interpretation developed by Ken West at Carlisle, and, with some modifications, this has continued to be the most common approach. The principal benefit for bereaved people is the unambiguous relationship between the tree (their tree) and the grave of the deceased and how this contributes to the creation of a shared memorial landscape. This model does, however, pose challenges in terms of tree establishment and future management and also the character of the woodland when users are permitted to choose their tree; the juxtaposition of large forest trees and smaller ornamental species, for example, can seem incongruous. However, the most obvious limitation of this approach is that the rate at which trees can be planted is restricted to the rate of burial. This is potentially problematic for users whose prior conception of a burial ground, which in many instances includes 'woodland' in its name, has little connection with their actual experience – put simply, they cannot see the wood. It is for this reason that some of the larger, private burial grounds have focused on developing sites in areas with mature trees and/or existing woodland.

Figures 4.9 and 4.10 show four sketch plans and an accompanying section of each plan to summarise the different approaches we have observed at sites creating woodland through burial. The plan shows how the distribution of the woodland and the differences in the size of each tree convey the passage of time. The sections provide an indication of how the woodland structure will evolve

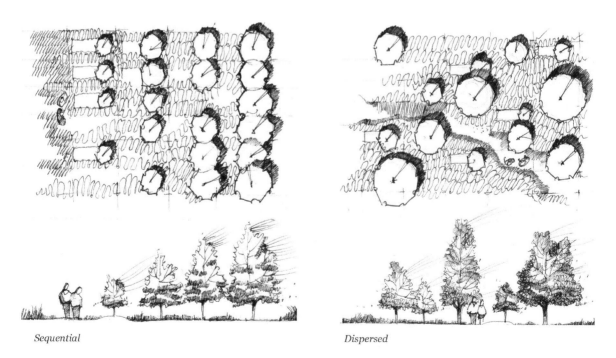

Sequential   *Dispersed*

Figure 4.9 *Sequential and dispersed models of woodland through burial.*

and what impact this might have on the emerging habitat as well as on access for visitors and burial ground workers. In order to reflect how the woodland is established, we have assigned names to each of the approaches we have observed and which we now go on to discuss.

Sequential is the most common interpretation of woodland through burial and is more typical of local authorities and early providers. Wisewood Woodland Burial Ground is an example of this approach, arranging the graves in relation to the existing burial plan and typically using them in sequence. Inevitably there are modifications to this strategy; for example, the council has adapted the allocation of graves in response to seasonal changes in ground conditions as the site is prone to waterlogging during the winter months. Gaps are also left in the sequence when a family reserves an adjacent plot.

Dispersed uses the same burial plan approach, but, here, users are encouraged to visit the burial ground and choose the location of the grave and therefore where the tree will be planted. This freedom of choice has a significant impact on how the woodland will develop and is characteristic of the approach that has been followed at Ulley. In the sequential model, the woodland progressively unfolds across the landscape, maturing as it does so. In the dispersed model, there is no such order. Trees are planted in response to individual preference and, as a result, with time, mature trees will stand alongside those that are newly planted. The development of woodland at Ulley is explored in more detail in Chapter 8.

Both of these approaches have their merits and constraints in terms of creating woodland. By planting sequentially, the adjacent trees will be of a similar age, and, while there may be differences between species in terms of how quickly they grow, it is likely that the establishment will be more successful as the newly planted trees will have access to space, light and water. The establishment of newly planted trees may become more of a challenge in the dispersed model as the canopy of much older and larger trees extends well beyond the grave to shade adjacent plots. In addition to choosing the grave, there may be other important advantages to the dispersed model for bereaved people. In a burial ground that is continually changing, the presence of some larger trees will provide useful landmarks from which to locate the grave, as we go on to discuss in Chapter 8 where we explore in more detail how the woodland has evolved at Ulley. In contrast, a sequential approach will soon restrict access, and the uniform age of trees may also make it difficult to distinguish one grave from another. For some users, however, this might not be an issue; and, from an environmental perspective, discouraging people from visiting or tending a grave can be beneficial to the development of a more ecologically rich habitat. The variation in the distribution and age of trees in the dispersed model can contribute to a stronger sense of an emerging woodland character and spatial structure that provides shelter and privacy for visitors. It does, however, raise important operational and management issues. Pre-purchased graves that might remain unused for many years could prove more difficult to access for both the gravedigger and family if trees on nearby plots are well established with a large canopy and root system. In the sequential model, this is less of an issue as the trees on nearby graves will be small. In the short to medium term, woodland that is dispersed across the entire site may also prove more costly to maintain because of restricted access for machinery and difficulties with annual mowing.

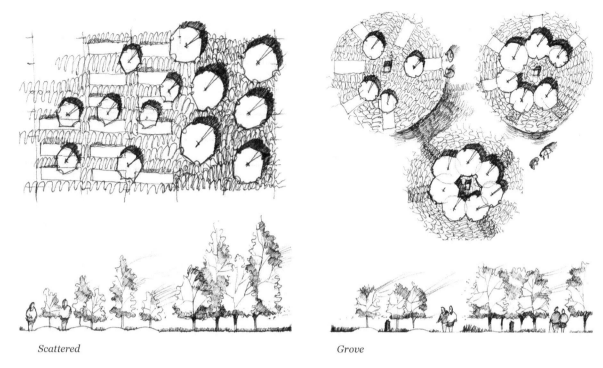

Scattered

Grove

Figure 4.10 *Scattered and grove interpretations of woodland through burial.*

In the sequential model the distinction between the emerging woodland and adjacent grassland is more clearly defined.

The remaining two models of woodland establishment – which we refer to here as *scattered* and *grove* – show developments which, while retaining a woodland through burial approach, attempt to resolve some of the issues we have identified. Following advice from their countryside officer, Ribble Valley Council Bereavement Services implemented a scattered model in their woodland section at Clitheroe Cemetery, where the vision is to create broadleaf mixed woodland. Planting is restricted to the dormant season when it is easier to establish young saplings, and the trees are evenly planted across the area of new graves without showing preference to any individual grave. This approach allows more control over spacing and species mix and addresses their concern that people can become emotionally attached to a tree that may, at some point, be removed as part of the woodland management. The countryside officer told us:

> [one thing] we were sure about with the woodland burial site was nobody would be able to buy a tree . . . we couldn't allow a situation where the next of kin felt they had custodianship over the tree. The worst thing you can do is cut someone's tree down, very emotional.

The *grove* model represents a creative adaptation of the burial plan to produce clusters of woodland planting, which gives less rigid and formal appearance than the sequential model. The burial plan is reconfigured to

Figure 4.11 *In this scattered model of establishing new woodland, the trees are planted across the area of graves but are not attached to individual graves. Waddington Road Cemetery, Clitheroe (May 2008).*

establish fixed points around which the graves are arranged. Carlisle no longer organise their burial plots on a sequential grid and, in their new section, have moved to a system of groves. At each evenly spaced intersection there is a wooden marker post around which the graves are arranged in a circle, with a tree planted on each grave. This approach retains a clear and logical framework for planning the burial space and looks far less regimented. The trees appear to form more natural clusters while also preserving space between each grove to allow access for the grave digger and for mourners to gather beside the grave at a funeral.

While each of these models tries to capture the different approaches we discovered during our site visits, there was one example we recorded that did not fit comfortably into any of the models that we have outlined above. Catherine Hunt, an independent provider at Great Bradley Cottage in Devon, had a vision of creating an orchard on land that she owns near to her house. She chose fruit trees not only because they were smaller and could be placed on each grave, but also because they would have a more immediate impact for bereaved families.

> Each grave could have a tree, I felt that was important. If you had all native trees, it's a bit boring because they don't do anything, in our lifetime . . . they're very slow growing, an oak we will never see mature, a beech we won't see mature but a fruit tree you see doing something, from its second year, it will blossom, it will come out into fruit, for crab apples, the fruit will stay on during the autumn, the wildlife will eat the fruit.

Figure 4.12 *Graves are arranged in a circle around a fixed marker. This approach creates a more relaxed woodland character and has important practical advantages in preserving access for staff and bereaved people. Carlisle Woodland Burial Ground, Cumbria (September 2012).*

Figure 4.13 *Fruit trees have been selected in preference to native trees because of their more immediate impact in terms of blossom, fruit and autumn colour. Great Bradley Cottage, Devon (May 2008).*

Our conversation with Catherine also revealed an important dimension of natural burial: the close relationship that can exist and is often sustained between the provider and the deceased and their bereaved families and friends, which we go on to discuss in Chapter 5. This relationship evolves from their initial contact, when arranging or attending a funeral or visiting the site to see if it is appropriate for their needs, and is sustained at Great Bradley Cottage by Catherine's ongoing presence in the burial ground as she goes about her regular tasks of managing the site. Figure 4.14 illustrates how Catherine initially only used alternate graves and has also missed out alternate rows so she can maintain access for the digger and also in anticipation that family members would like to be buried near to one another. In the plan, the larger trees show the first phase of burial and it can be seen how the space between the first two rows is gradually being infilled with new graves. The trees are also planted in alternate rows at the head and foot of each grave.

Figure 4.14 *The arrangement of graves and planting of fruit trees demonstrates a creative approach that retains some flexibility to allow family members to be buried alongside one another. Great Bradley Cottage, Devon.*

I have met, I should think of the eighty people that are here, I've probably met seventy-nine of them. Because it's small I've done all the burials and I know everybody, I can name everybody here, I know them all and I know who's got people to come back and visit, who comes back, who doesn't. I can always fit auntie in, if I wanted or plus auntie or uncle could go at the foot or the head end . . . And so it's personal.

(Catherine Hunt, Great Bradley Cottage)

Woodland independent of burial

In response to the challenges that we have identified above, some natural burial providers decided to completely separate woodland creation from burial. For example, Coventry Bereavement Services included a woodland and wildflower burial option, alongside areas of traditional graves, in a new cemetery they opened in 1995 at Lentons Lane on the outskirts of the city (see Figure 4.15).

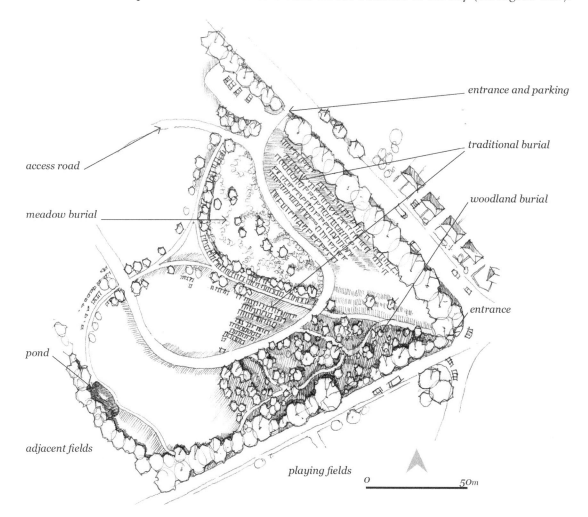

Figure 4.15 *Lentons Lane Cemetery, Coventry. A new cemetery that incorporates traditional burial sections with woodland and meadow burial.*

The woodland section was planted with a mix of native trees and meadow sown with wildflowers before the burial ground was opened. Graves are accommodated within the woodland, between the newly planted trees. The inclusion of the woodland and wildflower burial areas makes an important contribution for *all* visitors to this cemetery. The woodland burial section helps shelter the cemetery from the prevailing winds and screens it from the adjacent road. It also creates a more private area where visitors can walk within the cemetery.

The Arbory Trust, a Christian charity who own and manage a large woodland burial ground at Barton Glebe near Cambridge, worked closely with the Forestry Commission to convert 17 hectares of agricultural land into native woodland. Their design has resulted in a landscape divided into a series of woodland glades that are accessed by a central avenue and connected to each other by smaller informal pathways that lead through the woodland (see Figure 4.16). Their strategy was different to that at Lentons Lane because it completely separated burial from the newly planted woodland. The graves were restricted to the woodland glades that are managed as wildflower meadows where no permanent grave markers are permitted. The woodland consists of over 20,000 native trees that are indigenous to the area and was established in two phases. The first phase was in 2000, and a second phase was initiated in 2009 when the burial ground was extended.

For both Lentons Lane and Barton Glebe, because the establishment of the woodland is not restricted to the rate of burial or location of each grave, there is more control over the choice of tree species and how plant selection varies across the site. Planting the trees before the burial ground opened has also helped to draw users into the design vision and environmental aspirations of these sites.

At Barton Glebe, retaining control over the woodland species mix has meant that each glade can also have a distinctive woodland character, where selected species are more prevalent – for example, wild cherry, oak or lime. Recognising this variety in the woodland character helps visitors in finding the glade and grave of their relative or friend. While this model of woodland burial does not permit users to claim ownership of a tree, it does simplify woodland management. If required, trees can be extracted as part of the woodland management by removing them via the perimeter path without intruding on the burial glades.[8]

Mature woodland burial

Mature woodland burial sites, which we have defined on the basis that they include established trees, are relatively uncommon and include a wide variation in size, from less than a quarter of a hectare to over 20 hectares. There is no simple definition that defines woodland on the basis of size, number of trees or species mix. In the UK, for example, the Forestry Commission does not set a threshold on when a group of trees moves from being a copse into a woodland or woodland into a forest. Instead, they give a more fluid definition that recognises the tremendous variety of ways in which trees are situated in the landscape, defining woodland by the extent of the tree canopy, which must be at least 20 per cent of the site and include integral areas of open space.[9]

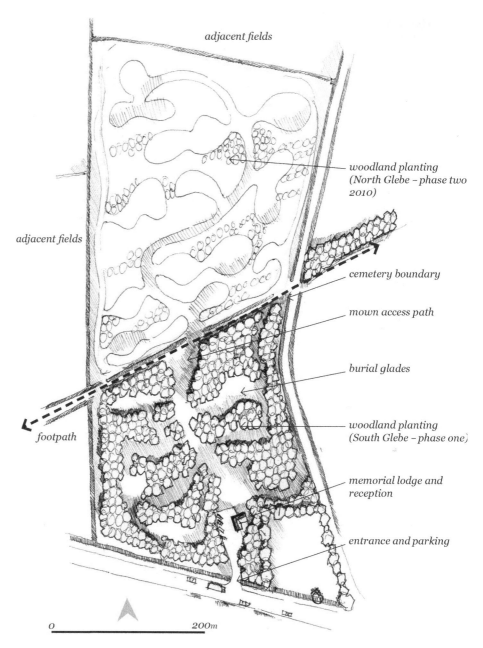

adjacent fields

adjacent fields

woodland planting
(North Glebe – phase two
2010)

cemetery boundary

mown access path

burial glades

woodland planting
(South Glebe – phase one)

memorial lodge and
reception

entrance and parking

footpath

0   200m

Figure 4.16 *Barton Glebe, Cambridge. The site covers a total area of 17 hectares and has been established in two phases. Over 10,000 native trees were planted in the first phase to create the wildflower meadow burial glades.*

Four of the 20 sites we visited, including East Meon, are mature woodland burial grounds. By virtue of the habitat that already existed, each of these four burial grounds has already attained their vision of natural burial. However, the woodland experience varies hugely between each of these sites, as does the extent to which the woodland is being actively managed. For example, as

Figure 4.17 *A new grave can be seen within the large stands of coppiced sweet chestnut that create a distinctive identity within the burial park. GreenAcres Woodland Burials, Epping Forest (April 2008).*

we discussed in Chapter 2, at Allerton Cemetery in Liverpool the woodland is restricted to a narrow strip of mature native trees that run alongside an access road. In contrast, East Meon offers a very different experience by virtue of its rural context and size that enables visitors to immerse themselves within the woodland. The woodland management at East Meon also reflects a vision that is about transforming what exists into a different type of woodland. Through the selective clearing of trees, burying of bodies and new planting, the existing conifer plantation will be gradually transformed into broadleaf native woodland that will include coppiced hazel. This model of transformation is a feature of many of the larger sites where the woodland may have been neglected for many generations. Epping Forest Woodland Burial Park has leased woodland that had not been actively managed for several decades. As a consequence, large areas of what was traditionally coppiced hornbeam and sweet chestnut have become overgrown. By reintroducing traditional woodland management techniques, including coppicing and thinning to let in more light, the owners intend to improve the species and habitat diversity, while also harvesting a supply of fuel for their woodchip boiler. Epping Forest demonstrates how natural burial is being used as a catalyst to help fund and regenerate existing woodland, while East Meon has transformed what was low-quality forestry plantation with limited amenity and ecological value into something far more habitat-rich and interesting.

Wildflower meadow burial

In many respects, the vision to create a wildflower meadow might appear to be the most easily achieved of the interpretations of natural burial that we have discussed. There are no complications of working around newly planted or existing trees when locating a burial or excavating a new grave. This interpretation also negotiates the concern that has been expressed by some providers that bereaved people may either become attached to the memorial tree or wish to plant a tree that is not in keeping with the character of the emerging woodland. A meadow is also relatively simple to manage in terms of cutting once or twice a year and preserves the original integrity of a field that might still be used for grazing, now or at some point in the future. Perhaps it is for these reasons that each of the 3 wildflower meadow sites we identified in our sample of 20 was developed by a farmer. That said, through extended dwelling within a local landscape of woodland and arable fields, individual farmers were also likely to be aware of the challenges that creating a meadow could throw up.

This deep appreciation of a need to protect and preserve the existing landscape was exemplified in our conversation with James Leedham at Usk Castle Chase Natural Burial Meadow. James' company, 'Natural Burial Grounds', works with landowners to jointly develop and manage sites and includes burial grounds in Scotland, England and Wales. At Usk Castle Chase, James spoke of how he and landowner Rosie Humphreys arrived at a key moment in defining their vision of the burial ground after a consultation with a landscape architect to consider how their large field, surrounded by woodland, might be developed. The conversation they had touched on how the designer could work with them to create vistas and arrange groves to frame views. James recalled how:

> Rosie took me to one side and said 'Do we really need any of this? Just look at what we've got, it's beautiful, we should just preserve what we've got here.' That was a fairly seminal moment for us in that we'd decided there and then that to bring in a landscape architect was probably not the right thing to do for a truly natural environment because there is inevitably going to be an impact that they make on that environment.

Rosie told us how the field is now *grazed by sheep, and it's topped as needed according to the season, to encourage flowers, wildflower management so it's more like a hay meadow*.

Ifor at Green Lane Burial Field and Alan Willey at Seven Penny Meadow each spoke of their desire to recreate wildflower meadows. Ifor felt this was an opportunity to do something more interesting and challenging than establishing a woodland: *'There's plenty of woodland around, that's easy to recreate in many ways but a meadow site with wildflowers growing is much more difficult to recreate.'* They each, however, recognised that their land had been intensively farmed in the past and, as a consequence, it would be difficult to establish wildflowers; as Alan comments: *'You see with it being arable it's too damn fertile.'* Wildflower species thrive on soil that has low fertility, which restricts the growth of the more competitive and aggressive grass species. Ifor was advised by the local wildlife trust to remove the turf in order to reduce the competition from grasses and to see what would grow: *'We were told the best way to get a hay meadow was to take off the turf and just leave it to grow.*' He felt that this was '*too radical*' and, after further advice, decided to sow yellow rattle, a native hemi-parasitic annual plant that gains its nutrients by feeding from the roots of other plants. This weakens the more aggressive grasses and creates a niche in which wildflower perennials may gain a foothold. In the first year after plough-ing the field, Alan had a fantastic display of annual poppies and cornflowers; this was, however, short-lived, and the more competitive grasses soon returned. Like Ifor, Alan has also experimented with yellow rattle but, after little success, has fenced off a large section of the burial field that he now grazes with Jacob sheep. In time, he hopes he will be more successful in promoting a richer and more diverse meadow:

> It was nice in the first year but it's grass now, so that's the problem we've got . . . but what we're going to do is fence the middle off and I'm going to put some Jacobs on . . . to keep it down and get the wildflowers up.

Each of these different approaches to designing for nature reveal how natural burial providers have adapted their approach as they respond to their own and other providers' experiences of providing natural burial. While the actions of bereaved people can impact on this process in terms of the trees and flowers they plant or their gardening activities at the grave, it is to the placing of more permanent memorials by bereaved families and friends that we now turn.

Memorialisation in the absence of a headstone

The aspect that many natural burial providers find most challenging in trying to realise their vision of natural burial has been the desire of bereaved people to preserve the identity of the grave by placing permanent memorials upon it. For example, in the sites we visited, we observed wind chimes, a wide variety of ornaments, plastic flowers, cards in plastic envelopes, Christmas decorations, benches, kerb sets and headstones. For many of the new providers we spoke with who had little or no experience of working with bereaved people there was an initial assumption on their part that the landscape and tree (where this was an option) would be the only memorial, as Catherine Hunt's (Great Bradley Cottage) comments reveal: '*I thought it would be just a tree and a grassed over grave and then everybody started planting things.*' For some providers there was also an assumption that people would not return to visit the grave:

> We had a vision of planting people there and just, oh well, that's it, they're not coming back . . . we thought the people that come will just have the tree and that'll be it . . . but they come every week, they put things on and, you know, they like to be there.
>
> (Cheryl Long)

For the providers, and also for many of the bereaved people that we have interviewed, it is the visible presence of grave markers that can shift the identity of a burial ground towards a tipping point after which it may appear no differ-ent from a traditional cemetery. Catherine Hunt at Great Bradley Cottage spoke of this concern and how she provides a small plaque that records the name and plot number, to be placed beneath a stone that the family is encouraged to bring from home. We asked Catherine why she did this:

> I don't want it to look like a cemetery . . . as soon as you have a name plaque or names it changes the feel of it . . . it feels like a cemetery because you've got, you know, in loving memory . . . I'm not knocking it but it just changes the whole feeling.

At one of the sites we visited where we were not permitted to take photographs, the 'headstones' were clearly visible among the trees. The manager's comments reveal that, for him, this tipping point had already been passed: '*It's kind of transposed itself, the woodland ethos has somewhat been diluted, let me put it that way, and it's more a private cemetery.*'

Before we consider why it is that some natural burial grounds attract memorialisation beyond that which is permitted, it is important to recognise that there already exists a wide range of different approaches among natural burial sites. Figure 4.18 attempts to capture some of this variety through a series of images gathered from different sites. These are arranged to reveal a gradient in terms of the permanence and prominence of grave marking and also the extent to which the memorialisation retains the identity of the deceased. The majority of sites permit a small stone plaque to be placed flat on the surface of the grave. Some of the managers we spoke with said this was originally only intended to record the grave number but has, in response to requests from bereaved people, been adapted to include more personal information.

> The original idea was the marker stone that we provide and this really was for us to identify the grave, not really for the family to identify the grave. In response to requests and pressure from bereaved families this has gone through a series of changes and now records the full name and year of birth and death and grave number.
>
> (Sue Nadin, Wisewood Cemetery)

From our experience of talking with managers, excessive or potentially inappropriate memorialisation can be attributed to a number of causes.

Figure 4.18 *Grave memorialisation at five natural burial sites reveal a range of different approaches. Some are more permanent and include the name of the deceased etched in stone, while others are made of wood that will gradually rot away.*

First, providers are often concerned about causing distress to bereaved families by removing items from a grave, especially where the grave is that of a young person. One of our providers spoke of the difficulty of making this judgement:

> It's all got to be biodegradable and if it isn't then we take it off, the day of the funeral we don't worry, we'll leave it there for a week or so, it's a question of stages . . . for a child's grave, a teddy bear on it we'd leave it there for a month or two . . . then we would leave a note to say look we've got to, we've got to. . .
>
> (Nicholas Taylor, Epping Forest)

Second, providers spoke of the importance of getting bereaved families to visit the burial ground before making any commitment so they could see for themselves what was, and perhaps more importantly, was not, permitted. Some providers, including Al at East Meon, insist on meeting the family before they will agree to a funeral so that they can be shown the burial ground (see Chapter 5). Such meetings are also an opportunity to ensure families fully understand the choice they are making. Where funerals were arranged independently with a funeral director, several providers expressed their concern that the site's regulations had not been fully explained, with the result that families left items that were not appropriate. This situation was also more difficult to manage because no prior relationship had been established between the bereaved people and the site owners and managers.

As noted in Chapter 2, it emerged from our study that the regular presence of providers at the site creates the opportunity for relationships with visitors to be formed, which in turn allows providers to quickly address any issues that may arise. Ifor at Abermule, for example, commented that as part of his daily routine he would take a stroll across from his farm to the burial ground:

> I probably have a walk around the field . . . once a day, you know, as a matter of routine, it's a nice little walk and you want to see if anybody, if anything's happened or any, any disturbances, or, you know, whatever has gone on.
>
> (Ifor Humphreys, Abermule)

In an effort to preserve a vision of the burial ground that is free from individual memorials, providers have developed different strategies that allow the family to record the identity of the deceased without impacting on the burial area. These have included the promotion of memorial websites, a book of remembrance and, as we have seen at Carlisle, a sheepfold, set apart from the woodland for memorial plaques (see Chapter 2). We have observed similar strategies for providing a location for memorial plaques at other sites; for example, Springwood Woodland Burials on the Isle of Wight has placed large boulders at the entrance for this purpose. Perhaps because of the visual connection with the traditional cemetery, where plaques are often displayed in a prominent position in the landscape, natural burial providers have looked for alternative approaches to make them less intrusive. For example, at Abermule, families can pay for a plaque to be placed on an oak post next to one of the trees in the adjacent woodland.

Christmas is perhaps the most challenging time for many providers because families often come together and visit the burial ground, looking to find ways of including the deceased at a time of festivity and celebration:

> Christmas time is the worst [time of year for memorialising] and we do find tinsel and balloons and Christmas trees and so on and baubles, we had a lovely tree this year which . . . fortunately I came up here on Christmas Eve, I've got a dog and I come up and walk her here deliberately around the major festivals because the amount of stuff that appears is really . . . unbelievable.
>
> (Patricia Banks, manager)

In response to this challenge, two of the providers we interviewed now host an annual carol service. Ray Ward at Herrongate Wood has planted a large Christmas tree, and each year they have a band and carol service that is attended by several hundred people. By providing a point of focus for memorialising and an event that the family can participate in, Ray is able to manage the amount of memorialising that would otherwise appear in the burial ground. He told us:

> They can write their name and a message to the person they've lost and hang them all over it no problem at all. And then we leave them there until the following January the sixth when all the Christmas decorations [come down] and take them all off.
>
> (Ray Ward, Herrongate Wood)

Servicing the natural burial ground: buildings, thresholds and processions

Here we consider the contribution of new buildings and structures at natural burial sites in terms of the facilities they provide and, perhaps more significantly, how their design contributes to the identity of the burial ground and experience of users. Only one of our four ethnographic sites, East Meon, has buildings. The building here was inherited from its time as a Royal Navy training college (see Chapters 3 and 5). This building is not particularly attractive or evocative but has proved to be a valuable asset in supporting the activities of the Trust as it includes office space for staff and volunteers, and has also enabled them to extend the service they offer to bereaved families. Rooms can be hired for a funeral service and there is a café that is open throughout the week and can also provide catering for a reception if required.

Whilst very few of the 20 sites we visited could support this range of facilities, 7 of them had invested in a building or buildings in order to provide a space for a service and/or possibly a reception. These were all independent providers, which is perhaps not surprising as many of the local authority sites may have a chapel on-site or can recommend alternative venues located nearby. The independent sites tend to be more remote, which means potential users might be discouraged from using the burial ground if there were no easy access to a suitable venue or gathering place.

The building may also be important in marketing the burial ground to people wishing to pre-purchase a grave, and indeed pre-purchasing represents a significant proportion of the income of many independent burial grounds. Some natural burial sites – for example, Memorial Woodlands Bristol – also

Figure 4.19 *A traditional green oak building creates a space for a simple service, a threshold to the burial ground and a place to shelter in bad weather. Similar to the sheepfold at Carlisle, it is also a place to display memorial plaques, thereby keeping them separate from the burial meadow. Usk Castle Chase, Monmouthshire (April 2008).*

market their facilities for weddings and other celebrations.[10] This is an interesting development, and, while uncommon, it does suggest how natural burial sites might capitalise on their buildings and landscape and return to a time when the burial ground was a familiar landscape in which other significant celebrations, including weddings, took place. From a design perspective, new buildings are an important opportunity to enhance the vision and experience of the burial ground. To illustrate this point we look at two contrasting sites that represent very different levels of investment and context but achieve similar outcomes: Usk Castle Chase Natural Burial Meadow and GreenAcres Woodland Burials, Epping Forest.

Near the entrance to Usk Castle Chase there is a simple timber-frame shelter that the owner commissioned to provide a space where an outdoor service could be held and where visitors could retreat in bad weather. The shelter has been carefully sited so that it is visible as visitors approach the burial ground from the parking area. However, it does not intrude on the meadow but instead sits below the earth bank at the threshold to the burial ground. The vision was about protecting the existing character of the landscape where no grave marking is permitted. The building was crafted from green oak in the style of those that would once have been a common feature of the agricultural landscape, used for sheltering livestock or storing hay. Only when the visitor steps inside and look upwards is its relationship to the burial ground revealed in the memorial plaques that are attached to the ceiling.

Figure 4.20 *There is a large circular paved courtyard at the entrance to Woodland Hall with sufficient space for a hearse to turn around in. The hall is set back from the parking areas and creates a threshold into the woodland. GreenAcres Woodland Burials, Epping Forest, Essex (April 2008).*

Epping Forest represents a much greater level of investment and includes a separate site office and two buildings, referred to as the Gathering Hall and the Woodland Hall, that are arranged around a central courtyard. Nicholas Taylor, who then managed the site, explained that the buildings were a refinement following their experience at Colney Woodland Burial Park in Norfolk, which they also designed and manage. He said '*they are about 90 per cent the same as Colney because we have incorporated improvements . . . especially on environment issues . . . here we produce our own fuel so we run off wood chippings* [produced from the wood extracted from the burial ground]'.

While the buildings at Epping Forest are more contemporary in their form and construction design than Usk Castle Chase, the use of wood, a *natural* material, is explicit in both designs. At Epping Forest the buildings have also been carefully sited within the woodland so that, from the entrance and parking area, they are partly obscured by trees. The Gathering Hall and Woodland Hall have also been arranged so that the funeral party moves through a series of spaces that culminate in the Woodland Hall. Large windows connect the building visually with the landscape, which also informs the materials and design of furniture within the hall. A monocular vision of landscape as panorama is thus encouraged, in contrast with the binocular vision likely to develop through grave tending and planting.[11] The lectern, for example, was fashioned from a branch. At other sites we have also observed the introduction of an iconography that replaces traditional religious symbols with paintings of trees and carvings of, for example, the Green Man.

Figure 4.21 *From within the Woodland Hall there is a visual connection into the surrounding landscape that is echoed in the detailing of the lectern. GreenAcres Woodland Burials, Epping Forrest, Essex (April 2008).*

> We've introduced aspects of the woodland environment into the Hall, as indeed the Hall reaches out into the woodland, so it's that journey that they can connect with, they see the evidence through the glass walls of the hall of nature at work.
>
> (Nicholas Taylor, Epping Forest)

At Usk Castle Chase and Epping Forest the buildings thus create important connections with the landscape and a threshold from which the cortège progresses into the burial ground. Procession through the burial ground is an important aspect of many natural burial grounds, particularly where the topography and absence of surfaced roads require the coffin to be shouldered or transported on a hand bier to the grave (see Chapter 5). At Penwith Woodland Burial Place in Cornwall, an oak lychgate defines the entrance to the burial ground. Traditionally symbolic of the threshold into the church graveyard, here it is also used as a shelter and a place to sit, and it makes an important separation between the woodland burial ground and the pet cemetery which the visitor must walk through before entering the burial ground.

Summary

From our visits to a sample of natural burial sites and interviews with burial ground managers, we have captured some of the richness and variety of different approaches to designing the natural burial landscape. These landscapes

Figure 4.22 *The oak lychgate, symbolic of the entrance to the church graveyard, here creates a clear boundary between the adjacent pet cemetery and the natural burial ground, as well as a sheltered place to sit. Penwith Woodland Burial Place, Cornwall (May 2008).*

reveal how providers have experimented in designing new alternatives for how to arrange, locate and memorialise each grave in order to create more 'nature'-like settings where trees are no longer confined to a regimented grid. Where new woodland is being created, some have come to appreciate the challenges of preserving sufficient space for trees to grow while also ensuring that there is access to the grave for the bereaved family and for the grave diggers to do their work. This has included the introduction of woodland groves (Carlisle Cemetery) and wildflower burial glades set within a newly planted woodland framework (Barton Glebe), or the creation of an orchard of small fruit trees (Great Bradley Cottage).

Excessive memorialisation has continued to be a challenge for many providers, and at one site the manager accepted that while it was called a woodland burial ground there was little to differentiate it from a cemetery and its neatly aligned rows of headstones.

During our visits we have also been interested to observe how buildings, whether it be a simple traditional timber-frame shelter or lychgate or the much grander Woodland Hall, are becoming a more common feature of these landscapes. These structures, the materials they are made from, the furnishings they contain or the carvings on their walls have become an important device in projecting the identity of natural burial.

What is exemplified here, then, is the creative and evolving nature of design within the natural burial ground. Rather than an externally imposed template, those who would provide a site and those seeking natural burial for themselves or someone close to them have entered into a creative entanglement[12] which leads them along particular pathways, not to conclusive destinations but to continuing journeys through inhabited landscape.[13]

5

Ethnography of a natural burial ground

This chapter draws on data gathered while Mark Powell was living at East Meon during the summer of 2008. It provides a grounded perspective on the day-to-day events that took place at the burial ground and an opportunity for readers to get a first-hand account of what it might mean to bury naturally.

This account is based on Mark's experiences of the South Downs natural burial site, East Meon, and provides the vehicle for making sense of the everyday world of the natural burial ground. We begin by briefly explaining how we chose East Meon as a site for our ethnographic research and the unique opportunity it presented. The chapter is then organised around a timeline that starts with Al, the site manager, and observations of his encounters with bereaved people when they requested to bury someone at East Meon. It also explores their initial reactions to the site. This provides an opportunity to reflect on how Al communicated the burial ground to them – its landscape and the ideas and values that underpin this, and how users might participate not only in the funeral, but also in shaping the landscape. The chapter then follows the sequence of events that take place at the burial ground, moving through each stage: grave preparation; the funeral procession; committal of the body; and backfilling the grave. These observations allow for reflection upon the 'doing' of natural burial, including the ways in which the burial ground landscape shapes these experiences. Finally we discuss Mark's experiences of working alongside the community of volunteers, which included people who had buried a family member or friend at East Meon.

Inhabiting the burial ground

Ethnography and participant observation are part of an anthropological research tradition of seeking to understand how and why people act as they do. It requires the researcher to find a role that will enable them to engage with and embed themselves in the community they are researching in an unobtrusive way.[1] Although other researchers have been successful in recruiting and interviewing participants in the cemetery, they focused on large municipal sites that were frequently visited and where staff were permanently employed on-site.[2] Finding a role in a natural burial ground was more difficult. Many of the sites we had visited were small and remote. Days or even weeks could pass without a funeral, and visitors were infrequent. Our feelings were that, at such sites, bereaved people might not

Figure 5.1 *Al and Mark visit part of the woodland that had recently been cleared of conifers and was in the process of being prepared for burials and broadleaf woodland planting. (East Meon, September 2007).*

welcome intrusion at the graveside and might well be suspicious of someone who appeared to have no obvious reason for being there. We needed to identify a burial ground where Mark could find a role that would legitimise his presence and, most importantly, provide him with a community to engage with.

Andy Clayden and Mark first visited East Meon in September 2007, when they met with burial ground manager Al Blake. As Al accompanied them on a tour of the site, they soon realised the unique opportunity East Meon presented for their research. It was a well-established burial ground with a large community of users, and funerals were a regular weekly occurrence. The visitor centre and café provided a central focus: a place to meet people and a venue for funerals and receptions. Most importantly, Al was enthusiastic about our project and was happy to include Mark in the day-to-day activities of the burial ground and introduce him to potential research participants. Finally, East Meon was most unusual in having its own on-site hostel, just a short walk from the burial ground. Staying there made it possible for Mark to develop friendships and engage with the day-to-day activities of the burial ground in an opportunistic way.

Fieldwork fell into a regular pattern of staying at the hostel for periods of 4–5 days throughout June, July and August 2008. Each morning Mark would meet with Al and his assistant Charlie at his office in the visitor centre, where they would discuss the day's schedule over a cup of tea. A critical first step of the research was developing the trust of our research participants and finding a way to inhabit the research space in an unobtrusive manner. This came about as

Mark worked alongside Al and Charlie, helping them set out a burial space or clear vegetation from a path, or assisting Charlie with preparing a grave. While Mark worked with Al, he told him he had no formal training or traditional background in the death care profession; instead his approach was informed by varied work experience and on-the-job learning. He grew up in a nearby village and before coming to East Meon had been a freelance designer and had later worked in a forest school with disaffected young people. His life story helped inform our interpretations of his unique contribution at East Meon.

Al's enthusiasm for DIY funerals also provided opportunities for Mark to find a role on the day of a funeral, working closely with the bereaved family and the rest of the burial team. Through this hands-on engagement Mark got to know the people who worked at East Meon and was able to develop a more relaxed and informal approach to his fieldwork.

Establishing research contacts was made easier by Al's outgoing and friendly demeanour and good rapport with fellow workers and site users. Assisting in preparation of the ground for burials and working alongside Al and Charlie in making arrangements for a funeral enabled him to meet funeral directors, celebrants and priests, as well as bereaved people. Through these meetings Mark was able to explain his presence at the site and introduce our research. Mark often worked with the volunteers in the woodland, and, during these times, he periodically recorded details of conversations on small pieces of paper stuffed in his shirt pocket, to be written up later as field notes. Where Al and Mark felt it was appropriate, Mark would invite some of the volunteers and burial ground users to meet to discuss their experiences. These conversations would often take place at the visitor centre or in Al's office or sometimes, at their request, by the graveside. The analysis that we present here is informed by some of Mark's observations when he worked at East Meon and the many different conversations he had with the people he met there.

Introducing bereaved people to East Meon

In conversations with Al, it became apparent that he was very much aware of how first impressions of East Meon could influence people's perceptions of how the burial site was run and maintained. Al was of the impression that many people were initially shocked and dismayed at the general 'run-down' appearance of the site. He went on to describe how new arrivals must first drive past the razor-wire-topped fences that cordoned off vacant buildings, a residue of the time when the site belonged to the Royal Navy, and might also find themselves parked next to a set of battered garages, with grass growing up through the cracks in the concrete. He felt that the collection of yurts and tipis they would have passed by on the way to the burial ground might contribute to a feeling that the site was managed by a 'bunch of hippies'. When he met prospective clients, Al therefore made what he described as a 'judgement call' on how to introduce them to the sustainability site. Sometimes he chose to emphasise the burial site within the context of the wider social ambitions of the Centre, presenting its good work with local schools and communities; alternatively he might choose to focus on his environmental objectives for the burial ground and explain how the existing conifer plantation was gradually being returned to a mixed native woodland. He also sought to reassure visitors that East Meon was responsibly run and financially secure, that there was a long-term commitment to the burial ground and that the site's membership of the ANBG and NDC required management's adherence to a national code of good practice.

At the time of our research, Al's initial meeting with bereaved people took place in his office, located towards the rear of the visitor centre beyond the café and reception area. Given Al's concerns about potential clients' initial responses to East Meon, Mark reflected on his own first impressions. When Andy and he visited Al's office for the first time, they were struck by the collection of muddy boots pushed beneath chairs, axes and spades propped against a wall and chainsaw files scattered across his desk. On the walls, the site burial plans competed for space with posters of woodland birds and wildflowers. Clearly, then, in Al's office the practical realities of managing a woodland and burial ground co-existed with often emotionally charged conversations with bereaved people. What this display suggested was Al's openness about what the process of burial entailed at East Meon: the visible display of tools that both prepared the grave and shaped the landscape. This was in contrast to the premises of a funeral director where such a meeting would take place in clean and tidy office. This observation resonates with Glennys Howarth's[3] ethnography of a funeral director's business. Howarth applies notions of front- and backstage; that is, a private back room of the premises where the body is 'humanised' (via embalming) and thus considered ready for viewing by family and friends and then moved to the frontstage area. By contrast, at East Meon everything in the manager's office was 'frontstage'. Al considered most people who buried at East Meon to have a passion for the natural environment and be supporters of conservation and environmental sustainability. Many of the enquiries he received came via recommendations from previous site users. Even so, Al only agreed to a burial once he met the relatives and or friends of the deceased and had accompanied them on a tour of the site. Indeed, encouraging people to visit the burial ground was considered to be extremely important for many of the providers and funeral directors we spoke with. They were anxious that people understood what it meant to bury at a site where no headstones are permitted and felt a visit would help them gain some understanding of the realities of burying naturally.

Walking people around the burial ground provided Al with an opportunity to address potential concerns directly, to show the different burial options and to explain how the landscape was being managed, where trees were being felled and planted and how the site changed with each passing season. On reflection, this interaction enabled Al to address not only the immediate issue of helping the family choose a burial place but, perhaps more importantly, to convey his primary responsibility – management of a woodland located within a National Park and an Area of Outstanding Natural Beauty (AONB). Al discussed how he would use this time to try and assess visitors' emotional state. In his view, those with a *realistic attitude* were aware that the person was gone, although he realised people had different ideas and beliefs about the body and its relationship to the person. Al said this first meeting was also an opportunity for him to understand what potential users knew about natural burial and to explain how they might be involved. He would also try to gauge how far he should encourage them to participate in the funeral; possibilities that ranged from what he described as a DIY,[4] to the appointment of a funeral director to make some or all of the arrangements. Al explained, *'the difficulty is . . . if I say . . .*

do this and do that ... I don't want them to feel they're having an inferior do ... doing anything lesser because they have chosen to have the funeral director there ... or the Minister'. Through our conversations, it was clear that Al did not wish to impose natural burial on people as a practice that occupied a higher moral ground. Another concern for him was that he did not want people and arrangements to go to pieces on the day of the funeral and felt it was his responsibility to look out for bereaved families and ensure everything went well for them. This was especially important when Al had both encouraged and agreed to a DIY funeral and taken on the role of facilitator. So while natural burial creates opportunities for a burial ground manager to adopt other roles, these are accompanied by a degree of risk and anxiety. Al's feelings of responsibility coupled with his role as 'facilitator' of DIY reflect Walter's argument that: 'If the individual is to die and grieve in their own way, they can be helped to do so by practitioners only if the latter listen attentively to the individual.'[5]

Al explained how he considered bereaved people's involvement in the funeral to be a cathartic experience that would help them work through their grief. If they were fit and active, he suggested they might participate by using the hand bier to transport the coffin and to assist in lowering the coffin into the grave, a task that Mark helped a number of families with. In one interview, a bereaved husband explained how Al suggested he might collect his wife from the funeral director and bring her to East Meon in his own car. He reflected on how this had enabled him to participate and find a role in a process he felt excluded from because other family members had taken on the responsibility of planning the funeral. Al also enquired whether family members or friends wished to speak at the burial service. At the same time as advocating that people made their own burial arrangements, however, Al was also conscious that not every family is able to support a DIY funeral, or is inclined to do so. Our data highlight how frequently people preferred the ceremony to replicate practices they were already familiar with. Al recognised the complexity of his role, explaining: '*What I'm supposed to do is just facilitate people to bury people in my woods ... but obviously I'm an events manager as well, because I have a duty of care, as soon as people are on this land ... this is my gig.*' It was this recognition of having a 'duty of care' that we later reflected on when we sought to understand what motivated Al to act in this way. It became evident that he was not merely concerned with the practicalities of burial, but was also aware that East Meon's reputation as a burial venue was very much linked to the success of a burial performance, his 'gig' and the site's capacity as a mortuary landscape to shape people's experiences in positive ways.

Digging the grave

At the time of our research, all the graves at East Meon were excavated by hand, and this remains the practice at the time of writing.[6] While Al said there had been occasions when the family and friends had dug the grave at East Meon, this did not occur while Mark was there. Graves were dug according to the measurements provided by the funeral director and marked onto the ground using pegs and tape. Charlie took a great deal of care to shape the grave precisely to these measurements so that the coffin would fit snugly when lowered into the ground. He would take a whole day to dig a single grave, and on some days Mark worked with him on this task. After removing the first six inches of top soil, the remaining white chalk was hard to cut and required considerable effort with a mattock, iron bar and pick – shoring up and boarding the grave-sides to stop them collapsing was not necessary. The chalky soil was loaded into wheelbarrows, pushed a short distance away from the grave, and piled onto timber boards that would make it easier to shovel when backfilling the grave. It was necessary to use the wheelbarrow to avoid placing earth on an adjacent grave and to allow space to manoeuvre the coffin and accommodate the mourn-ers. Al explained his belief in a spiritual connection that linked the physical graft and care of digging a grave at East Meon with the Bronze Age tombs still visible on the hills surrounding the site. For Al, digging by hand provoked a notion of there being a 'naturalness' to burial at East Meon that was not found on sites where graves were dug by machine. While hand digging was slow and physically demanding, it allowed Al and Charlie to work within the constraints of the existing woodland without the fear of damaging trees with heavy machinery or disturbing the tranquillity of the site.[7]

In one area of the burial ground, among the mature woodland, the graves were dug to fit into the space between the trees and then marked on the burial chart in Al's office. We were interested to observe that while Al made a con-nection with the surrounding Bronze Age landscape, he also maintained the convention of arranging the graves on an east–west axis. This highlighted the complexities that exist in natural burial practices, where tradition, custom and the legal requirement to locate each grave might override opportunities to respond to the landscape and surrounding views.

Funeral days

Al would not agree to what he deemed to be unusual requests, such as burying the dead with an uncovered face. Although a limited number of shroud burials had been carried out at East Meon, Al was not keen on these as he feared they might be more upsetting for mourners than they anticipated and, as we have discussed elsewhere, this to some extent revealed his more personal concerns.[8] This exposure of the body of the deceased, its shape and form potentially changed Al's relationship with the grave and, more importantly, how he expe-rienced and visualised the landscape.[9] On the day of a funeral, Al and Charlie had a well-rehearsed plan of action. After morning coffee, they walked down to the gravesite to clear away the tarpaulins and boards they had placed above the pre-dug grave and covered the pile of earth with branches gathered in the wood-land. It is interesting to note this practice of hiding the soil, given the importance that natural burial attaches to the earth and how the use of biodegradable willow and cardboard coffins are used to help accelerate the decomposition of the body through contact with the soil, air and water. At East Meon, cover-ing the soil had taken on a creative twist in its response to the materials that could be found in the surrounding woods. At the other sites we visited, where graves were dug by a contractor, artificial grass was often used for this purpose. In trying to understand this difference in approach we turn to Ingold[10] and Olwig[11] to explain how Al and Charlie's practice was shaped by their experi-ence of inhabiting this landscape and a desire to preserve the coherent vista of the woodland, rather than drawing attention to what lay beneath its surface. In

Figure 5.2 *The grave is made ready on the day of the funeral. The earth from the grave is covered with branches gathered from the woods. Wooden putlocks are placed across the grave to support the coffin before it is lowered into the grave using the strops that are positioned beside them (East Meon, June 2008).*

Figure 5.3 *At natural burial sites where contractors excavate graves the earth is typically dressed with synthetic grass. Wooden planks secure the grave edge on which the putlocks and strops are placed (Ulley, May 2008).*

Figure 5.4 *Al and Charlie check the dimensions of the grave on the morning of the funeral after clearing away any leaves to expose any potential trip hazards (East Meon, July 2008).*

contrast, the contractor's visit is short and focused on the task in hand, shaped by the experience of working in other cemeteries and graveyards and, through the use of a mechanical digger, physically separated from the land.

Al and Charlie always appeared more focused on the day of a funeral; for example, they were anxious that coffin measurements were correct for they had the experience of the funeral director's staff forgetting to pass on information about prominent handles and sometimes received incorrect measurements of the coffin. Conversely, at another site visited, the funeral director expressed the same concern and said that he always visited the burial ground on the morning of a funeral to check that the grave had been dug to the correct dimensions. As part of the pre-funeral preparations, Al and Charlie would carry out the same checks; and both admitted to being greatly relieved once the coffin was safely sitting on the bottom of a grave.

Other pre-funeral preparations included sweeping the area around the grave clear of leaves to reveal any roots or other trip hazards. The putlocks,[12] wooden poles that support the coffin, were positioned over the grave and the lowering strops placed alongside. Al would then brief Charlie and any other staff or volunteers assisting with the funeral on how he expected the service to proceed, where the hand bier or horse-drawn cart would stop, where the relatives would be standing, and finally how the coffin would be manoeuvred into place. The terrain – the location of trees and stumps and roots – appeared important in shaping the way Al coordinated and arranged each funeral and how, as a consequence, each burial at East Meon represented an individual response to this landscape.

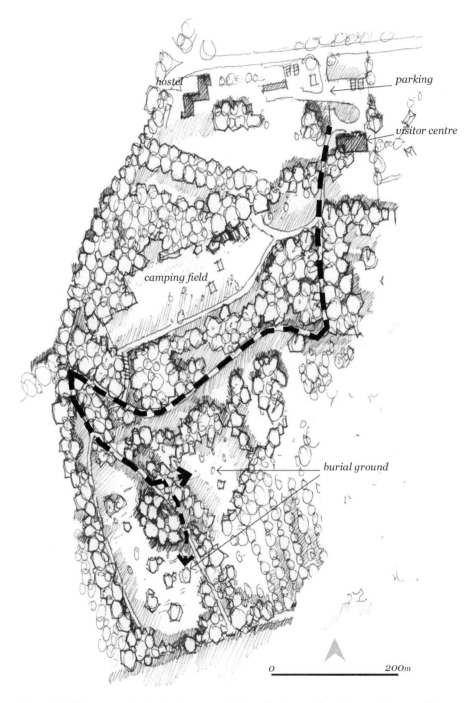

Figure 5.5 *The procession leads along a track through the woodland, beneath the camping field and down to the burial ground.*

Figure 5.6 *The hand bier is used at East Meon to transport the coffin from the visitor centre to the burial ground (East Meon, June 2008).*

Procession

Having returned to the office after their site check, Al and Charlie usually made themselves another coffee before they headed off, still in their work clothes, to greet the funeral party. Charlie waited at the main gate, coffee and cigarette in hand, to direct the cars, a task Mark would often assist with. Al waited near the entrance to the visitor centre to greet the funeral party, occasionally hugging people he had met previously. The informality of these occasions contrasted with that of the funeral directors and their employees, who appeared more reserved and distant in their formal dress. One of the funeral directors explained how he did not feel it appropriate for him to adopt a similar approach to Al and that the thought of not wearing black to a funeral made him feel '*strange*' and somehow '*less in charge*'. He described how, '*these clothes are your barrier ... [and] they're your badge of office ... If you haven't got a black tie you're not a proper funeral operative.*' There was a sense among funeral directors of being somewhat disempowered, therefore, when requested to move away from well-rehearsed and accepted codes of practice, and we explore these issues in more detail in Chapter 7.

At funerals attended in East Meon, some bereaved people made use of the meeting room and catering facilities at the visitor centre for the service and reception, while others made independent arrangements. However, because vehicles were not permitted to drive down through the woodland, unless someone was infirm or had a disability, all funeral parties were required to walk the 500-metre journey to the burial ground. This took approximately 10–15

Figure 5.7 *The horse and cart were occasionally requested to transport the coffin from the reception centre to the grave (East Meon, August 2008).*

minutes and led along a track past the camping field, tipis and yurts and then descended down into the woods. The coffin was usually transported with the hand bier or occasionally some families requested the service of a horse-drawn cart. Some of the funeral directors' pallbearers refused to use the hand bier, pre-ferring instead to shoulder the coffin to the grave. This procession and the time and space that it created were an important aspect of burial at East Meon. The coffin was accessible when it was transferred from the hearse and placed on the hand bier. Family and friends had the opportunity to place flowers upon it and help in delivering the body to the grave. This journey also allowed time for quiet reflection and, on occasion, conversation as the cortège slowly wound its way down and into the woodland.

At one of the funerals Mark attended, a bereaved son brought his father in a VW camper van, the cardboard coffin sitting on the folded-down bed beside him. On arrival, friends and family lifted the coffin out of the van and onto the hand bier. Al usually stood amid the crowd and explained to the funeral party how they were the only ones burying that day, so they could take as long as they liked. On this particular occasion, as they stood waiting to push the hand bier to the burial ground, one of the mourners turned to another and said: '*You know, this is almost natural.*' We interpret his comment as not only being a reference to the woodland but also to how family and friends had come together to care for their dead, something that 'came naturally' to them.

At another funeral, the mourners pushed the hand bier down the tree-lined track while Al guided the remainder of the party along a narrow woodland trail, a more direct route to the open grave. As they made their way a young girl struggled to prevent her stilettos from sinking into the soft ground. One of the funeral directors, a regular at East Meon, described how some of his colleagues disliked the site because of this long walk and the muddying of their shoes, especially when they had another funeral to attend that afternoon. Similarly, an Anglican priest explained that while he was happy to attend burials in the woods, many of his colleagues were not because it took longer than they were used to and frequently meant coping with '*difficult weather*' and '*extremely nasty mud*'.

On one occasion Charlie prepared a space in an existing family grave for the interment of cremated remains. Later that afternoon Al joined the funeral party, which included two sisters and their children, on the walk to the grave. The children fought among themselves to carry the urn containing their grand-dad's ashes and while one carried the urn, the others laughed as they ran among the trees and jumped over burial mounds. As the group moved through the woods to grandma's grave, the two sisters maintained light-hearted banter with the children, joking and laughing about grandad and grandma. At a later inter-view they spoke of suppressing their sadness at losing their father while the children were with them. When gathered around the grave, one of the sisters said a few words; then Charlie, with the help of the children, covered the urn with soil. The children were then encouraged to '*go off and explore*', being told by their mothers they wanted '*a few moments with grandad*' alone. Finally, the sisters were given a chance to express their emotion and offer comfort to each other. There was a noticeable ease with which the sisters allowed their children to roam 'free' in the burial ground, which they may not have felt so comfortable to do in a traditional cemetery. In terms of our research, we can identify mul-tiple readings of the same place. The women were at the site in order to inter the ashes of their father, a sacred place in which they had previously committed their mother. By contrast, the children responded to the woodland as a place of adventure.

Committal and backfilling the grave

Al preferred to have the coffin left on putlocks over the open grave so the family had a few reflective moments prior to the committal. He also officiated at some of the funerals while, at others, a priest or celebrant took on this role. These occasions were often marked by storytelling, the recital of favourite poems, or music. On one occasion, there was a recording of the deceased playing his guitar and singing. These services were a mixture of tears, laughter and applause, with Al on hand to step forward if needed to help guide proceedings.

When the coffin was lowered by family or friends at a '*DIY funeral*', an additional third strop was used. This helped to secure the coffin for those who were inexperienced in this task and at the same time allowed more people to participate. Al would direct this process, making sure that everyone was ready and would guide them in lowering the coffin into the ground.

Once at the bottom of the grave, Al said '*thank you gentlemen*', and the strops were laid down on the ground. Al kept a pot of dried earth close at hand and at the end of a service he would invite mourners to throw some of the soil into the grave to mark the end of the funeral. This signalled the time for mourn-ers to leave the graveside and make their way back through the woodland to

Figure 5.8 *Preparation for a DIY funeral. An extra strop is placed in the middle of the grave to help secure the coffin and allow more people to participate in lowering the coffin. A small pot of earth is also visible at the foot of the grave, available for those who wish to cast earth after the committal (East Meon, July 2008).*

the visitor centre and car park. We did not observe family or friends backfilling a grave, but Charlie acknowledged that when this happened he would offer to help. Al explained how he had introduced the scattering of earth as a means to guide people towards the end of a committal.

At no time was the grave left unattended after the funeral. Charlie waited until people left the graveside before starting his work, aware that some might choose to return. The process of backfilling began by his removal of the strops and moving any flowers to one side of the grave to be placed on top of the grave once filled. If it was raining, he covered the earth with a tarpaulin to prevent it becoming sodden and more difficult to move. When backfilling, Charlie first filled the space between the coffin and the edge of the grave, and he then continued to lay the broken chalk around the edges of the coffin and worked inwards, backfilling in layers. He tamped as he progressed until the grave was completely filled. Some of the remaining earth was neatly mounded on the grave. Although Charlie explained how this was to allow for the future settlement of the grave, many of the older graves still retained this form, preserving the location of the deceased within the landscape. Backfilling took several hours and, when finished, surplus soil was removed by wheelbarrow. Having removed the soil from the plywood boards, a clean grassed area adjacent to the now filled grave was revealed. Charlie finished by sweeping around the grave with a broom then headed back to the office with his wheelbarrow and tools for a cup of tea.

Figure 5.9 *A willow coffin fits neatly into the hand-dug grave (East Meon, June 2008).*

While natural burial seemingly offers a chance to bury in new ways, fieldwork observations and interviews suggested that funerals at East Meon continued to abide by certain traditions and expectations around appropriate burial practice. Although bereaved people were given a degree of freedom to arrange a funeral as they wished, the practices observed at East Meon shared similarities with those of traditional funerals This is not wholly unexpected for, as Al explained, he guided people towards a '*Judeo-Christian burial cere-mony*', advocated carrying a coffin feet first and buried bodies in an east–west

Figure 5.10 *Charlie fills the grave, taking care to consolidate the chalky soil with a tamper in order to minimise any later settlement (East Meon, August 2008).*

orientation. Some users of East Meon wished to personalise various aspects of the funeral, but many continued to identify with a '*proper*' way of doing things. This reveals how cultural habits or 'habitus'[13] has a significant influence on individual choice. In the main, and despite having some degree of freedom to bury as they wished, our fieldwork observations suggest that people were reluctant or unable to completely re-invent the way they buried their dead. This resonates with Walter's arguments regarding a new revival of death that nonetheless incorporates a mix of older customs.[14]

These cultural habits are also apparent in the activities of funeral directors and other death care professionals, and illustrated in a conversation Mark had with the priest who regularly officiated at East Meon. He recalled one occasion where he agreed to a non-religious service and suggested to the bereaved family they might prefer him to wear a shirt and tie rather than his usual 'dog collar'. His suggestion was met with, '*I think you'd better wear your collar, just in case they think I've dragged some old boy in off the street to take it!*' While there is no requirement for a priest to officiate at a funeral, people might continue to be constrained by the notion of what is appropriate or indeed legally permitted.

It is important to acknowledge that there might be good reasons for people deciding not to reject tradition completely, especially in the emotionally charged moments immediately surrounding a death. Knowing what to wear and how to act during a funeral provides bereaved people and professionals alike with a degree of emotional comfort. It may also allow them to accommodate unresolved thoughts and ideas they may hold in relation to both themselves and the deceased concerning life, death and immortality.[15] Overall, Al had adopted a traditional framework for each burial: the procession, the placing of the coffin on the putlocks and finally the committal. Bereaved people were then invited by him to embellish this structure as they wished. In a recent article, Al discussed how there are occasions when families and friends choose to prolong the time they spend at the burial ground and centre by booking into the hostel or camping in the field above the burial ground.[16]

Memorial landscapes: a place for bereaved people

Al and Charlie's work in the woodland involved them journeying along different interlinked pathways, and these regular everyday movements familiarised them with the activities of other site users and how they engaged with the graves and wider landscape. They took a keen interest in those who had buried there and regarded themselves as having an ongoing '*duty of care*' towards users of the burial ground, a duty that extended beyond the day of the funeral. They noticed aspects of landscape that infrequent visitors might be unlikely to observe; for example, when a grave was unusually clear of fallen leaves or when objects gathered in the woods had been arranged on a grave, suggesting regular visiting. These kinds of behaviour were also observed at the Ulley site during the longitudinal survey Andy conducted, which is the focus of Chapter 8. As Mark spent more time working in the burial ground, he too began to notice subtle changes that indicated how people were engaging with the burial landscape even though he had not seen any visitors.

If someone spent long periods at a graveside, Charlie and Al became concerned, interpreting this as a sign of emotional distress. At one point during the fieldwork, Charlie and Mark noticed a man regularly sitting alone by a new grave. This was adjacent to where Charlie's wife had been buried several years before. Charlie explained how he recognised something of himself in the way this person was dealing with his bereavement. There was a familiar pattern to his memorialisation activities, the regularity with which the grave was swept clear of fallen leaves and the lighting of candles. The grave space was also adorned with a multitude of small wooden ornaments and flowers, and, most tellingly, the man spent long periods at the graveside, obviously distressed.

As Charlie went about his woodland tasks, he took the opportunity to engage the man in conversation. His approach was very informal as he gently enquired about 'how he was doing'. In different circumstances this intrusion might be unwelcome or feel somewhat forced, but both Charlie and Al were familiar faces to those who regularly visit the burial ground. It was probable they would have helped with the arrangements and facilitated at the funeral. What emerged was not only how natural burial enabled continuing bonds between the living and the dead,[17] but also how this landscape facilitated bonds between bereaved people and those who worked in the burial ground.

Bereaved people's desire to memorialise the dead was revealed, or indeed perhaps not revealed, at East Meon in different ways. On first impressions, the majority of graves in East Meon appeared empty of memorabilia, but a closer inspection revealed a range of subtle, discreet and what Al described as '*organic*' forms of memorialisation there too. Al and Charlie could identify memorialisation, such as arrangements of twigs, leaves and pebbles on graves, or plants not typical of this woodland, which for others would go unnoticed. Indeed, interviews with bereaved people also revealed that the desire to memorialise was as strong in this site as in others we visited during our study. Charlie, for example, told us how he had surrounded his wife Terry's grave with large chalk stones so 'you could see it from the moon'; Ros Eastman, whose husband Bill's grave was in close proximity to Terry's, had done likewise. It was only over time, and through conversations with Al, that such desires were tempered and their memorialisation practices became more discreet and at times concealed; in her interview, Ros explained how she had hidden a small Buddha in the long grasses of Bill's grave.

Al chose not to enforce strict rules that forbade memorialisation in the immediate aftermath of burial and would leave flowers and funeral items on a grave. In subsequent days, however, plastic toys were removed and placed in a box in his office for bereaved people to collect. Mark helped Al with stripping plastic wreath formers and oasis from bouquets to create small flower bunches that were returned to the grave. On one occasion Al found a large sunflower in a pot on a new grave, and, while happy to leave it *in situ* for a while, he knew the people who had buried nearby would complain if it remained there. Al was a close friend of the deceased and a member of the same social crowd. He removed the sunflower in its pot from the grave and took it to the local pub and gave it to one of the regulars, who was '*chuffed*' to learn it came from the grave of their mutual friend.

Burial ground communities

As the sunflower example demonstrates, Al searched for innovative ways to keep East Meon free from what he saw as excessive or inappropriate memorialisation. However, he was conscious that people often needed to tend the grave as part of the grieving process and was keen to facilitate this process, while retaining a landscape of minimal grave marking. What most alarmed Al was when bereaved people continued to be fixated on the gravesite and appeared unable to engage with the wider landscape. Al described how, on such occasions, he would talk to them and introduce the idea of working with the volunteers to take care of the woodland. Charlie described how Al had approached him at a point when he had felt '*lost*' at the side of Terry's grave; and he in turn encouraged Ros Eastman to join the volunteers. Ros said she was '*glad he kept on at me*'.

The group of volunteers do not work exclusively in the burial ground or for Al but right across the sustainability site at East Meon, under the direction of Sean, the general woodland manager. So, while there was a small group of bereaved volunteers, they worked alongside others who had not buried at East Meon but who were there to support the environmental aims of the trust. Mark worked with this group nettle bashing, bramble clearing or assisting with the felling of small trees and shrubs. As he worked alongside Ros, she explained how being in this group had led her to renegotiate her emotional links to the burial ground and to her deceased husband. '*When I first started volunteering, I would sit over lunch time [at his grave] . . . but now I see him when I first arrive.*'

Ros' willingness to change her routine from sitting alone over lunch at her husband's graveside to spending her lunchtime with the other volunteers provides an example of how being practically immersed in the landscape and developing new friendships might enable bereaved individuals to renegotiate their relationship with the burial ground. At the same time, their identities as volunteers allows them to legitimise their presence there. Another of the volunteers, Mark, said he was '*moving on . . . I don't go down there [to the grave] every time I come here . . . [but] . . . periodically . . . to make sure it's tidy.*' Speaking about his relationship with the volunteer group, he noted: '*It's become an essential part of my life now . . . it's not the most convenient place . . . I could volunteer [elsewhere] . . . Probably the same work . . . but I choose not to.*' When asked why he decided to keep coming, as there are places closer than East Meon, and whether it is because this was where his wife is buried, Bob replied: '*It's bigger than that . . . it's the place and the people.*'

These conversations illustrate how, through active engagement in working in the landscape alongside others, their focus shifted from a binocular, or close focus perspective, to a monocular, or broad frame view, one that positions the grave in its wider context.[18] We would argue that this is not about the erasure of the identity of the deceased within a collective memorial landscape because the location of the grave remained important. Rather, we suggest that a reframing of the grave occurs and appreciation develops of how it contributes to this environment as a whole. Over time and through their volunteering, bereaved people's understanding of burying naturally became more nuanced:

> I walk past her, and I brush the leaves off. If I've got to go with some tools, with the wheelbarrow, I'll walk across past Terry. Terry doesn't stop me working or slow me down . . . but I still see her every day. I can go there and I can be there, and I can do all of that [caring for the grave] and it's lovely, but I can also come away from it and close the door on it, and outside [beyond the graveside] the sun's actually shining now.
>
> (Charlie)

Summary

The underlying reason to undertake ethnographic research at East Meon was to understand the various perspectives people have of one particular burial ground and to witness the activities that take place there. In spending time at the site,

Mark was able to observe the day-to-day activities and relationships at East Meon. One of the most important features of the East Meon burial site was the presence of Al as an on-site facilitator fully engaged with the management of both the burial ground and the woods. Through his approach to burial, Al had a major impact on the experiences of burial ground users. Although the funerals attended were not radically different from what one might expect to see in a traditional cemetery, after careful assessment of their capabilities, Al was offering bereaved family and friends the opportunity to engage in all aspects of the funeral process, should they so desire. Al was not a trained death care 'professional', so he was able to approach not only natural burial but bereavement with new ideas and a fresh perspective not constrained by historical tradition or training.

His focus on the woodland also impacted on his approach to site users because his ultimate aim was to return the area to a native broadleaf woodland; he regarded the bodies buried there as adding to the 'earthy substrata' that encouraged growth and added to the above-ground vista. Opportunities to work alongside Charlie as well as Al deepened our understanding of the importance of grave preparation and how, while Al related this to the historic landscape and was influenced by his interests in and respect for approaches to death and burial during the Bronze Age, Charlie took pride in the precision with which the grave was dug, an activity through which he demonstrated his care and respect for the deceased and the bereaved in the present day. The act of grave digging also revealed how the landscape, the trees and topography shaped how Al and Charlie were able to work; for example, decisions around the location of graves, and how this was further influenced by custom and practice, as well as the need to adhere to legislation.

Talking with death care professionals who worked at this site allowed us to contemplate the ways in which natural burial might present challenges to their usual working practices. These were revealed in the adjustments they had to make in order to operate in this landscape – for example, manoeuvring the coffin over rough terrain – and the time a funeral at the site might take, especially when compared with those at crematoria. A key marker of difference between Al and funeral directors was Al's willingness to actively encourage and facilitate bereaved people's participation in all aspects of the funeral, regarding this as a hugely important part of the grieving process. He was also relaxed and unceremonious with his clientele and, although not disparaged by funeral directors, there was a certain reserve on their part over whether such informality was 'professional'.

Al and Charlie made a significant contribution to the experiences of those who chose to bury at East Meon and offered continuity of care beyond the time of the funeral. Al adopted a pastoral role and provided a personal connection and degree of normality to his clients at a time of emotional upheaval, adjustment and distress. Most importantly, it was clear that bereaved people trusted Al and Charlie to be looking out for their best interests. It is for these reasons that we perceive Al as a 'new' kind of death care professional. For those engaged in these landscapes, then, natural burial seemingly offers new and unexpected experiences and opportunities.

Our ethnographic research provided a unique perspective on bereaved people's changing relationship with the burial ground. This perhaps was most significantly revealed from working alongside the volunteers. Their regular engagement with the landscape enhanced their understandings of natural burial and enabled them to modify their approach to memorialising and tending the grave. In the same way that the bodies of the dead were returned to the nutrient flows of a woodland system, so the emotional dimensions of bereavement appeared naturally remedied as people engaged practically in the physical landscape.

Perhaps more importantly, while the significance of the grave did not diminish, some of the bereaved people were able to anticipate the grave's future within a wider landscape, or collective memorial (an objective of the Natural Burial Movement). We have observed evidence of a change in focus at other natural burial sites as new woodland slowly emerges or a meadow is established over time, and Chapter 8 presents a visual representation of one site wherein this appears to happen. At East Meon, however, this shift in understanding seemingly took place quite quickly for the majority of site users. This was partly due to the scale and maturity of the woodland that enabled bereaved people to experience an established nature and so immerse themselves within it from the time of their first visit. It was, however, through the role of volunteer, and a sustained engagement with the site and activities of the Centre that bereaved people were invited to actively engage in the site's 'becoming' and, in so doing, shape the landscape and help realise the Trust's vision.

6

Choosing, doing and living with natural burial

This chapter focuses on how natural burial was chosen as a disposal option by our research participants and how they planned and enacted burials at the sites. It also explores bereaved people's experiences of the sites in the aftermath of burial and beyond. The chapter is divided into three broad sections that reflect its title, each of which draws extensively on data from our interviews with bereaved participants from the four ethnographic sites. The chapter thus begins to further unravel bereaved participants' motivations for choosing to bury naturally and explores how this choice played out with wider family and friends. To do so, the chapter considers whose choice natural burial was (deceased/bereaved/both) and what it was that attracted people to use a particular site. We discuss how burials were planned and carried out and follow our research participants' experiences of the day of the funeral in order to explore how these were anticipated and experienced. We also consider how bereaved people felt when they visited the sites and what they did in these places wherein graves remain relatively unmarked, in the traditional sense, so that the identity of the deceased is obscured. In order to present as full a picture as possible of natural burial as a process, we have chosen to focus on the natural burial journeys of four bereaved people, one from each of our ethnographic sites. They are: Ros Eastman, whose husband Bill is buried at East Meon; Allan Holbrook, whose father George is buried at the Abermule site; Maggie Carter, whose son Adam is buried at Ulley; and Marie Cooper, whose husband Jonathan is buried at the Wisewood site.

In selecting our bereaved participants, we were keen to explore experiences of different burial ground environments that the four ethnographic sites present and the different approaches they have taken towards what is permitted by way of memorialisation. At the same time, we wanted to investigate any differences that might manifest if burying a parent, a partner or a child, as this might have implications in terms of bereaved people's enduring relationship with the burial ground and their emotional investment in the site of the grave. We also selected people whose experience of burying naturally was more recent alongside those who have had a longer period of time to reflect on this experience so that we could explore how engagements with the burial ground might shift. Hence our selection of these four individual case studies from our sample of 40 bereaved participants helps convey how familial relationships between the living and the dead might be renegotiated and redefined through the process of natural burial over time. In order to direct readers to the 'bigger picture' of natural burial, throughout the chapter we also make links to other of our participants' experiences.

Four natural burial journeys after bereavement

Ros Eastman, East Meon

Bill Eastman died from a degenerative neurological disease in September 2007 and was buried at the East Meon site four days later. We interviewed his wife Ros one year after Bill's funeral. The interview took place in the hostel of the burial site one late afternoon, on a day when Ros had spent the morning working as a volunteer. The hostel common room was really busy and noisy so a quiet space was found at the bottom of some stairs in a corridor leading to a glass fire exit door, through which there was a view of the grounds. We drank our mugs of tea and chatted about Bill and how Ros had buried him with his hat, door key and unread book. It was dark by the time we finished, and the heating had come on.

Ros told us how her decision to bury naturally had emerged from an article in the magazine *Country Life*. She had clipped the article and kept it with wills and other documents, '*never thinking we'd need it so soon*'. In the final stages of his illness, Bill was not aware his death was imminent although Ros was; as such, there was no opportunity to discuss his own funeral arrangements, as Ros said, '*as far as Bill was concerned, he wanted to come home, he was getting better*'. However, Ros told us the subject had cropped up previously because her son had been to the natural burial of a friend and had talked very positively about it to his parents. Ros said she was then able to ask Bill what he thought, saying she herself would '*quite fancy being food for a tree, it seems like a good idea*', to which he agreed. Because of this conversation, Ros was able to satisfy herself that she had made the right decision for Bill and told us: '*I thought, thank God you said that, because I can go ahead with this idea and actually think that he actually agreed with it.*' Concern that they had 'done the right thing' for the deceased emerged several times in our interviews with bereaved people and it might be that doing something that is or appears to be 'different', that is, choosing and doing natural burial, requires users to seek further reassurance for their decision.

Ros described Bill as:

> A very interesting person. He was a professional photographer, he was a teacher, he was a scientist on the biology side, interested in lichens and what have you, and he was also interested in archaeology and he would field walk and we have thousands of flints.

The interviews we conducted with bereaved people revealed that Ros was also not alone in relating characteristics akin to the deceased with her decision to bury naturally. This was often linked to their work histories, their likes and dislikes and/or their beliefs. It is also the case that some natural burial sites in the UK allow bereaved people to choose the site of the grave of dying or deceased family members/friends; this was the policy in three of our four ethnographic sites. As we highlighted in Chapter 5, at the East Meon site, Al the manager spends time with family members and friends getting to know them and through such conversations gains a picture of the character of the deceased. Interviewees who used the East Meon site said they welcomed the way Al enabled their involvement in decision-making around funeral plans and so on and showed support for the choices they made. Ros told us how she had contacted Al before her husband died to enquire about the possibility of holding his funeral there and then again after Bill's death, at which time Al invited her and her son, Jack, to the site, a visit they made the day after Bill died:

> Al said, I know exactly where Bill's going, he's going in the Agincourt Wood [laughs]. He said, I know exactly, took me down there, took us down there, you know, he said, I know that's a bit dark but, he said, the sun in the afternoon shines right on this bit, and he's so exactly right, he knew exactly what happens and I said, that's fine, so that's what we went with.

Participants often talked about the lack of dogma that enabled scope for an unstructured funeral, which they felt natural burial offered; this was particularly strongly articulated by our participants from East Meon. Ros Eastman told us she had not been involved in the funeral of her parents, who were cremated, and said she remembered each of their funerals as '*a non-event . . . I don't look back on it and say, oh, that was a really nice send off*'. In contrast, she said, '*you can have what you like with natural burial*'. Ros described how, during their walk around the site, Al informed her she was free to choose how Bill's funeral was organised:

> We sat on the bench and nattered but he explained that, you know, you could do whatever you like, you could have whatever sort of service you wanted and that, you know, you can have a picnic if you wanted or what, that it was totally up to you, and told us about Sam the horse and I thought, oh yes, that sounds wonderful, we'll have Sam the horse please [laughs].

Because of the support from Al, as well as the funeral director, who Ros described as '*absolutely brilliant*', Ros said she felt able to take control of all the arrangements for her husband's funeral. The funeral party met at the visitor centre:

> When we were organised we just sort of, Al leading the way and then Ian [the funeral director] and then Sam the horse and then Jack and me and everybody else trawled along behind. Jack had the ghetto blaster.

Once at the graveside, all ten mourners spoke before Bill's coffin was lowered into the ground:

> I just decided who was going to talk first and who was going to talk second. I went into teacher mode, absolutely brilliantly [laughs]. Oh, I organised the whole thing. It's your turn now I think, would you like to say something? [laughs] and I'd asked everybody to bring a bunch of flowers from the garden,

I didn't want flowers from florists, I wanted, you know, it didn't really matter, I said whatever you happen to have in the garden in September, bring it. It was a natural burial site and so I wanted things that were natural and I wanted, I suppose I wanted things that were personal, I felt it was far more personal if somebody went out and picked a bit from the garden and brought that along. I didn't want fuss, I didn't want bother, I wanted simple.

Ros told us that once Bill's coffin had been lowered into the ground the funeral party '*stood there sort of looking rather dismal and then we wandered off and then we went, we went over to Old Winchester Hill and had a picnic; absolutely lovely*'. It was clear from our interview with her that, overall, Ros felt that Bill's funeral was a celebratory and uplifting occasion. In the weeks that followed, she visited the site on a daily basis to spend time at the graveside, and it is perhaps here that we can see how Ros' choice of natural burial, which made perfect sense to her in the run-up and here-and-now of the funeral, seemingly began to unravel and expose unexpected consequences.

As discussed in Chapter 4, the desire to mark the grave of a deceased relative or friend is a common feature of many of the burial grounds we have visited and a significant point of discussion in our interviews with bereaved people and burial ground managers alike. Several tensions played out across our data, not least with regard to users' compliance with, as well as resistance to, site owners' rules and regulations regarding memorialisation in the aftermath of burial and beyond. Managers frequently mentioned their continued frustration at having to address what they perceived to be 'inappropriate' memorialisation and the difficulties this created when they dealt with the family members and friends of the deceased. Bereaved participants' narratives revealed how they had placed objects on the grave so that they remained undetected. Indeed, personal items were often placed inside the coffin, which might not be considered acceptable nor indeed biodegradable by natural burial providers. Ros Eastman told us Bill was a keen historian and archaeologist and he was buried with his archaeological equipment, as well as a front door key '*in case he wants to get back in*'. Although Ros told us she '*certainly wouldn't put up a headstone because that, that's the sort of thing that you expect to see in a graveyard or a cemetery*', she did speak of her own experience of marking her husband's grave and her awareness that her actions, like those of other bereaved people she met at East Meon, were going against the Sustainability Centre's aim to create an anonymous memorial landscape:

> Both Mick and I and a lot of other people unfortunately, had put flints, we put discreet flints around [our partners' graves]. Bill's got his name, Bill, in flints as well and a little Buddha and a little metal rose that I gave him for Christmas. We put these stones round and unfortunately, I mean you're not supposed to demarcate the graves, which is difficult, that is a bit hard, I see their reasoning, but we thought, well, it's natural, but other people abused this and poor Al was getting [laughs] large flint cairns being built with really big rocks and what have you.

After talking their actions through with Al, both Ros and Mick removed their memorials; however, as Ros further indicated, the continuing need to tend

Figure 6.1 *Lumps of chalk and sticks have been gathered and arranged around the edge of the grave and mark out the initial of the deceased (East Meon, July 2008).*

her partner's grave meant compliance with the site's rules and regulations was to some extent resisted:

> Al had a word with both Mick and me and, ooh okay, course Al, I'll move them, so I, I did, but what we both did, we sort of moved every alternate one and took them away so there's a few there but you can't see them now because there's leaves all over them; the Buddha's there, hidden in amongst the flowers.

Like many of our bereaved participants, Ros highlights the tensions that are at play within the natural burial landscape, not least the myriad of understandings that surround the term 'natural'. What is clear as well was her awareness of others' memorialising activities; knowing that they were going against the site's rules, but nevertheless attempting to meet their own needs and desires to tend and care for the graves of their loved ones.

Ros told us that, at the time of Bill's illness and her subsequent realisation he was not going to recover, she felt a complete sense of isolation. Her parents and her only sibling had died several years previously and she had few close friends. She described '*a very, very severe sense of, of loneliness, of not having, not having a group of people*'. As mentioned earlier, Ros was a volunteer at the East Meon site. She told us that this came about because Al had noticed she spent a long time sitting alone at her husband's grave. Her narrative revealed how she suspected Al harnessed her skills on the site in an attempt to help her work through her grief. Part of Al's strategy was to introduce Ros to a group of similarly placed people. After some initial difficulties, Ros became a member of the volunteer team and worked on the site two days a week clearing thistles, brambles and other invasive vegetation. At the time of our interview with her, being part of this group and working the land had become an important aspect of her life, as she put it: '*the whole purpose, the ethos of this place, you know, was that it was trying to return, albeit a small bit of land to what it used to be.*' Like others at the site, her volunteer status provided Ros with a legitimate reason to be there, as opposed to making a visit sparked by her desire, as she expressed it, to '*sit with Bill*'. As a volunteer she was able to be near her deceased partner and care for his grave; at the same time, she was able to care for the wider landscape wherein his grave lay.

Ros described site manager Al as '*wonderful, such a caring person*', and indeed, at the time of our study the East Meon site was unique in its provision of this kind of aftercare for its bereaved community, perhaps to some extent because Al and others of the management team of the Sustainability Centre worked on-site on a daily basis, rather than being located remotely, and the site offered activities other than burial. Several of our bereaved participants from this site were also volunteers who, in their turn and through their relationship with Al and other volunteers and workers there, were concerned for the future of the landscape. As discussed in Chapter 5, at the same time our data also revealed how users at this site watched over newly bereaved people, and it is perhaps interesting to contemplate the complex balancing act that underscored Al's actions with the bereaved community when set alongside his dedication to the landscape he was striving to return to that of its South Downs surroundings. These inherent contradictions and complexities were perhaps succinctly summed up by Ros, for whom the grave '*is where Bill is*' and because of this had difficulty in accepting the East Meon site would one day become an anonymous deathscape:

> For all that I want it to be returned to downland, to as it was, well, you know, as it might have been, I suppose there is a bit of me that would like there to be something somewhere that says, this is a special place, there are special people here.

Allan Holbrook, Abermule

We interviewed Allan Holbrook in the kitchen of his small cottage in Abermule, Powys, which was located approximately two miles from the natural burial site. Also present at the interview were Allan's wife Josie and Allan's mother. There was also a very large and friendly dog who tried to get our attention for the duration of the meeting. The five of us (six with the dog) sat around the kitchen table nursing mugs of tea and coffee while Allan told us about his father George's death and subsequent burial at Abermule. Although, for the majority of our interviewees, ecological reasons were not their priority but part of the natural burial package they had bought into, this consideration was uppermost in Allan's mind when he planned his father's funeral, with whom the decision to use a natural burial site was made. Like his father and paternal grandparents before him, Allan was a Pagan; he told us his father was '*always updating, he always thought of the new [he was] unconventional in his hobbies [and] search-ing for something*'. Again we can observe how the character of the deceased played its part in the decision to strive for what Allan termed '*unconventional*' through the choice to bury his father at the Abermule site.

Like several of our interviewees from this burial site, Allan's family were 'incomers', that is, they were not from the area. Indeed, he and his family had moved around England and Wales for several years before settling in there. We have suggested elsewhere[1] that natural burial might at times offer a sense of belonging and rootedness to a place. This seemed to be the case for Allan's parents who, through their employment, had settled in nearby Newtown in the 1970s. As he explained, '*In those days, if you got a job here, you got a house to go with it.*'

In January 2007, following a bout of illness and a prolonged stay in hos-pital, Allan brought his father home where, four days later, aged 74 and with his family around him, '*He died, in the front room in the bed, where he'd sat in all the years, used to come in the door like that and dad'd be sitting there with his books all round him.*' Allan told us that, although his father was very ill, his death was unexpected because throughout his lifetime he had suf-fered periods of illness from which he always recovered. Our impression from speaking with Allan was that the father–son relationship had been extremely close: '*We've always been keen gardeners and always outdoors, done camping and so forth, we'd talk about everything, every single subject you can think of.*' Ostensibly his father's sudden death was a shock from which he was still recovering. As said, Allan was a keen gardener and after his father's death he started a veggie-box scheme in the local community, which was something he and his father had planned to do together. When we asked Allan why he had chosen natural burial, he explained he was '*a green person*'. He told us how his childhood and upbringing were couched in a belief in the force of Nature and that his ancestors' actions and beliefs were the foundation of contemporary environmental politics:

> We've always been sort of green, I suppose, my grandfather and grandmother and that, which all were traditionally before the word 'conservation', in other words it's just an innate feeling that Nature is right, I suppose, isn't it? And Nature is all powerful. You've just got a connection in a way, which is unbroken.

Indeed, Allan's father felt his connection with nature so strongly that, although he had a fear of burial, he had eschewed cremation *'because of the damage it would do to the environment'*. Although Allan and his family were interested in green burial for themselves, this predated the opening of the Abermule site. When the site opened in 2003, Allan, Josie and Allan's mother went to the open day, although his father was unable to go. Their attendance emerged from curiosity rather than with a view that they would need the site in the near future; *'not knowing dad was going to obviously die quite soon after'*. Allan's first impression of the site was that it was *'not that much different from that field to be honest, or to anywhere else round here'*. Allan's observation is an interesting one as Eira and Ifor, the owners of the Abermule site, strive to make the burial field as anonymous as possible so that it merges with the surrounding landscape. Ifor's skill at 'fixing' the site of the grave after a burial is something we observed ourselves when we attended a funeral there. Once the funeral party left the site, the grave was backfilled manually by Ifor and the soil flattened, a process that required Ifor to pack the soil in the grave very tightly. Once the soil was replaced, the squares of turf that had been carefully removed by Ifor prior to the grave being dug were placed back on top, rather like a patchwork quilt. Once completed there was very little evidence of the ground being disturbed. Indeed, we returned to the site one week later and it was quite difficult to locate the grave, even though we had been present at the funeral.

Allan told us he *'knew dad would want everything to be green'*, and took responsibility for his father's funeral, a decision which was partly due to his rejection of *'somebody else comes in from outside and does it all for you'*, alongside his belief that a celebrant would be unable to provide an adequate summation of his father's life: *'I ended up just doing the funeral all myself because there was no ceremony I could imagine for dad ... he'd followed this path that was unique.'* Allan's wife Josie added: *'His spiritual path was definitely single journey, wasn't it, a lone journey.'* In planning the ceremony, Allan consulted the *Natural Death Handbook* and *Journey to the Summerland*, which, as Allan explained, *'is a Pagan book about the afterlife'*; alongside this, he sought advice from someone from the Pagan Federation.

Some natural burial sites in the UK allow bereaved people to choose the location of the grave; this was so at three of our four ethnographic sites. Several of our bereaved participants talked about how this decision was made. Again, this was often linked to personal histories of the deceased and bereaved. Allan had walked the surrounding countryside of the Abermule site with his father, stopping to eat a packed lunch in particular spots that afforded them the best views. He said he chose the plot up the hillside for his father's grave *'because I knew Dad would like to look around over the valley'*. Allan went with his family to choose the plot for his father's grave – although it was he who had the final say on where it should be – which in the aftermath of burial Allan connected with each time he visited the site:

We picked the plot and that was quite high up when we got there because I knew dad would like to look around over the valley. I was thinking, if we were out walking, me and dad used to do a lot of walking when he was younger, where would we stop for our cheese and onion sandwiches and cup of tea? So I

Figure 6.2 *View looking across the valley from the top of the burial field. Daffodils temporarily reveal the location of two adjacent graves (Abermule, April 2008).*

walked around the field and I thought, this is where we'd stop, we'd actually sit down there and just have a, a look around, yeah, we would sit here.

A local funeral director agreed to keep the body of Allan's father at their premises in the interim period between death and burial; and on the day of the funeral George's body, in its wicker coffin, was transported by the funeral director to the burial field, where Allan said a few words around the coffin to explain to the coffin bearers, a group made up of family and friends, what was going to happen *'because obviously no one knew what was going on there'*. They then carried the coffin, leading the procession of 40-plus mourners to the graveside, the route of which was also planned by Allan:

It wasn't straight up, we just curved around a little bit so that people could follow, because you want to be a bit ceremonial. So we carried the coffin, which is a lot heavier than you think it is to be honest. We had to put it down halfway up the hill [laughs]. But they'd warned us of that; someone had said that they're heavy, so be prepared to actually have a resting place up there, rather than actually all start stumbling.

The opportunity for the procession of mourners to follow the coffin as a feature of funerals in natural burial grounds emerged strongly from our interviews with bereaved people. There is not much opportunity in traditional cemeteries or indeed in crematoria for a procession to be included as part of the funereal ritual. Figures 6.3 and 6.4 are reproduced from photographs one

Figure 6.3 *Family members and other mourners weave flowers into the wicker coffin (Abermule; source: Craig Bradbury).*

of our bereaved participants gave to us. They show family members and other mourners weaving flowers into the wicker coffin and the funeral procession up the hill at Abermule, a similar procession to that described by Allan.

Allan prepared a reading that he recited at the graveside, although at the time of the interview he said he found it difficult to remember exactly what he had said. He told us he had striven to be inclusive of everyone attending and

Figure 6.4 *The funeral procession informally follows the coffin bearers up the hill towards the grave (Abermule; source: Craig Bradbury).*

so knew that he had begun his eulogy with the words: '*My dad was Pagan, and these are the words of his goddess, ye, they are also the words of the divine reality and I ask you as you listen to hear the words of your own god and draw comfort from them.*' His decision to create a ceremonial atmosphere again hinged on aspects of his father's personality:

> I just tried to get something I thought that dad would like most, dad was quite, I suppose, a ceremonial person, he quite liked that aspect of things, so I had a candle in a lantern which was meant to sit inside the light, and you carried that before you and so forth and then when we went to the pub afterwards, we snuffed it out after the ceremony; we did it right at the end.

Undoubtedly, there was a ritualistic core to the funeral service and wake that Allan prepared for his father. The importance of ritual and ceremony emerged throughout his description of the funeral and was constantly linked to his father's life and beliefs; as he put it, '*just different ceremonial things that I thought chimed with what dad wanted*'. The wake took place at a local pub, '*the last place me and dad had a drink*'. Allan told us that his father had kept several journals throughout his lifetime and in his final months had condensed these into one journal that held significant events and people from his life. During one of their talks in the last days of his father's life, Allan was given this final journal, which he used to prepare his father's wake:

He'd given me this book of his life and all the other stuff he'd wanted, he'd given me his journal so I just put, took bits out of that and went through his life basically. I was trying to keep it open and some of the words I used was trying to include people, I wanted to bring people in because dad had always wanted to open his life and help people.

Allan said he '*tried to make the ceremony really as much about dad as possible*' and had ordered a couple of cases of mead, his father's favourite drink, to be served at the wake, which was also accompanied by skiffle music. Allan also ensured everyone who attended the funeral and wake was mentioned in his eulogy, and Josie described an activity they had prepared for the wake:

We got a big red box and lots of different coloured pens and different coloured paper and we got people to write a memory or a comment on and then, and put them in the box, and we started off the wake with Allan pulling them out.

Children were also present at the funeral and wake, and those too young to write down their memories were asked to draw pictures that reminded them of George. Allan told us he '*really liked that because you got (what) everyone thought of dad, not just your own views*'.

As discussed in Chapter 3, at the Abermule site memorialisation is discouraged, and there is no memorial plaque or planting on the grave provided by the owners. Instead, a numbered stone is sunk into the ground to identify the grave

Figure 6.5 *The grave has been back-filled and the turf neatly replaced. When the floral tributes are finally removed, the grave will be almost indistinguishable from the surrounding landscape (Abermule, July 2008).*

and tree adoption is offered on the periphery of the burial field. The majority of bereaved people choose to have an oak peg affixed with a memorial plaque placed among existing trees. There is then very little opportunity to demarcate the grave, although several of our interviewees told us that they had themselves planted daffodils and wildflowers on the graves of their loved ones; in some instances with Ifor and/or Eira's assistance.

Allan and his family intended to plant some wildflowers on his father's grave; as he explained, this was '*mainly to identify the grave, it's getting a bit overgrown there now, I don't mean in a nasty way, I just mean the grass is actually getting thicker so the stones that have dad's number on it, you can't really see anymore.*' As other interview data attest, knowledge of the location of the grave emerged as a key concern of our bereaved participants; and this was no less so for Allan and his family who also planned to plant a tree at the site, the choice of which was, like other participants' choices, linked to the preferences, characteristics or life course of the deceased:

> He wanted to be somewhere and a tree planted over him, which you can't do at the green burial site, and I've been thinking about planting a tree and I've talked to them about it there. I was thinking of planting a Newton Wonder because that was the first tree he planted [but] because it's quite rocky an apple tree I don't think really is going to flourish, so I think probably the other two trees he'd like the most were either oak or Scot's pine.

In the aftermath of his father's death, Allan told us he visited the site quite regularly but that there was no pattern to his visits; he told us: '*I go there and stand there and talk to dad as such, but I know he's not there.*'

Maggie Carter, Ulley

Maggie Carter was interviewed in the kitchen of the house she shared with her partner Kim. She had six children, including her son Adam, who was fostered and later adopted by Maggie and her husband during their marriage. A photograph of blonde-haired Adam, aged two, hung on the wall above the kitchen table, the only family photograph in evidence. Maggie made a cup of tea then spent some time looking out of her kitchen window at her garden, where several large birdcages housed the rare birds she and her partner bred, before joining the interviewer at the table to begin her story. Adam had multiple and severe disabilities and at the age of ten, following a prolonged bout of illness; and, with his large family around him, he died at home in Maggie's arms: '*We brought his little bed downstairs and I laid him in his little bed and I laid at side of him and I just stroked his forehead like that and said, it's all right if you want to go now lad and he, he did, he went.*' The decision to use the Ulley site for her son's burial emerged from Maggie's perception of Adam's enjoyment of the outdoors, and, like other participants, the characteristics of the deceased clearly played their part in Maggie's choice:

> Adam was never able to express himself but he loved the outdoors, did Adam and he loved, you could see it on his face, he loved the wind. We used to go into Belvoir Park every weekend with kids because they all loved playing in woods

and that and then we used to have a game of football and I used to take a big picnic, we used to lay Adam on a blanket under a big beech tree just halfway down drive at Belvoir and he used to love it, he used to love watching the light flicker in through the leaves.

The involvement of family and friends in tasks associated with preparation of the body for burial, such as dressing the deceased in their own clothing, rather than a shroud from the funeral director, or other tasks associated with the funeral, were often perceived by our interviewees as a way of coping with grief – a view held by bereaved people and natural burial providers alike and also present in much of the natural burial literature. Indeed, the majority of our interviewees were involved in the funeral service for their relatives in some capacity, ranging from organising the whole day to playing particular roles such as coffin-bearing, reading and singing at the graveside, playing musical instruments and so on.

Of course, it does not follow that participation happens in the majority of natural burials, but in our sample of bereaved participants this seemed to have been the case. In some instances, as well, bereaved people we spoke with rejected the traditional hearse and used their own cars to transport the coffin to the burial sites. Again, some of these activities are not unique to natural burial. As we discuss in the following chapter, our interviews with death care professionals revealed that bereaved people are becoming increasingly keen to individualise or personalise funeral services, despite their choice of disposal. Indeed, a shift in how funerals are planned and a movement away from mourning death towards celebration of life has been evident in the UK for several years.[2]

It could, however, be suggested that natural burial allows for more freedom of expression as well as involvement of bereaved people as its ethos is under-pinned by that of the Natural Death Centre, which advocates a 'hands on' approach to death and dying and encourages those who are bereaved to wrest control of the body and the funeral from traditional death care professionals.[3] This also relates to the role of many independent burial ground providers who are a constant point of contact for the bereaved community and so are able, as Chapter 5 illustrates, to play a key role in supporting the involvement of family and friends.

The most common activity bereaved people we interviewed had engaged in was coffin decoration; as Figure 6.3 shows, wicker and willow caskets in par-ticular rendered this quite straightforward and with visually stunning results. Daniel Armitage, whose wife Gail is buried at the Abermule site, described some of the healing effects of this activity:

> We planted all the daffodils up there in the September before she died and she never saw them come up, so my daughter and my sister, and two sisters-in-law went and adorned the coffin with daffodils. My sister-in-law, came up to me and she said, I didn't really want to do it at first [but] she said that was lovely, I actually said goodbye to my sister [at the church]. I was expecting to see this horrible box, like we all do, and I saw the daffodils and I went ooh, that's nice. I actually smiled as it came down and everybody said it was the most wonderful coffin they'd ever seen . . . The whole coffin was completely covered in daffodils . . . it was a nice feeling, if you can understand when I say nice.

As Daniel also intimated, a hands-on approach to death and burial is nothing new: '*When you look at it, people used to do that. They used to dress the body and prepare it and I think we've lost all those things in this modern life we live in.*' As he and other of our interviewees pointed out, these kinds of activities have been 'lost' in a modernist approach to death that normalised the removal of the body from the care of the family and the home. Maggie Carter told us how she had encouraged her daughters to decorate Adam's coffin as she thought it would help them deal with the loss of their brother; although, in this instance, it raised unanticipated difficulties for Maggie:

> We had a willow basket made for him and we wove it all with flowers so the girls came with me and they, now decided they wanted him in one set of clothes and then they changed their minds they didn't want him to be buried in, they wanted him buried in his Leeds United kit so I had to take him out of coffin and re-dress him and everything, you know. Then put him back in and so I had to keep it all bottled in and acted as though it was perfectly normal, for girls, you know, so they didn't go to pieces.

Maggie told us how, in life, Adam was unable to express his wishes but had displayed his enjoyment of Mahler and hip-hop music through the movements he was able to make with his arms, which Maggie described as '*windmilling*', and which he had done when laid under the trees in the park. The choice of a natural burial for Adam was perceived by Maggie to accommodate this latter love; the funeral and service at his graveside the former:

> We played Gustav Mahler as we walked with the coffin to the grave and then we played some hip-hop for [my daughter] and for Adam because he loved it, and then we were all going to say our little bit but the kids, none of the kids could do it so they just put their notes in with him, [my ex-husband] read a poem and I can't remember what it was now. Oh, I think it was Keats, but I'm not sure and I'd written a piece about him and I read that and then popped it in with him and we'd got, we just had white roses, one each that we all, and [my partner] was there as well, and we all put a white rose each on coffin and then played Gustav Mahler again and that was it. But it was, it, I don't know, it somehow seemed right for Adam.

Like many of our interviewees, taking on an active role in the funeral ritual was underpinned by Maggie's rejection of a stranger conducting the funeral ceremony for her child: '*I don't want some vicar or anybody who's never met him in their lives talking about him as though they knew him.*' Maggie told us she felt unable to release her emotions at the time Adam died because of her felt need to support her children, something which clearly emerged when she helped her daughters to decorate his coffin which inadvertently led to a change in Adam's burial clothing; it was at the side of the grave that Maggie was overcome by the feelings she previously masked:

> It was only when we lowered him and we'd all said our little piece that we suddenly realised that, you know, he'd gone sort of thing, and I went to pieces then; but I suppose I had to keep it together for them when he died and everything. I nearly passed out when they put him in grave but that was just me and seeing

him go down into dark earth I think, you know, I fell over backwards. I think, I think they all thought I was going to fall in grave with him poor lad but he, I knew I was going to faint so I'd sort of sat myself down, you know, so I didn't, didn't faint and I couldn't see either, so.

Several of our bereaved participants spoke of the difficulty they experienced at this stage of the burial process – that their relatives were to be placed below ground and covered with earth and left to the elements was very difficult to come to terms with and particularly strongly felt by participants who had buried a child. However, one of the ways people were comforted was through an imagined future for the body of the deceased. Indeed, from our interview data and in keeping with natural burial discourse, a sense emerged from our bereaved participants that natural burial allowed for above-ground growth to occur naturally and that the body of the deceased would become part of the above-ground vista. This was in contrast to the majority of participants' views of traditional cemeteries, wherein it was perceived that managed gardens, mown lawns and slabs and stones suppressed new life and indeed nature itself. The notion of the body feeding the above-ground vegetation thus allowed the deceased to 'live on' after death, and this belief was a recurring theme in our data.

As well as the body nourishing and becoming part of the landscape, however, in some instances natural burial held possibilities in death that had been denied in life; as Maggie said of Adam:

He's free, I mean he can be in the countryside like everybody else now, he doesn't have to be carried there and laid on a blanket on the grass and not be able to do anything but just lay there, you know, to me he's, he's, he's part of the environment now and he's, you know, he's gone green eventually. Well literally but, you know, he's, I think he would have, he would have been a kid who really enjoyed outdoors if he'd been able to run and, you know. He always, he always seemed to take great pleasure from being out. You can hear the water as well, can see it, you can hear it tinkling along; he will like that as well because he loved, he loved water. I'm more happy that he, knowing that he would be happy where he is and that, that makes it easier for me, I don't need the trappings of a grave if you see what I mean, I know that that would have been the best possible place for him to go.

Although Maggie commented that she did not need '*the trappings of a grave*', nevertheless the place where Adam lay remained important to her. Indeed, the vast majority of bereaved people we spoke with visited the graves after burial, although the frequency of their visits varied greatly. Most visited on a regular basis, for example weekly, monthly, seasonally, as well as on anniversaries of deaths and at times of celebration such as birthdays; a small minority had visited very few times, and in one instance a father had not returned to the site of his son's grave at all as he felt his presence was in the home rather than at the burial site. In most cases visits began as daily or weekly vigils to the graveside which, in most but certainly not all cases, lessened over time. The weather also dictated when visits would or could happen and, due to the sometimes rough terrain of the burial landscape, visits were not always possible for the less able, such as the very young, the infirm or the elderly. Nevertheless, as said, the vast majority of our bereaved interviewees spent some time visiting the sites in the aftermath of burial, and for many these provided a sanctuary wherein they could express themselves and commune with their dead. Maggie Carter told us how her son's grave, a small space within the wider burial landscape, continued to hold emotional significance: '*You can go and talk like I do, you know, go and talk to Adam and it doesn't matter what, you know, there's nothing there, it's just a bit of grass and a tree.*'

However, Maggie perceived her sons and daughters felt differently with regard to the site of Adam's grave:

> My kids will go and won't know, remember where he is, or won't know where he is but I don't think it'll matter so much to them then because they'll just be going to be where Adam's buried if you see what I mean, whereas I go to see Adam still. To them, Ulley is Adam whereas to me it's still, I've got to find Adam, you know, I still think I need to go to that tree and talk to him, you know. I've got to find Adam still.

Adam was buried in 2001, and, at the time of our interview with her in 2009, Maggie perceived he was '*part of the environment*'. However, the account she gave of her journey revealed how her ability to accept her son's status took time and indeed was ongoing. Maggie talked about the importance of knowing the location of his grave and how, in the first months following his death, she would sit there and talk to him. She also told us that at one point, because of a leg injury, she was unable to visit the site for some months. When she did return, seasonal changes meant that the grasses at the site were waist-high and the landscape visually so different from her previous visits that she was unable to find Adam's grave; it was an incident that caused her some distress, as she said: '*I thought I'd lost him.*'

Adam's presence was symbolised by an oak tree; as Maggie explained, '*he's part of the tree now*'. It was the tree she talked to when she visited. Indeed, Adam's burial at Ulley was the cause of several complicated and conflicting emotions for Maggie regarding the desire to retain a graveside space within the site alongside her acknowledgement that the burial site was a collective memorial landscape. Other of our data attest that the majority of bereaved people interviewed held very similar views with regard to the site of the grave and the desire to retain the individuality of the deceased. So, and like many other participants, the wish for the woodland to thrive and acceptance of the burial site as collective memorial raged against Maggie's need to preserve the uniqueness of her son's identity and her memories of him through her access to and knowledge of the whereabouts of his grave:

> You want it to go back to a wood and you want it to be just a copse of trees but then there's a bit of, at back of your mind wants to know which is your tree, you know what I mean? It's a bit, bit difficult. There's just a little piece of wood leaning against tree with his name on, that's all, but apart from that he just looks part of field, you know, and I think once you've got over the shock and the grieving period, I think then if you're going for a woodland burial then you should let it go back to the woodland.

Jennifer Davey, whose father was buried at Abermule, talked about the grave as a wound in the body of the earth that gradually healed over in parallel with the 'healing' of grief. So for her it was not any kind of instant disappearance. The natural landscape is then perhaps especially amenable to many interpretations and can stand for several kinds of emotional orientations towards a death, as Maggie pointed out:

> I think as long as they give [bereaved people] the, a little bit of time to get over their grieving. I think things, taking things and things on the, where they've been buried are important at first. I don't know why but they do. You need to take something with you and you need to have a, a sign that they're there, you know what I mean? But after a while it doesn't, that's not so important.

Marie Cooper, Wisewood

Our interview with Marie Cooper took place in the flat she rented from the council, where she had moved a few months before we met with her. The flat was within walking distance of the Wisewood site. Marie had previously lived in a large detached house from where her husband Jonathan ran his business. When Jonathan became ill, Marie told us they had sold their house, '*thinking, we'll use the money for his illness, because he was self-employed, he'd got to stop work and everything and we thought, oh we'll buy again afterwards, and afterwards didn't come*'. One year after being diagnosed with lung cancer, and aged 64, Jonathan died. Since her husband's death, Marie told us she had '*discovered e-bay*', and the windowsills and shelves of her compact living room were bedecked with the ornaments she had begun to collect. Marie was 59 at the time of the interview, and she was employed at a local primary school four days a week. As well as searching e-bay, she filled her spare time with caring for her five grandchildren and busying herself with various arts and crafts. We shared a pot of tea at her dining table, which overlooked the local bowling green; Marie said she enjoyed watching the matches from the window. On her small balcony, Marie was growing tomatoes in growbags, and several other plants adorned this outdoor space. When asked how she had made the decision to use the Wisewood burial site, Marie told us she first heard about it from reading the local paper and it had occurred to her that the location of the site chimed with Jonathan's life course:

> I just managed to say to him one night, I've found out that there's a woodland area in Wisewood Cemetery, which is, you know, just over the hill really and it's opposite Jonathan's school that he used to go to when he was younger, there's a, it goes down to a valley with a river, he used to fish in the river as a child, up the other side of the valley is Howell's brickyard that he used to work from leaving school and it just crossed my mind that he would be near where he was when he was a kid, near where he used to work and he'd be up the hill to the pub, so it was near the pub that he used to go to when he finished work, sort of thing, and I just said to him, what would you think of that? And he said yeah, sounds all right, and that was all we were able to talk about, we didn't go back to it but I'd got the idea in my head then, didn't talk much to the girls about it or anything, I just thought, that's what I'm going to do and, you know, left it at that.

As Marie intimates in her narrative, although she and her husband knew his illness was terminal, in the time that passed between knowing he was going to die and his death, the couple did not discuss in any depth his imminent passing, nor did they make any of the arrangements for his funeral. Like Ros Eastman, as well as other of our bereaved participants, Marie comforted herself that she had made the right choice for her husband based on their brief discussions of woodland burial. As she said, Marie kept the idea of the woodland in mind and explained that '*it wasn't really because of, of being green or anything like that, it just seemed traditional but less formal, not all sort of pomp and circumstance and big stone tombs and all that sort of thing*'. As with others we interviewed, evident in Marie's narrative are some clues that might highlight why she felt natural burial was the right choice: '*traditional but less formal*'; and the absence of '*pomp and circumstance*', alongside her rejection of the traditional cemetery through a desire to shift away from '*big stone tombs*'. Several of our participants made comparisons similar to Marie's between the traditional cemetery or crematorium and the natural burial site.

The location of the site was also strongly felt by Marie, and, on the day of the funeral, the journey from home to burial site took in areas that sparked memories of the life she had shared with Jonathan. In some cases, the journey of the cortège from home to burial site passed through places that held meaning for the bereaved; as Kenneth Davison told us, on the day of his wife's funeral at Ulley, the cortège '*followed a route of my life going backwards, past the woods where I'd played as a young child, it was a journey back in time*'.

The importance of accommodating the perceived needs of the living as well as the dead also emerged from our interviews with bereaved people; a mixture of the traditional and the less conventional through, for example, the inclusion of a religious element by non-believers in order to accommodate the needs of other mourners with some religious beliefs. Marie Cooper clearly articulated her desire to meet the needs of others as well as her own and her husband's when she described the choices she made for Jonathan's funeral:

> He'd been a churchgoer as a child and I know he was basically religious, I know he believed in God, and it wouldn't have been right for me to put my views and say, right we're just having a graveside committal and we're having poetry instead of prayers or whatever because it, as I say it was really sort of conventional and I think he would have wanted it to have been done the proper way so that's why we did, you know, we sort of covered all, all the angles really, you know, having a proper traditional church service with hymns and then the committal with poetry and things instead, you know.

It is not usually possible to choose the site of the grave at the Wisewood site; as discussed in Chapter 4, these are allotted by the city council's Bereavement Services, who are typically responding to a request from a funeral director. Even so, it was more often the case that those we interviewed who used this site had visited prior to the burial or were familiar with the cemetery itself. Although Marie knew of the cemetery and its location in the wider landscape of the Loxley valley, she did not choose to visit the woodland area before the funeral:

I'd stood at the cemetery gates and looked down but somehow, the girls kept saying do you want to go in? And no, no, I don't, I assume it'll be all right, I don't want to go in, so I didn't actually see it until we stood at the graveside; that was the first time that I saw it.

As her previous narrative illustrates, the location of the site with its links to Jonathan's life was of utmost importance to Marie and underscored her decision to use the woodland; however, she chose not to visit her husband's final resting place before his funeral. In some ways, this decision throws light on some of the anxieties she later experienced once Jonathan's funeral had taken place and she returned to the site to visit his grave: '*It just wasn't maintained, wasn't kept tidy. I thought somebody would go round and tidy it up every now and again.*'

In defining a burial ground, Julie Rugg notes the visible iconography of the cemetery landscape, wherein each grave is clearly located within a predefined grid and accessible via roads and pathways and each burial, with the exception of public graves, is identified by a headstone.[4] As we discussed in Chapter 4, many natural burial grounds permit a stone or a wooden plaque on the grave, as well as a tree, whereas others forbid memorialisation of any kind. In this example, only the burial ground management has an overview of the whereabouts of the deceased, guided by the site plan, burial register and discrete fixed markers that locate the precise position and orientation of the grave. In contrast to Rugg's description of the traditional cemetery landscape, then, the natural burial ground might seemingly have no order; and, though they do indeed allow for graves to be located, which is a requirement by law, graves are seldom accessed via designated roads and paths. In Chapter 4, we discussed in more detail the issue of finding the grave in nature. At the Wisewood site, a small stone marker bearing the name of the deceased and their dates of birth and death is laid flat on the ground at one end of the grave, and a tree is planted which users can choose from a list of native trees.

Marie Cooper's perception that the Wisewood site was unkempt and mismanaged arose from her attempts to walk through it to find Jonathan's grave, as brambles, weeds and couch grasses made her journey difficult. Marie's discontent with the woodland might also have emerged because of its proximity to the traditional cemetery, whereby differences between the two different burial options are clearly displayed. We discussed this in more detail in Chapter 4, and in Chapter 3 we provided a plan view of the site. Only a road and lawned section separates the woodland area at Wisewood from the neatly regimented rows of headstones and well-defined graves. The two types of site can be viewed in terms of their pros and cons over the long term. For traditional cemeteries, expectations may be more easily matched in the short term as gravesites are maintained following burial. However, what was once a fine headstone and well-maintained site can become neglected and overgrown over time. In contrast, woodland sites which are not fully matured may fail to match expectations in the short term – reflecting Marie's disappointment in the stark reality of a newly emerging woodland site, rather than the mature woodland the burial ground's name implies. Her awareness that the site will continue to develop, becoming closer to the ideal, is set against the close proximity of the traditional counterpart which is in its ideal state now. This contrast seemingly cuts to the very heart of a tension for the bereaved and their experience of natural burial sites, and perhaps especially for those sites where the landscape identity or vision is yet to be fulfilled.

In the same vein as the vast majority of our bereaved participants, when Marie contemplated the future she was able to accept, albeit at a different pace from Bereavement Services officials, the eventual anonymity of her deceased husband through the incorporation of his grave into the wider landscape:

> In years to come, maybe when I'm not here sort of thing, the trees will be big and the names will be, I mean we don't like the name plate getting grown over, that doesn't seem right, but everything will be grown over one day and that'll look better then. An ordinary cemetery when the descendants aren't there and the stones are falling down and they're neglected; they look so unloved, don't they? Whereas that will go back into its natural habitat and that's what I always said was good about it. If you don't go, there are some people who don't go back at all, I've some graves roundabout and people have never been back since the funeral and it doesn't matter because that's, you know, and that and that's the other good thing that I thought about it, that's what I expected.

Summary

This chapter has explored how some of the bereaved people we met during the course of our study chose natural burial for a deceased relative, how they planned and performed their funerals and how they later negotiated the space wherein their relatives were interred; its management, rules, regulations, other users and terrain. Our decision to ground our discussions in data from four participants has enabled us to provide an in-depth investigation of the complexities that surrounded their expectations of a funeral in a natural burial ground during its planning stage and its lived experience and aftermath. Discussion of their particular experiences has also enabled us to provide insight into a bigger picture of what our participants in general have chosen, experienced and later reflected upon.

As their narratives have demonstrated, our bereaved participants chose to inter their relatives in a natural burial ground based on notions of the character of the deceased coupled, in many cases, with a belief that a natural burial landscape offered the possibility for the deceased to 'live on' in some form after death. This was a common theme across the interview data from bereaved participants, although, as we have shown, while Allan Holbrook talked of sharing the views with his father, at the same time he acknowledged that his father was not there. His narrative helps highlight some of the contradictory emotions and experiences that might manifest at times of bereavement, and which we acknowledge can be ascribed to any disposal option. Using a natural burial site also offered bereaved people an opportunity to shift away from traditional forms of disposal; although we should comment that, of the 40 people we interviewed, very few chose natural burial based on their environmental/ecological beliefs – see Davies and Rumble for contrasting findings on this issue.[5] This is not to suggest that environmental considerations were absent from our participants' choices, but rather to note that these were often secondary to their desire to individualise and display the uniqueness of the deceased, and indeed themselves, through their choice to bury in a natural burial site.

Our discussion of the aftermath of burial explored bereaved participants' everyday experiences of a natural burial site over time, their visits to the sites and what they did when they were there. We chose to do this partly through the lens of memorialisation because this aspect of natural burial emerged from our interview data as the most contentious; many of our bereaved participants had struggled with the lack of scope for memorialising. As discussed in previous chapters, one characteristic of the natural burial ethos is a commitment to a burial landscape that contains no headstones or non-biodegradable memorial objects and which appears, as far as is possible, to be natural – although, as this and other chapters have shown, interpretations of 'nature' and 'natural' differed across our whole sample of research participants. In this chapter we have revealed the ways in which bereaved people sometimes countered such requirements in order to satisfy a personal desire to mark the graves of their relatives and that these actions were in turn linked with emotions that shifted over time. That the sites would eventually become shared (mourning) spaces was not held in contention by our bereaved participants, however. In most cases they were able to anticipate that the sites would in time become anonymous landscapes and that their own needs had or would change. It is their insight that this acceptance takes time, perhaps a generation, that will help foster understanding between those who choose to bury in a natural burial site and those who provide these relatively new deathscapes.

The discussion thus highlights different views of what is natural and, in so doing, adds a further level of complexity to memorialisation practices in a natural burial ground. Many of the sites we visited are still very much in a process of becoming and as already noted, at both East Meon and Abermule, this proves less of a challenge possibly because of the strength of the landscape, a less confusing context and indeed a very different management regime. Attached to this is an acceptance among some of our bereaved participants that memorialisation is often temporary and that while providers may be frustrated with how this competes with their vision of the landscape, for some of our bereaved sample, this was less of an issue. We return to the ways in which individuals found new and creative approaches to memorialising their loved ones in Chapter 8.

Just as preceding chapters have explored the diversity of interpretations of natural burial, this chapter has illustrated the heterogeneity of the people who choose to use these sites. As we have said, natural burial has no one model, and among our bereaved participants there was no common understanding of natural burial, nor indeed of nature. By virtue of their location, habitat, ownership/management structure and bereaved community, natural burial grounds each present an entirely unique experience.[6] What we can further attest is that each of our bereaved participants found ways to encapsulate the unique identities of their deceased loved ones through choosing, doing and living with natural burial.

7
Natural burial: new endings, old habits?

Earlier chapters have discussed the design and management of natural burial sites; managers' and bereaved people's relationships with those sites; and the close bonds that are forged with these memorial landscapes. This chapter explores the implications of natural burial for funeral directors and celebrants, two discrete groups of professionals who also play a part in the natural burial process. Both of these groups could be described as fairly remote or perhaps less emotionally connected to the burial sites and in relation to the landscape or the bodies buried therein. As such this discussion presents a somewhat different perspective from that covered in previous chapters. Elsewhere we have defined natural burial as a culturally creative endeavour and considered the landscapes and practices that constitute natural burial as the outcome of engagements between a range of individuals and their environments.[1] To this end, we propose that the natural burial ground is a new arena for death care professionals and, as such, could be considered a heterotopic site that is invested with a diversity of meanings, understandings and practices that are at times contested and might be considered contradictory and/or conflicting.[2]

As previous chapters have discussed, since its conception in 1991[3] and manifestation as a woodland burial section within Carlisle Cemetery in 1993, an array of different models and approaches to the concept have emerged and, with this, a variety of different landscapes, management styles and practices. Thus, there is no one model of the natural burial site, and indeed our data also indicate that there is no one 'type' of natural burial ground user. Certainly in two of our four ethnographic sites, 'incomers' made up the majority of site users, while the other two evidenced a more localised clientele. One of these latter two is owned and managed by a funeral director and the other by a local authority. It might be suggested, then, that differences in ownership and management style, alongside the sites' very different geographical locations, impacted on bereaved people's decision-making processes. For example, staff from the funeral-director-owned site offer natural burial as a 'third way' to their bereaved clients, with as equal an emphasis as cemetery burial and crema-tion; in consequence, natural burial is a 'normalised' disposal option. The local authority site is set within the boundaries of a traditional cemetery located in a suburban area on the outskirts of a bustling city. Once within the grounds of the cemetery, the woodland area is visible and easily accessible. In this way, then, these two sites offer a more 'localised' consumer option than their counterparts in that they are embedded within already existing and therefore familiar disposal processes.

One of the aims of this chapter, then, is to highlight the challenges and indeed the opportunities natural burial might present for the twenty-first-century funeral director who remains, more often than not, the first port of call for bereaved people.[4] The chapter also explores how celebrants – those from religious denominations and Humanism – might perceive natural burial. We offer a discussion of their experiences of working at these sites and with the families and friends who used their services. The chapter thus provides some understanding of how natural burial is positioned within the wider context of contemporary UK death and disposal from the perspective of those who have worked in all disposal locations.

In each of the four ethnographic sites we interviewed two funeral directors, either from family-run businesses or larger establishments, and two celebrants. In the case of the two sites near Sheffield, the funeral directors and celebrants we spoke with had worked at both sites. We spoke with funeral directors because we were interested in finding out the wider ramifications for them of natural burial, such as how this new disposal option was perceived and understood by this professional group and whether this might have changed over time through an ongoing relationship with a site and those who managed it. We were interested in changes to their working practices – for example, embalmed bodies are not allowed in the majority of natural burial sites, so we were interested to know how this might impact the professional status of the funeral director. As well as this, the use of different types of coffin and the format of funerals were areas of inquiry for us. Finally, we were interested in funeral directors' observations of funeral rituals to explore if and how they felt these differed from more traditional funerals in crematoria or cemeteries and whether any such changes impacted their role.

Like funeral directors, each of the celebrants we interviewed had worked in other burial sites and crematoria before natural burial was introduced into their repertoire. We were interested to find out from them how natural burial was perceived and understood and, again, how this might have changed through their experiences of officiating at a site and their dealings with mourners and site managers. We also hoped to gain insight into how traditional and new spiritual practices operated within the context of natural burial and whether celebrants' experience of funerals in these sites differed from those in the cemetery, churchyard or chapel and, if so, in what ways. To begin with, the chapter considers the narratives gathered from our interviews with funeral directors.

Funeral directors' perceptions and experiences

As the introductory chapter of the book described, the funeral profession as we know it today emerged from individuals who previously combined the skills of woodworking and undertaking. Many funeral directors started off as coffin makers and through the acquisition of coach and horses, and later motorised transport, were later able to transport bodies from home to cemetery. The majority of people died at home, where the body was laid out. The upper classes later started the trend of body storage elsewhere and the lower classes followed. This included the request of families to view the deceased in the

undertaker's premises, which in turn called for improved facilities to accommodate the family as well as the body. Embalming processes sealed a professional
status for the funeral director, putting them on a par with some aspects of the
medical profession.[5] Although the professionalisation of the industry was a
seemingly rapid transition, it was nevertheless hard fought and accompanied by
a concerted effort to remove the social stigma surrounding those who handled
and cared for the corpse.[6] It is important, then, to consider these issues in order
to gain a deeper understanding of the implications of natural burial for the
contemporary funeral industry.

Several of the funeral directors we interviewed were from family-run
businesses and had experienced first-hand the shift in their professional status
from part-time undertaker to full-time funeral director, as the quote below
highlights:

> We used to work in the furniture shop because they were old-fashioned house
> furnishers and undertakers. You'd put a note on the desk in a little office saying
> 'funeral directors, please call next door', people would come and say, I've come
> to arrange a funeral and you'd say okay, you'd just whip, change your jacket,
> change your top, say if you'd like to come this way, you know, it was a bit
> Heath Robinson really but then beginning of eighties [the town]'s grown quite
> a lot and so, so we moved then to having, you know, staff on the funeral side
> only, rather than dash between the two.
>
> (Ron Southwell)

Although through their business the funeral directors we interviewed were
connected to the areas in which they operated, this group of participants had
no relationship to the natural burial landscapes in which they had worked other
than that they were local to them. Indeed, locality to the natural burial site was
often given as the reason for their involvement:

> I think the majority come via, via the, the site first. Very few actually come here
> and ask us without already having spoken to [the site manager]; if anything
> he, he directs them this way. I think from a territorial point of view, if they're
> within our unwritten boundaries, then he says right, there's the funeral director
> that's going to look after you. They come to us as a third call, or they come in
> having heard about it. I can't say that we have people come in here saying, what
> are the options?
>
> (Jamie Lane)

Several respondents identified being local as one of the strengths of their
business; it was through their belonging to an area and build-up of family
loyalty and trust over time that they enjoyed a steady stream of local custom for
all disposal options. Other interviewees were from larger corporate, rather than
family-run, funeral businesses serving several areas. Anthony Phillips was based
in Powys and Karen Timms in Rotherham, and both had worked as funeral
directors in large companies for more than 20 years:

> Funerals are more personal now than when I first came into it 24 years ago.
> People are requesting far more things than they did then, non-religious funerals,

when I first came into it, it didn't happen; funeral directors said, you've got to have a vicar involved. I've always believed it's up to the family what they want to have.

(Anthony Phillips)

Funerals have changed over the years, they have gone more towards celebrating a person's life; everything's changed, people will ask us for all sorts and if we can do it we will do it, and I much prefer it that way.

(Karen Timms)

In Anthony's experience, the funeral director should no longer 'direct' what happens but should listen and respond to the needs and wishes of the family. As the examples we present in this chapter evidence, this was a general trend that emerged from our interview data, and not only pertinent to natural burial. The two quotes above also indicate recognition of the shift from mourning a death to celebrating a life; and for Anthony and Karen it seemed paramount that the funeral director should meet the requests made by bereaved families and friends. As Karen told us, '*within reason*' they carried out the family's wishes. She related the following story:

We were once doing a service and I think the chap that had passed away was quite flamboyant and a bit of a showman; the minister said, 'as the curtains come together, if a black glove was to come through and wave to everyone, the family thought it would be quite funny'. So I'm sat there in the vestry, service is going on, I thought, oh, I'll do it. I ran right round the back of the crematorium, sneaked through the side doors, and as the curtains came together I walked with them and as they totally closed, I just put my hand through the curtains and waved to everyone! Oh and the whole place was absolutely, I pulled my hand back, ran right round the chapel to the doors to let them out and the family, they thought that were great.

(Karen Timms)

We use Karen's story here to indicate how funeral directors might willingly respond to a family's wishes, however unusual they might seem. Indeed, the local funeral directors we spoke with described their job as one that relied on the ability to react in appropriate ways to diverse groups of people in a fairly short space of time; as one told us, in the initial meeting with a bereaved family, '*you only get two hours*'. Clearly one of the skills the funeral director must have is to ensure they gather enough information in order to meet a family's needs. Even so, as Karen's narrative shows, there might be times when they were requested to 'think on their feet' and make decisions at short notice.

It was evident from the narratives of this small group of respondents that getting things right for bereaved families was integral to their provision of a good and professional service:

I think it's important for the family because they feel that they've done something, because quite often funeral directors come along, take everything away from you and all you're doing is just answering a few questions, filling in a few forms and some of the family feel that they've done nothing. They feel they want to show something because they love the person.

(Ron Southwell)

Family members' requests to be involved in funeral arrangements were encouraged by several of the death care professionals we interviewed, whichever disposal option was chosen, although the extent of family involvement encouraged/permitted varied across this cohort. A funeral director who had worked at the East Meon site spoke very positively about the benefits for bereaved families and friends of taking part in the funeral process and endorsed this himself, as did all of the funeral directors we interviewed – although perhaps not to the extent that the NDC advocate did. What can be drawn from these interview extracts is, however, that our interviewees felt they were responding to shifts they perceived happening within the public realm, and they had altered their working practices accordingly to meet the changing needs of bereaved people. As they also identified, the changes they talked about were seemingly recent and as such they correspond with the emergence of natural burial.

Such changes cannot be attributed to natural burial itself, of course, but perhaps they are related more to a general unease within the bereaved population that their needs have not been met in the past and so they are becoming more assertive about what they are purchasing: a different model of consumption, perhaps. In our focus group interviews, for example, there was evidence that people had been deeply unhappy with funerary practices for some time but had not felt empowered to 'do their own thing'. In these interviews, natural burial emerged as an opportunity to offer them something more empowering. Our interviews with natural burial providers that we discussed in Chapter 3 also highlight how their experience of a family funeral was often a significant motivation to offer a 'better alternative'. Natural burial, of course, comes with its own sets of rules and regulations, although masked at times by a rhetoric that implies freedom of choice; but nevertheless it is located within its own set of guidelines and parameters, in particular around the issue of memorialisation, which we discuss in other chapters.

Promoting natural burial to bereaved people

For the most part, the funeral directors we spoke with perceived their role as to present bereaved families with the range of disposal options available. What we wanted to find out, then, was if, when and how natural burial was introduced into conversations with bereaved families as one of the choices they might make. One funeral director we interviewed commented that natural burial had not changed his practice at all – however, he displayed only willow coffins in his window explaining that '*they look better*'. Although originally very sceptical about the burial site opening, at the time of his interview he had officiated at more than 20 funerals there and was very popular with bereaved people and the site owners, as both funeral director and celebrant. It also emerged in some of our data from bereaved people that the window display had attracted them to this particular funeral director.

Christopher, a funeral director who worked for a large corporation, said he did not tell bereaved people about the natural burial option. This was not because he was opposed to it, but rather that he only talked about it if and when the customer brought it into the conversation. In his experience this did not happen very often. He was unaware of how people found out about natural burial and assumed it was '*off the telly*'. It is worth noting here that the majority of bereaved people we interviewed had chosen natural burial before they visited the funeral director, either as pre-death choices made with relatives and friends, in the aftermath of an unexpected death or the death of a young person, or at times when an unusual bereavement had occurred. To this end then, bereaved people had already decided on natural burial before visiting the funeral director. It therefore begs the question of when natural burial will become normalised within the funeral profession as a whole so that it becomes a 'third option' that is offered to all of their bereaved clientele.

In the instances when natural burial was not already decided upon, some funeral directors told us they might suggest it when the character of the deceased was discussed with bereaved families. As Karen said: '*When you're arranging a funeral, you can start and read people and, and, oh, he loved his nature and his walks and listening to the birds.*' It would be this kind of narrative that led Karen to suggest the burial site at Ulley to her clients. Paul Masters, who ran a family business in Sheffield, told us he advised his clients to visit all of the options available if they had the time, including natural burial sites; several others said that if a customer came to them wishing to use a natural burial site they would always advise them to visit if they had not done so already: '*My immediate reaction is that if they haven't been there, they must go there ... they need to be aware that it is different*' (Jamie Lane). It was not clear, however, whether Jamie would advise people to take a look at the cemetery or the crematorium.

What is perhaps interesting is that funeral directors did not direct bereaved people to natural burial websites, and, although they had pictures of local cemeteries and crematoria in their offices, none of them had images of natural burial sites to show clients. It might well be that increased dialogue between natural burial providers and local funeral directors would enable natural burial's acceptance as a legitimate and indeed conventional choice for bereaved people.

Delivering the funeral

Although funeral directors told us they responded to bereaved clients' requests, it was evident they continued to feel responsible for ensuring funerals went well. As we discussed in Chapter 5, such responsibility was also strongly felt by natural burial site owners/managers. This was, however, a particularly pertinent issue for funeral directors because their loss of control over the funeral process was seemingly much more ambiguous, as illustrated in the experience of Eileen in Abermule, whose husband George was a classic cars enthusiast. When George died, Eileen wanted to transport his coffin to the burial field in his favourite vehicle, Primrose, a bright yellow Volkswagen camper van:

> I thought it'd be rather nice for him to have Primrose to take him to his last resting place; our son-in-law drove it. He picked the coffin up and came back to the house, and all the other cars followed. The undertaker said, 'well, you'll still

need us', and they took one or two cars and their staff and they said, 'it's best if we go to make sure everything goes smoothly.' I'm glad they did.

In the above scenario, the funeral director continued to direct from a distance, overseeing but, nevertheless, seemingly less powerful. His presence was not unwelcome; rather a case of give and take was clearly in play, for both funeral director and bereaved family. There was, then, evidence in our data that funeral directors felt anxious when expected to let go of their control over proceedings yet ultimately were left feeling responsible that the day went well, as a funeral director who had worked at the East Meon site, explained:

> If they want to use the hand bier, I'm quite happy for the family, you know, explain what to do and we'll put one of each of the family on either corner, but I have my men standing by them to assist them all the way, you know, they walk beside them like nannies.
>
> (Ron Southwell)

Ron also talked about health and safety issues for family members and for his staff. He explained he had a duty of care for both and obviously experienced certain anxieties in situations where bereaved families and friends were also proactive participants, not least because this would take place in an 'unfamiliar' setting. Although Karen Timms stressed that the practicalities of a funeral in the natural burial ground were no different from those of the traditional cemetery, she also felt the need to ensure the safety of the funeral party in an environment that might include hills, mud, no paths, long grass, seemingly randomly planted trees, and so on:

> It's a bit more overgrown, you know, natural, that's the only difference. You just have to tell them to watch where they're stepping because they're probably near a grave, and with it being a bit uneven, not all beautifully mown with paths, we do have to keep an eye on them, make sure they're not going to tread on something or fall down.
>
> (Karen Timms)

Time and emotion

Many of our interviewees referred to cremation as a 'conveyor belt', and this included funeral directors. During our conversations with them, time emerged as one of the major differences between the natural burial ground and the crematorium. The description below highlights the stark differences that might be experienced between these two environments:

> There is pressure on a funeral director because you're conscious that you've got your eleven o'clock slot, the next one's eleven thirty, you've got to get the people in and the people out within that allotted time, you're always pushed for time. With the natural burial site, you arrive at ten or twelve or whatever and I know that I can't book another funeral at eleven because it's a slower process, very much slower, but it seems very laid back.
>
> (Ron Southwell)

From our observations of attending funerals at three of our four study sites, we are able to state that a funeral at the natural burial ground can indeed be a time-rich process. The journey from hearse to grave at some sites is much longer than that of a traditional funeral; and, with one burial a day at most sites, there were seemingly no time constraints. This freedom was acknowledged by funeral directors as very positive for the family of the deceased, but, as Ron Southwell pointed out, '*sadly, we're all here for business*'. In this context then, time really is money. With this in mind, it might be reasonable to suggest that when a funeral director is required by the family to stay on-site for the duration of the burial, which was the case in the majority of interviews we undertook with bereaved participants, there could also be some acknowledgement of the cost of this much slower process, because from a business perspective, as our data would attest, this could prove problematic. Perhaps to counteract this as well, burial ground owners/managers could accept more than one funeral a day onto their sites. Although this might not be ideal from a natural burial perspective, it has been shown to be manageable at some sites.[7] It is also easy, perhaps, to overstate the fiscal element of the funeral industry, while simultaneously understating the business side of natural burial. Although sometimes perceived as such, natural burial is not a 'cheap option'; like their funeral director counterparts, site owners/managers earn money from the services they offer their bereaved clients.

All dressed in black?

Even though their narratives indicated that funeral directors' practices were changing to meet the public shift from mourning death to celebration of life, more often than not these changed practices happened within the confines of the crematorium, a relatively controlled environment with obvious routes into and out of the space and a carefully managed timescale. This location might then suggest particular boundaries around the performance of funeral rituals. As well as this, the bounded space of the crematorium, and indeed the cemetery, might suggest particular ways of dressing and behaving for mourners and death care professionals alike.

In the natural burial ground there are no confining walls to enclose the 'flock' and ensure ministering words can be heard; no shelter from the elements, so the weather encroaches on the process; and overall the funeral ritual takes place on a terrain that suggests 'sensible' footwear such as walking boots, thus lending itself to dressing down rather than up. The natural burial ground therefore presents a very different scenario to a profession that is often identified and indeed, as our data indicated, also described through its formalities of dress. Similar issues to these arose for the celebrants we spoke with, and we return to this below. Paul Masters, a funeral director from a family-run business in Sheffield, said that care should be taken when making decisions to perform differently in traditional settings:

> If you turn up at the crematorium dressed as clowns and bump into another funeral, nothing wrong with dressing up as clowns, that's fine, absolutely fine, absolutely fine, dressing up as clowns and carrying a coffin, absolutely fine, but if you turn up at the crematorium dressed as clowns and anyone from that

previous funeral or the funeral afterwards sees it, you've ruined their funeral, you've really ruined their funeral!

(Paul Masters)

Paul later commented that as fewer funerals happened on a daily basis in a natural burial ground, dressing as clowns would be acceptable. There are some similarities here with Karen Timms' willingness to wave her hand through the curtains as they drew in front of the coffin at the crematorium, and both are perhaps indicative of the funeral director's observance of the shift from mourning death to celebrating life. Despite these accommodations, it was clear from interviews with local funeral directors that the uniform was part and parcel of their ability to display their professionalism, described by one as his '*badge of office*' and by another as a source of '*power*'.

Although seemingly out of place in a natural burial ground as opposed to the more regulated environment of the cemetery or crematorium, then, the uniform might well be here to stay for the funeral professional. One respondent explained that if not for his uniform, he might be mistaken for a mourner – something he did not want to happen because: '*they [mourners] know they're safe because they've got you there if they need you ... I've always done that in the 30 odd years, and I think it's right.*' It might be as well that bereaved people would prefer funeral directors to remain separate from the funeral party, or at least to remain identifiable. Data from our ethnographic study (Chapter 5), for example, draw attention to a respondent's preference for the priest to wear his dog-collar even though officiating at a non-religious ceremony, so that others would be aware he was not '*some old boy off the street*'. Evident in these data as well was that interviewees perceived the funeral director to be someone who directs those who, because of their emotional state, might be directionless. This again resonates with burial site manager Al Blake's commitment to 'stepping in' for the families at East Meon if proceedings began to 'fall apart' (see Chapter 5).

It would seem from their narratives, then, that the uniform not only separated funeral directors from mourners, but also detached them emotionally from the realities of death and bereavement. In their interviews, funeral directors presented themselves as rational rather than emotional figures, available to give assistance to mourners as and when required. It could also be argued that funeral directors are accustomed to wearing black and being smart at funerals as this is how they have presented themselves, and indeed have been represented, traditionally. Instigating change might prove difficult and provoke unease, meaning that funeral directors choose to continue to dress in a way that, rather conversely, they find emotionally as well as professionally comfortable. As well as this, shedding an 'official' persona might have links with the ways in which funeral directors performed their role with bereaved families, described by Ron Southwell, among others, as offering emotional comfort and support while, as Ron highlights, simultaneously carrying out the 'backstage'[8] work:

The thing is with funeral directing, it's a privilege for us to be entrusted with somebody that's loved by somebody else. We try and care as much as we can for the families and the bereaved when somebody comes and trusts you to do, to look after somebody and take that responsibility on because it is a responsibility for us to, to make sure that we get there on time and make sure that, you know, we, we have the right body, make sure that we make sure it's dressed or whatever. There's lots of work behind the scenes as well as in front of the family.

(Ron Southwell)

Keeping their distance?

Glennys Howarth comments that becoming emotionally involved makes the funeral director's job more difficult.[9] Indeed, when their role is compared with that of natural burial managers/owners, for example, funeral directors deal with many more bereaved people and remain, for the majority of the general public, the first port of call when someone dies. Paul Masters, for example, who managed a family-run business, told us his company arranged more than 450 funerals per year. Moreover, the main concern of the funeral business is death and bereavement, unlike the manager of the burial ground at the East Meon site who has his woodsman persona and other activities of the Sustainability Centre that might at times shield him from some of the 'rawness' of death. Farmers and landowners we interviewed similarly had other distractions and, in consequence, other emotional outlets.

The majority of the funeral directors we spoke with told us they learned on the job. This meant their ways of working with bereaved people had been passed down over the years, through experience in large companies or through smaller firms and family businesses. Undoubtedly, this is where the funeral directors we met learned what was expected of them by their employers/family predecessors in terms of how to organise funerals. With little previous experience of natural burial, they might then lack the confidence to know when they are doing things right which, as we have said, was one of their major concerns. Natural burial has therefore introduced a degree of uncertainty and unease to what was previously a relatively stable world of work. Although we were assured by our interviewees that their priority was to get things right for the family, working with bereaved people who are active rather than passive, or indeed enabling a more active role for their clientele, were fairly recent phenomena that signified different ways of working with clients, whatever disposal choice. Moreover, as noted, this would engender a shift in working practices that might well have been entrenched for several generations.

The body: between death and burial

One major exception to increased family involvement that emerged in our research was care of the body after death. In all instances, funeral directors were employed to look after the deceased in the interim period between death and the day of the funeral. Indeed, as related above and in the introductory chapter of the book, one of the ways in which this workforce achieved professional status was via their care of the body, which included the embalming process.[10] As previous chapters have outlined, although we discovered some exceptions, the vast majority of natural burial sites do not inter embalmed bodies and state this rule in their guidelines. It would be no wonder if funeral directors might experience some anxiety that they are returned to a role of undertaking the care of the body, and nothing else. Alongside this, while a family might agree to have a funeral director keep the body refrigerated in order to adhere to natural burial regulations, there were certain tasks such as dressing the body and transferring the body into the chosen coffin that in the large majority of cases, in our study at least, was not done by the bereaved family. Funeral directors we interviewed thus continued, for the most part, to undertake this 'hidden' work.

As well as these issues, it is perhaps worth commenting here how natural burial discourse positions the deceased as adding to the above-ground vista of the burial landscape. Their being part of a collective memorial is emphasised and is, as we discovered, part of its appeal. We have argued elsewhere[11] that such a discourse denies the decomposition of the body over time and as it merges with the earthy substrata, the fetid mass that engenders life above ground.[12] Although advocates of a 'no embalming' policy, natural burial owners/managers do not on the whole engage with the body itself and, indeed, might at times go to great lengths to detach themselves from the reality of the 'body in the box'.[13]

Howarth comments that the removal of the body from the home set in train a series of actions that led to the professionalisation of the industry. Not least of these was the perceived necessity for embalming.[14] However, the eschewal of embalming in natural burial discourse (and practice) means that what happens to the body after death is no longer masked. As Howarth indicated in her ethnography, the 'backstage' work of funeral premises meant that this was hidden and the body only appeared in the 'frontstage' areas of the funeral director's premises when considered ready for viewing by bereaved family and friends;[15] thus the bereaved client was protected from the realities of death and subsequent decay. Although embalming was not carried out in all instances by the funeral directors we spoke with, the alternative of keeping the body in cold storage was perceived to hold several other problems, not only related to viewing. Although being aware of the ecological arguments against embalming, Paul Masters, for example, raised interesting questions about the 'green' credentials of alternative methods of body storage:

> There's a practical side going on here and there's an emotional side. I want to see Mrs Smith looking really nice in a coffin, probably embalming is the best way forward, then people can come and go from her room all day, whatever, or the body can be at home, they can come and go as they please, without having to refrigerate or anything like that. So yes, formaldehyde is not a good solution, use of refrigeration, is that good?
>
> (Paul Masters)

There was, then, little to suggest in our data that, unless they were also funeral directors, natural burial ground owners/managers engaged with what happened to the body in the period between death and burial. To discuss the condition of the body with bereaved family and friends in order to prepare them for viewing the deceased does, however, require a specific set of skills; effectively, the funeral director must reveal what were previously considered their 'backstage' working practices.[16] As such, the task of dealing with all aspects of the body remained the remit of the funeral director. Some data indicate that bereaved people's visits to the natural burial site prior to their meeting with the funeral director enabled the latter to take a more candid approach:

> As funeral directors we can't do things without explaining to the family, because it's their loved one and not ours. Quite often most people's been to the natural burial site first so [the manager's] had them against the wall and right in their face grilling them hasn't he? So they come in and they know what they're expecting, so that's quite good really, because it helps us when we're explaining to people, you know, we can't carry out hygienic treatment, that's what we call it. A person might be in a road accident where we can use cosmetics to rebuild and all this sort of stuff. You need to embalm to do that. So, so you have to explain, you know.
>
> (Ron Southwell)

The funeral directors we interviewed were on the whole positive about the changes they had experienced in their professional lives. From our conversations with them, there seemed no reason why their enthusiasm would not extend to embrace the promotion of disposal options that are underpinned by a commitment to environmental issues and concerns. This would add to their expertise in matters of death and disposal, as well as increase the choices they are able to offer their bereaved clientele. As discussed in Chapter 3, during the course of our study we discovered a blurring of the boundary between burial ground ownership and funeral directing and indeed, for funeral directors who were also burial ground managers or at least had good connections with local sites, several new possibilities were seemingly opened up. Through their environmental knowledge and interests they became more involved in the care of the land alongside care of the bereaved person. Perhaps in these groups there are real opportunities to revisit the service that they provide in a more coordinated manner, although, as this volume makes clear, this was not without its complexities and not least personal as well as professional status might be affected. It would seem to us, though, that a funeral director, or indeed burial site owner/manager, with another 'string to their bow' might acquire a more fulfilling working life and greater job satisfaction.

Celebrants' perceptions and experiences

We turn now to discuss data from our interviews with celebrants. We focus on their awareness of and engagement with natural burial; their relationships with bereaved families; and the comparisons they made between the natural burial ground, the cemetery and the crematorium.

Engaging with natural burial

The majority of celebrants we interviewed had first learned of natural burial through a call from a funeral director asking them to provide a service; although Susan Watson, an Anglican priest, first heard of it through her work in the hospice in Sheffield. Five years before our interview with her, a patient asked for her help with plans for a woodland burial; at the time of her interview, Susan had officiated at four funerals in the local natural burial sites. John Redding, an Anglican priest located in a village that borders Ulley, knew of the burial site from its inception. He described natural burial as:

A really comforting way of approaching death; the sense of identity with nature. People encounter this lovely setting with trees and the wildness of nature and not everything neatly trimmed off and the borders kept perfect, but something a bit different that resonates with feelings of belonging to the earth and that sort of sense of being part of the totality of things.

(John Redding)

John contrasted the wildness of the natural burial ground with the neat and perfect borders of the cemetery, intimating how the natural burial ground might promote feelings of continuity as well as change, rather than the constraint and stasis he identified as part of the cemetery landscape. Susan thought people who chose natural burial were those who 'had the courage to face their mortality'; like John, she described how she imagined the body blending with the environment:

I think those who go for woodland burial really thought about their life and their remains and what it's all about and where they are with it; it appears to me they may be more at ease with their death, that they are made of material matter, and it will just become part of the countryside, and just to have a tree remembering them is a rather beautiful thing.

(Susan Watson)

John also perceived that some of those who chose the natural burial option based their decision on 'what's right in terms of the environment', and recalled the funeral of one of his parishioners:

One lady whose funeral was in church here at Springley who was buried in the Woodland Cemetery was in a wicker coffin, yeah, so I guess that's, you know, it's more, yeah, biodegradable, yeah, and, and was taken to the cemetery on an open horse-drawn cart.

(John Redding)

The celebrants we spoke with felt that people who chose natural burial were concerned with the environment, although interestingly our data from bereaved people indicated that ecological concerns were often secondary considerations – the majority of our participants desired a 'nicer place' for their loved one to lie and for them to visit, alongside a narrative that often revealed a perception of the natural burial site as a very personal space. Our data therefore suggest a more individual rather than collective significance for those who make natural burial their disposal choice. As one of the Sudbury brothers in Abermule said:

Mum died in October and we went there in November, it was her birthday. So it was only a month later we went up there, dusk and we got a candle and there was just a candle burning and you could see this little light flickering on top of that hill, but in your mind you think that she's the only person there.

(Ed Sudbury)

Like funeral directors, the celebrants who participated in our study were aware of environmentally friendly disposal options other than natural burial.

Mavis Appleby, a Humanist in Sheffield, talked about promession[17] although, like funeral director Paul Masters, added the caveat that, '*you'd still need all the chemicals of course to freeze you*'. Mavis offered her own version of an environmentally friendly burial, which we present below alongside that of Paul Masters, who reflected on the historical records of his own business to assert that present-day natural burials had come '*full-circle*':

> If you're going to be truly, truly kind to the environment you should be wrapped in a sheep's fleece and just laid in the ground. You don't need anything, you know, as long as you've got, they can carry you and tip you in off a trolley; that would be truly friendly to the environment, yeah. [laughs]. Well of course that's what they used to do. You were wrapped in a winding sheet or a linen sheet or something like that.
>
> (Mavis Appleby)

> This is natural burial as you get, died at home, stayed at home, coffin was made here, English Oak, English Elm, Pitch Pine, okay, that's what was made, horse-drawn hearse up to the house, body remained in the house, the service was held in the house. Right, coffin was then taken by horse-drawn to the, to the cemetery, to Firpool Cemetery, which is our closest cemetery, buried in the ground. Now that, that is as natural burial as you're going to get, and that's about the most traditional funeral you're going to get. So actually, this is where, everyone is, oh I love these modern green funerals, and actually it isn't. The most, the most green is probably the most traditional.
>
> (Paul Masters)

Both Paul's and Mavis' reflections on historical burial practices also echo Al Blake's perception of Bronze Age death ritual that informed his mode of burial at the East Meon site that we discussed in Chapter 5. Thus our respondents' assertions might well act as reminders that natural burial as landscape as well as practice is, perhaps, not so new.

Meeting the needs of bereaved people

Celebrants told us that, more often than not, their first encounter with a bereaved family happened after they had met with the funeral director and, as such, the disposal choice had been made. None of the celebrants perceived it to be their role to question and make suggestions that might be at odds with these arrangements. In consequence, John Redding said natural burial had not caused '*a dramatic change; I don't know that it has affected our approach to funerals to any great degree really. When people have opted for this type of natural burial, that decision has been made before they come to us.*' Conversely, Seb Wells, a Humanist who had worked at the Abermule site, told us he always directed bereaved people to the funeral director in the first instance, before agreeing to officiate for them, seemingly to maintain good relationships across these different professional groups:

> I get phone calls from families now saying will you do this funeral? But I always refer them back to the funeral director because I'm not a funeral director. So

you have to say to them, would you please go and speak to whoever, and I always have to be careful, I don't recommend anybody, but it's the funeral directors that pay my wages.

(Seb Wells)

Richard Wright, a cleric in Powys, first became aware of natural burial through a local funeral director who knew of a parishioner whose request for a particular religious service had been refused because he was not a churchgoer:

He wished his wife to have this natural burial, which I must admit, it's a term that I do not fully understand, but I said I'm more than willing to carry out any clerical duties there because I think, if the people need the Church, we should be there for them. I met this family, he was a lovely chap and that is what he wanted, that is what put him at peace, and I think that's what our job should be, to help.

(Richard Wright)

Although Richard had no prior knowledge of natural burial, he nevertheless felt it his duty to respond to the needs of his parishioners, whatever their disposal option or religious persuasion. Indeed, like the funeral directors we interviewed, the celebrants we spoke with told us that their priority was the family of the deceased and articulated a commitment to getting things right for them; as Humanist Audrey Baker said: *'it's the last thing you can do for somebody who's lost their loved one.'* She continued:

My role is to celebrate the life of the person that's passed on, to be there with their family and friends, and I always say, would you like the service to be totally non-religious or would you perhaps like the Lord's Prayer or a hymn included. I always give them that option.

(Audrey Baker)

Several of the interviews with celebrants, both religious and non-religious, as well as funeral directors and bereaved respondents, revealed the hybridity Audrey described:

There's certain funeral directors know what you can do and what you will do for them and so. I get all the difficult ones normally; quite often a funeral director will phone me up and he'll say oh Dennis, can you do a funeral next Thursday? They're not religious so, so we thought of you [laughter]. Whether that's a compliment or not, I don't know.

(Dennis Thompson)

Evidently our celebrant research participants tailored a mix of religious and non-religious services to meet the needs of their bereaved clientele, as well as the deceased,[18] and often accommodated choices that appeared to be at odds with their own beliefs. Accounts of 'being there' for family and friends was further echoed by Humanist Greg Lewis:

The delivery of the ceremony is all very well but it's that gaining the confidence of the family that they needn't worry on that day, that, you know, that they can approach this awful day, with a bit of confidence that somebody is going to, is going to just get them through it all.

(Greg Lewis)

Greg commented that Humanists provided '*bespoke services*', and again parallels can be drawn here with data from clergy as well as funeral directors. From our interviews with celebrants, it was clear that their practice of creating scripts for services was very similar regardless of background or belief; they all spent time with bereaved family members, gathering anecdotal evidence about the deceased who, in the vast majority of cases, they did not know personally.

Working in the natural burial ground

Like funeral directors, mode of dress was an issue that this group of research participants discussed when we met with them. Greg Lewis told us he and his celebrant colleagues had '*a dress code and we stick to it*'. With striking similarity to the funeral director's dilemma regarding appropriate clothing, however, when talking of his first experience of officiating at a natural burial site, Greg told us how he and the mourners had been '*covered in mud*'. This led him to ponder: '*Do you wear like, you know, your wellies, or do you wear shoes?*' As he later acknowledged, wearing waterproofs might have been the best option in this instance. Seb Wells said he would be guided by his bereaved clients: '*I wouldn't necessarily go in, dressed shabbily or in a sort of hippy style just because it was a green burial, I would go in whatever I considered appropriate for [the family of the deceased].*' Mavis Appleby told us that in order for her voice to be heard in the burial ground, '*it sometimes means you're actually standing on the earth from the grave; that's quite exciting because you think if you slip you might go the wrong way [laughs]*'. Again, protective clothing would perhaps not go amiss in this scenario. These narratives indicate how the natural burial environment provoked thoughts around appropriate clothing for officiants and their funeral director counterparts that in all likelihood would not have emerged in more traditional settings.

As data from our funeral directors indicate, the general public is becoming more proactive in their approach to funeral rituals. This was also commented on by the celebrants we met:

It's like the kind of mushroom effect of realising that you don't have to have a standard religious service, in fact you can have a non-religious service, you can even have something that's kind of halfway, not from us but, you know, but even like within Humanism there are, there are kind of schisms. We can't necessarily sing All Things Bright and Beautiful because of the content of it, but we could maybe play it as a tune, you know?

(Greg Lewis)

In comparison with Audrey's narrative above, however, Greg seemingly drew the line at any verbal religious content at the graveside, indicating how practices and procedures can themselves be tailored to fit both the celebrant and the bereaved family. At the time of our interview with him, Greg had just qualified as a Humanist celebrant. He was interviewed one week after he had performed a service at the Ulley site, which was his first encounter with natural burial. He visited the site before the service in order to familiarise himself with the landscape. This was Greg's second funeral service as celebrant; his first was at the local crematorium, so he was able to offer the following comparison:

> Being in a crematorium you know you've got a half-hour slot and basically whatever you put together with the family has got to fit into 20 minutes of you speaking with 5 minutes for ins and outs at the end . . . you've just not got those time constraints at Ulley. So when I was writing this script . . . you weren't as tied to those same constraints.
>
> (Greg Lewis)

Similarly, Seb Wells commented:

> [In the crematorium] there's the catafalque, there's the lectern and there's the pews, whereas the green burial ground people can stand around and they can stand wherever they feel like it, I tend to stand one end of the, of the grave and they do what they like.
>
> (Seb Wells)

Again, there are similarities here with funeral directors' interviews and their experiences of being released from the bounded space of the crematorium, although, from the celebrants' perspective, this difference was seemingly embraced more positively. In Greg's experience, in the natural burial ground the weather also played a role:

> They had this Johnny Cash number that was nearly five minutes long and I said if you don't mind, which was kind of, you know, going off-script a bit, I would like to just shorten the music a little bit given the weather and they were all like nodding thank goodness for that. They didn't want to listen to Johnny Cash for five minutes in the rain either, you know!
>
> (Greg Lewis)

However, rather than being perceived in negative terms by the funeral party, Greg told us how:

> Quite a few of the family said, well we really are back to nature here aren't we? Because we were getting blasted by the wind and wet by the rain and they were very like positive about that, it wasn't like, you know, they were very upbeat about the whole thing really.
>
> (Greg Lewis)

John Redding described how it was difficult to gauge the end of a funeral service in the natural burial site, and we have come across this in other of our interview data as well as from our own observations of natural burials. John explained how traditional rituals were often used to signal this time:

> The funeral director is ready to throw soil onto the coffin at the point when you say earth to earth, ashes to ashes, dust to dust and when that's over people

often want to throw their flowers or petals down as an expression of, a way of saying goodbye, a letting go, of doing something that's a gift, you know, a special moment.

(John Redding)

Seb Wells told us he was able to perform his celebrant role more easily in the natural burial ground. He not only felt more at ease in a place where he was able to merge with the bereaved party, but also perceived the burial site was more enabling for mourners who wished to actively participate in burial rituals:

The big difference is the feeling of, of community. I like it because I've got people around me and I'm one of the, I'm one in the crowd as opposed to declaiming to a group. It's more comfortable for me, although I quite, I quite enjoy declaiming to a group, I don't mind 500 people in front of me. In fact I quite like it but at a funeral it certainly, how do I put it? If, if I'm taking a very big funeral at the crematorium I can feel everybody leaning on me they, they need me to be good, that's why everything I say at a funeral is written down, even though I've said it 100 times before, I feel that everybody is offloading their, their sense of, of occasion and trauma and uncertainty, it's all on me because I'm down there at the front and I'm in, I'm in charge. But at green burials you'll find that people are far more relaxed, they feel comfortable, they're in a group, they're close by and it's easier for somebody over there to say something rather than me say to somebody and here is daughter who's going to say that so it's very much more comfortable.

(Seb Wells)

In her role as an Anglican priest, Susan had also observed certain differences between officiating at burials at traditional cemeteries and natural burial grounds:

I think there's more participation, I think [mourners] are less spectators in a way, and I have noticed whoever's organised it in the family will give them all a flower each and people will all throw their flower in or place their flower on, in the woodland setting. I would say it's more inviting for people to get closer, because certainly at burials in an ordinary cemetery. We usually have to encourage them to come nearer to this hole in the ground.
[...]
   But somehow in a woodland, it's a bit chaotic, you've got grasses, you've got trees and it doesn't feel as austere, you haven't got these headstones looking at you. I think people aren't so overwhelmed – it's just how it struck me, that this felt nice. People were less on edge.

(Susan Watson)

Although Susan described the woodland as chaotic, it was her perception that the 'chaos' alongside the absence of headstones '*looking at you*', softened the environment and made it less grim than the cemetery. In her view, the natural burial ground provoked a more relaxed ambience that invited family and friends of the deceased to participate in the burial process – coming close to the grave/coffin; saying farewell with their flowers. As her narrative intimates, the absence of headstones might also have instigated feelings of being the only mourners there – and, as we have said, this was a theme that emerged from our data with bereaved people and resonates with the suggestions made in earlier chapters that natural burial sites might offer a place that allows for individual emotional expression and connection with the deceased.

Seb Wells similarly commented that natural burial environments '*draw people to express themselves much more than your bare blank crematorium chapel*', although he added that he encouraged people to participate by reading poetry and playing music in whichever disposal location. Like Al Blake at East Meon and other of our interviewees, Seb also talked about the importance of 'being there' for bereaved people who were active participants in funeral rituals:

> It's very important that no one is, no one is put into a distressing situation because they've started to burble or dried up or forgotten what they were going to say or whatever. You want people to feel safe so you have to be there to step in if necessary or to, something as simple as saying breathe or whatever. To make sure that they get the fullest part of it, yeah, which could, it's a, it's a very important thing.
>
> (Seb Wells)

The natural burial site wherein, as Seb put it, '*the only roof you've got is, is the sky, the only carpet you've got is the field*', was experienced differently by the celebrants we spoke with. What was striking, however, was the contrast they articulated between the burial ground and that of the crematoria or cemetery. In most cases, the celebrants felt liberated, somehow becoming less a performer and more part of a community where bereaved people were involved. Perhaps it is here that we perceive how the landscape supplemented the church or crematoria when a religious belief no longer had relevance or where a secular building failed to reflect any personal identity or belief. The opportunity to participate is also mapped differently across these two environments. In our participants' and our own experiences, funerals at crematoria seldom have any collective act of singing; instead mourners listen passively to piped music, albeit chosen by close family and friends. There is then no real opportunity to outwardly declare support for the bereaved and pay respects to the deceased. Perhaps the challenge of entering the natural burial ground, negotiating the landscape, exposing themselves to the elements, demanded something of them and in so doing revealed a collective commitment beyond the convenience of the crematorium. The distraction of leaves rustling, birds singing, wind blowing and rain falling filled the awkward silence when the celebrant might feel a need to step in and also perhaps offered the opportunity for informal conversation. By coming together in this way, the work of the celebrant became a shared experience that was less dependent on a somewhat artificial and rehearsed 30-minute stand-up routine where the audience are the experts and the presenter the novice.

As we have said, all of the celebrants we interviewed focused on meeting the individual needs of bereaved family and friends. Alongside this, they perceived the deceased to be an individual who, over time, would become at one with the surrounding landscape, a shared understanding summarised below by John, an Anglican priest, and Mavis, a Humanist:

I think there is something there that meets a, meets a need, you know, that, a need to accept death as, you know, part of the natural process and the natural setting reinforces that, you know, facilitates it but, so that the, kind of, grimness of death, you know, the grimness, it is grim, you know, there's no getting away from that. But seeing this bigger picture of being part of the natural process there's nothing to fear in the end, you know, that that, that is facilitated more in a natural setting than in a, you know, in a, maybe than in a crem or in a, in a cemetery.

(John Redding)

I like to think that when people are buried in a natural burial setting there's a kind of feeling or rightness about it that they're, that they are quite literally returning to mother earth, you know, they're asleep in the bosom of Mother Nature, they're safe and they're surrounded by good sounds and the wind is blowing free.

(Mavis Appleby)

Summary

This chapter has explored the challenges as well as the opportunities that natural burial presents for contemporary death care professionals, particularly in terms of raised awareness among bereaved people of having different choices in how they decide to dispose of the body of a deceased relative or friend and the kinds of funeral rituals they might choose to engage with. It might be that death care professionals are being forced to 'raise their game', as they encounter increasing competition for business from people drawn into the industry through engagement with natural burial, as well as broaden the range of options they decide to offer their bereaved clientele.

Jones[19] defines natural burial as confirmation 'that the days of undertakers and the religious communities having a monopoly over funerals are coming to an end' but adds that he is 'quite sure the undertaking profession will adapt to these new ways'. The data we have presented in this chapter do indeed indicate the ways in which death care professionals, both funeral directors and celebrants, might be responding to this new disposal option. Indeed, and as Jones asserts, our interviewees indicated a degree of adaptation to their usual practices when on these sites, although it must be added that changes to practice were not restricted to natural burial.

Even though care of the body is increasingly being undertaken by some family members, such practices are in the minority; and, although some of our study participants washed, dressed and/or transported the body to the burial site in their own vehicles, no one we interviewed kept the deceased in their home until the day of the funeral. At the time of our study, then, people seemingly continued to prefer the body to be cared for by others outside the home. This preference resonates with work undertaken by Hockey (1993). Although perhaps 'prefer' is the wrong term – it might be that, through entrenched traditional practices and expectations around death rituals, bereaved people let the body go to 'professional' others. Nevertheless, our study revealed that the funeral director remained a key player in death and disposal processes. Indeed, all of our bereaved respondents used the services of a funeral director to some extent, with a small minority using them for storage of the body only. The funeral director does, then, remain the custodian of the dead body, which Howarth, Parsons and Walter have interpreted as the source of the funeral director's power.[20]

As the first port of call in most instances, funeral directors occupy a key position because they are in effect the gatekeepers of disposal knowledge and, as we have said, several death care professionals we spoke with were aware of alternative disposal options. However, if natural burial continues to gain momentum to become a more mainstream disposal choice, the funeral director who is not directly associated with a natural burial ground might face certain challenges, as they could stand to lose some of the roles and responsibilities they and their predecessors fought for in order to confirm and retain their professional status. Indeed, that the funeral director is reduced to storing the body and nothing more could well be perceived as problematic by some in the funeral industry, as reduction to storage and 'body handling' equates with a loss of power over the funeral process as a whole and with it, perhaps, a return to a stigmatised non-professional identity and a deskilling of the funeral profession.

However, such issues could in turn be perceived as opportunities; for example, good relationships with site owners/managers might lead to their recommending funeral directors' services to bereaved people whose initial encounter with disposal is the natural burial site manager rather than the funeral director which, as our data attest, was the case in several instances. Individuals are beginning to face their own mortality, evidenced in the fact that funeral plans are becoming more commonplace. This is occurring in a climate of ever-increasing public knowledge regarding environmental issues and an increased erosion of belief in the afterlife.[21] It would seem, therefore, that the continuity of their role as death care professionals might require funeral directors to forge good relationships with local as well as national natural burial ground owners/managers.

There is evidence within our data at least that the funeral profession is responsive to change, and we would argue there is much scope for dialogue between natural burial ground managers/owners and funeral directors. Alongside this, the celebrants we spoke with evidently felt 'at home' in the natural burial site and with those who also wished to be active participants in funeral rituals. Celebrants we spoke with seemingly felt less distanced from the bereaved people they worked with even though, in the majority of cases, they had no prior knowledge of the deceased and had met relatively briefly with the bereaved family to gather anecdotes and so on for the service. In the absence of relationships that might previously have been fostered by regular church attendance or being part of a smaller community, natural burial ostensibly removed some of these formalities and helped negotiate this limitation by encouraging people to be involved and, in so doing, to share the load. This was partly due to the removal of time pressure imposed by a 30-minute slot at the crematorium, not least the ability to deliver a meaningful service and at the same time remain aware of the needs of other funeral parties waiting to enter the space.

What was also evident was a response to the landscape; of inhabiting a living space that chimed with the motives of site users to bury naturally, immersed as they were in the welcome distraction of sun, leaves, wind and rain – a very different environment from the crematorium where, from our participants' perspectives, bereaved people were rarely encouraged to sing or participate in any meaningful way. It is worth noting, however, that although funerals at natural burial grounds might take the whole day, or more,[22] this richness of time could be at risk if natural burial becomes a mainstream choice.

Importantly, our research has raised several issues different groups could debate around the assistance each can provide to bereaved families and friends in order to more fully facilitate changing needs and desires. What also arises for natural burial providers is the question of where natural burial grounds sit within the idea of pre-paid funeral plans, which are becoming more commonplace. Indeed, conversations we had with our participants about what people were expected to do in the past when it came to disposing of the deceased revealed this was informed by certain traditions and social expectations underpinned by ideas around respect and dignity. What was evident in much of our data was that some individuals had gained increased confidence from observing how others have chosen to deal with death, so that they no longer felt constrained by social conventions. It could be assumed that natural burial has acted as a catalyst to free up and empower bereaved people, perhaps regardless of disposal choice.

Contemporary funeral directors and celebrants thus engage with a bereaved community that is becoming more aware of how a funeral service might be arranged and how they themselves might participate; a situation some death care professionals could find disconcerting. However, several of these professionals are incorporating natural burial into their repertoire in response to bereaved people's requests and the growth in public knowledge. Although it was not the case in any of our interviews with bereaved people, it might also be that natural death discourse has contributed to a desire for people to maintain full control of the body after death. As this chapter has shown, while the majority of the population still choose 'traditional' disposal, natural burial practices and landscapes coupled with the bereaved people who had chosen this disposal option undoubtedly had an impact on the work of death care professionals we encountered during the course of our study.

8

Ulley: natural burial through time

This chapter focuses exclusively on the woodland burial ground at Ulley, near Sheffield, and is divided into two sections. In Part I we explore how the burial ground has developed since the first burial, which took place on 13 October 1995 and was marked with the planting of a rowan tree. As we have already discussed in Chapter 3, Peace Funerals, who own and manage the burial ground, permit users to choose the location of the grave. The woodland at Ulley therefore presents an interesting opportunity to explore how users have responded to the site and the changing context of the natural burial landscape as what was once a farmers field is gradually transformed with the addition of each new burial into an emerging woodland. Figure 8.1 reveals how the density of the woodland has changed over 2002–2012, during which time there have been approximately 400 additional burials. The field has given way to a landscape in which trees are now the dominant feature. They tower over the visitor and in summer their leafy canopies screen out the surrounding views. Using data from the burial register, we show how the distribution of the woodland has developed at five-yearly intervals up until 2011.

From our analysis of the site's burial register, which records the choice of tree for each burial, we go on to discuss how the character and identity of the woodland is being shaped by individual choice as well as changes to the burial ground's policies. Until recently, Peace Funerals had a permissive approach to the choice of memorial tree, which was not confined to a prescribed list of native species that bereaved people had to select from. The burial ground is therefore an eclectic mix that, while dominated by native species, also includes many exotic trees and shrubs. In response to the increasing woodland density, and in order to preserve space for the established trees to grow, Peace Funerals have adjusted their burial provision to include plots at a reduced fee where it is not permitted to plant a tree. In 2012 they also restricted the choice of memorial planting on half-size cremated remains plots to a small fruit tree or shrub. These changes reflect how they have adapted their early vision of natural burial in response to the choices made by their customers and through a growing understanding of what it means to bury naturally.

In Part II the chapter presents Andy Clayden's personal reflections of his experience of visiting and photographing the burial ground over five years. This photographic record, which was started in December 2007, was initially included in our research to identify if and how bereaved people memorialised

Figure 8.1 *Reading from left to right and top to bottom, these images illustrate how the burial ground has changed. Taken from approximately the same position and during late spring or summer in 2002, 2006, 2009 and 2012 they show how the woodland has become more dense and blocks out the surrounding views.*

the grave. It was soon expanded to include photographs of a series of selected views that would also trace how the burial ground changed with each passing month and season. For the first three years visits were made to the site each fortnight. Since the official end of our study, these have continued on a monthly basis. This means that approximately 100 separate visits have been made to the burial ground, and each time the same journey is followed, with the same graves and views photographed. Through this familiarity and attention, it has been possible to develop a sensitivity in reading this landscape that has enabled some of the less overt ways in which bereaved people are memorialising and shaping this landscape to be recognised – and these are included here in this reflection. For example, in February 2012 a snow angel appeared at the entrance to the burial ground, an imprint left by a small child and an evocation of a figure that is traditional in churchyards and cemeteries. This simple playful act, soon to melt away, was a reminder that children are also a part this community, although they were rarely visible during visits.

Figure 8.2 *A snow angel, formed at the entrance to the burial ground and soon to disappear, records the recent visit of a young child (February 2012).*

Part I: creating a woodland

The establishment of the woodland at Ulley, and the form and character that it takes, is largely determined by the preferences of those who have chosen to be buried there or who have made the choice for a family member or friend. Peace Funerals estimate that over 90 per cent of users will choose the location of the grave and the type of memorial tree. The emerging woodland is therefore effectively a collective endeavour that brings together many individual choices in a single landscape expression. Over time this expression has continued to develop as the trees mature and also as new graves and trees are introduced into the burial ground. The location of each grave therefore provides an interesting record of how each user has exercised their preference in response to the natural burial landscape, and the woodland is the record of their preferences. As noted, the choice of trees was initially restricted to a list of native species, but Peace Funerals have not enforced this and many users have chosen more exotic cultivars and non-native trees and shrubs for their memorial.

Grave and woodland distribution

In 1996, the first full year the burial ground was open, there were 11 burials, which included one ashes plot.[1] By the end of 2000 there had been a total of 87 burials, including 20 ashes plots. Figure 8.3 shows the distribution of graves for this period. The most popular areas were: the perimeter of the burial ground, the area next to the stream and the top right corner of the site. This pattern of occupation is very different to what we might expect in a traditional cemetery, where the oldest graves are typically found towards the centre of the cemetery, near to the main path and buildings and where the most recent graves have been pushed towards the perimeter of the cemetery where space is still available. We would argue that this choice reflects both a pragmatic and aesthetic dimension. We must recognise that these early adopters were very much at the vanguard of the Natural Burial Movement, when there was little public awareness and burials were less frequent. The hedgerow by the stream, where the banks are colonised by alder and willow, provided an immediate connection with established nature and an anchor in the landscape to return to when locating the grave. For these users of natural burial, there was no guarantee that others would follow their lead and make the same commitment to creating a new woodland. Graves located towards the centre of the field were therefore at risk of remaining isolated if natural burial proved to be only a passing fad. The top right corner was the most popular area in the first five years, accounting for a quarter of all burials. Users may have been attracted to this space, partially contained by the adjacent hedges and mature trees, because it offered the most shelter and privacy. While it is not the highest point in the burial ground, it nonetheless offers a panoramic or monocular view[2] of the surrounding landscape and the least visual and noise intrusion from the road that services the burial ground. It is also the furthest point from the entrance and car park. Visitors to these graves must journey through this landscape and immerse themselves within it and in doing so inhabit[3] the natural burial ground.

Between 2001 and 2006 the total number of burials had more than doubled to 182, of which approximately one-third were cremated remains. Figure 8.4 shows how the substantial increase in the rate of burial is reflected in a more rapidly expanding and dispersed woodland. Burial near the hedge and stream continued to be popular, but the most significant increase was towards the top left corner. This is the highest point in the burial ground that arguably has the best views across the surrounding landscape, again reinforcing the importance that users attach to the value of the panoramic or monocular perspective of the surrounding landscape.[4] Throughout this five-year period there was a noticeable

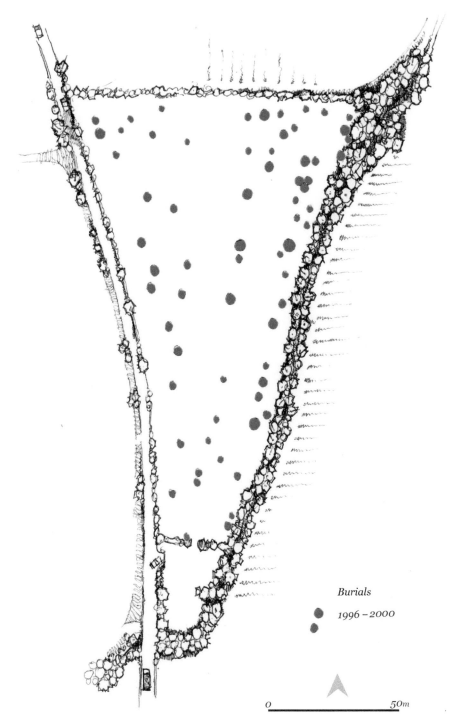

Burials

1996 – 2000

0 _____ 50m

Figure 8.3 *Plan showing the distribution of graves and tree planting for 1996–2000. The size of the tree symbol is an indication of how the burials developed over this five-year period; larger symbols indicate older graves.*

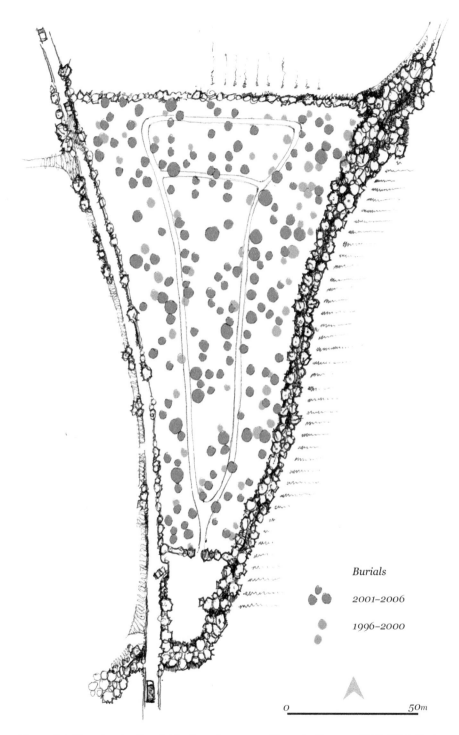

Figure 8.4 *Plan showing the distribution of graves and tree planting over 2001–2007. During this period the rate of burial more than doubled, which is reflected in the expanding woodland. In 2000 a mown path was included that forms a loop through the site along which graves are now clustered.*

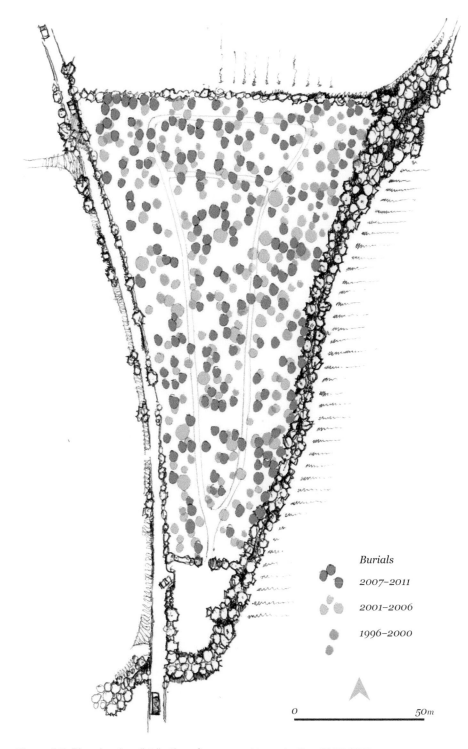

Burials

2007–2011

2001–2006

1996–2000

0   50m

Figure 8.5 *Plan showing distribution of graves and tree planting, 2007–2011.*

increase in the number of burials towards the centre of the site, an area that had previously been unpopular. This shift can be accounted for by a change in the management of the burial ground in response to requests from users who were finding it difficult to access graves through the long grass. Since the summer of 2000, a mown pathway has been maintained to provide access for funerals and visitors. The inclusion of this path has introduced a noticeable element of order that shapes how people move through this landscape. It performs a similar role to the hedge by giving bereaved people a fixed reference point from which they can locate a grave in an otherwise changing landscape.

Between 2007 and 2011 the rate of burial continued to grow from, on average, one burial each month in 1996 to one burial each week in 2011. The total number of burials during this period increased to 248, of which one-third were cremated remains. Figure 8.5 shows how the distribution of graves is much more evenly dispersed across the entire site in this period, with the exception of the area next to the road which continues to be less desirable. In terms of the choice of location of the burial plot, the landscape that people encountered from 2006 onwards was very different to the experience of those who first came to Ulley. There is increasingly less choice, so people are constrained to where the burial plots are available. However, although more than 500 burials have taken place at Ulley, these still represent less than a quarter of the total available burial plots. The important change for first-time visitors is that the landscape they encounter is no longer a field. While there still remain open spaces within the burial ground, the structure and character has changed significantly; and so has the experience of moving through the landscape. The hedge and mown path that initially provided the primary landmarks from which to locate a grave have been supplemented by a network of semi-mature and mature trees that stretch across the entire site. As the vegetation has continued to mature there is also a much greater sense of a more intimate and private landscape that can be immediately accessed when entering the burial ground. The panoramic views that may have initially contributed to the popularity of the far corners of the burial ground are gradually being lost as the woodland canopy extends across the site.

Changing woodland character

The wood at Ulley is not a native broadleaf woodland, typical of the region. Instead it is a unique collection of trees that reflects the complex range of individual motivations and preferences that have informed the choices of its users. A walk through the burial ground reveals this complexity for, among the native silver birch, alder, oak, ash and rowan, there are Japanese maples, magnolias and even a large monkey puzzle. Previous research at Ulley, when bereaved people were asked to identify their motive for choosing a particular tree, revealed that this was often informed by a desire to reflect something of the character and identity of the deceased.[5] For example, oak, with its sense of Englishness, strength and durability was a common choice for men, while silver birch was often chosen for women because of its perceived grace and elegance. There are also trees that were selected because they record the name of the deceased: ash, rowan and hazel. Our research participants also spoke of choosing a tree that reminded them of their childhood, the garden and street where they played. For others it was an opportunity to mark the time of birth or even death of the deceased through the seasonal display of blossom or fruit. For example, on the grave of one child there is a fir tree or what we would recognise as a Christmas tree. It recalls his death on Christmas day and each year small trinkets are attached to its branches. The choices of trees demonstrate a degree of creativity around how bereaved people continue to maintain a bond with the deceased that often only they understand the significance of. Natural burial, for many of our participants, was therefore not the erasure of the deceased's identity within a collective memorial landscape but instead an opportunity to express their identity in a more personal way.

Looking back through the burial register, we can observe subtle changes in the tree preferences of burial ground users. In the first five years the selection is dominated by familiar native trees including oak, rowan and silver birch, which account for almost half of all the trees.[6] There are also smaller numbers of cherry, willow, crab apple, hawthorn and hornbeam. They are almost exclusively native trees, although there are also a small number of cultivars that include copper beech and Kilmarnock willow, a dwarf tree with a weeping form that is more reminiscent of suburban gardens than a woodland.

Between 2001 and 2006 the burial register reveals a change in the order of popularity. Oak, rowan and silver birch remain common choices but have all been surpassed by cherry, which in this period accounts for approximately one-fifth of all the trees planted. A visit to the burial ground in May reveals the impact that this has had on the character of the woodland through the presence of bright splashes of pink and crimson blossom that are typical of these ornamental varieties. Native cherry trees (bird and wild cherry) are far less showy and have a much paler blossom. The growing appeal of cherry as a memorial

Figure 8.6 *Ornamental cherry trees have grown in popularity in preference to less colourful native varieties (Ulley, May 2013).*

tree, and particularly the more ornamental varieties, might be for a number of reasons. As we have already noted, they are often familiar trees and are frequently a feature of private gardens, parks and suburban streets. As a memorial they outperform many of the native trees with their seasonal display of blossom, fruit and autumn colour. Their increasing popularity might also suggest that natural burial has broadened its appeal to a wider audience who may be less familiar or concerned with the distinction between native and non-native trees and their respective environmental merits.

From 2006 onwards cherry has continued to gain in popularity but throughout this period there was also a noticeable shift towards smaller trees

Figure 8.7 *Small fruit trees have become a more common feature of the emerging woodland in response to changing burial ground regulations (Ulley, October 2013).*

and shrubs and a decline in large native trees, especially oak. The change in species selection reflects a change in policy by Peace Funerals who, from 2007, restricted the choice for ash plots to either a small fruit tree or shrub. The ash plots are half the size of the burial plots, and, with the increase in the number of graves and subsequent tree cover, they could no longer accommodate the planting of the larger native trees on each grave. As a consequence the woodland has taken on a different tack and now incorporates apple, pear and damson and familiar garden shrubs including *Photinia*, *Mahonia*, *Pieris* and shrub roses. The burial plots were not restricted in terms of the tree that could be chosen, but to a lesser degree these also reveal a growing appetite for more exotic species, including *Ginkgo* and *Camelia*. While many of these smaller trees and shrubs will ultimately struggle to survive in the shade of the much larger native trees, the burial register also records more recent examples of holly and hazel, native species that can thrive as part of a shaded woodland understory. While uncommon, their selection would suggest that users are responding to the changing woodland and how it seems likely to develop in future. If the new memorial plant is to survive, it must either compete successfully for space and light or be happy in the shade of much larger trees.

In summary, the burial ground at Ulley reveals how a woodland can evolve when individuals are given the freedom to make their own choices and where this choice is also informed by their engagement with the changing landscape and changes to the regulations. Each user must respond to a different situation that is determined by the maturity and character of the woodland and the availability of burial plots at that time. What began as predominantly native woodland has evolved into a more diverse eclectic species mix that now includes many flowering non-native trees and shrubs. More recently Peace Funerals have introduced alternative burial options as they look towards the future of the burial ground. From 2012 burial and ash plots were introduced at a reduced cost but with no rights to plant a tree or shrub. These graves will help to maintain access for future burial and preserve space for established trees to grow.

Part II: observing and inhabiting the burial ground

The rest of this chapter is written in the first person and draws exclusively on Andy's experience of visiting the burial ground each month for the past five years. It is an opportunity to present his own experience of inhabiting this landscape and is a personal reflection of what he has observed and experienced. In order to take the reader into the burial ground in a more immediate sense, then, the point of view of one particular visitor is offered.

Winter, spring, summer and autumn: the changing year

Winter

In winter, the burial ground can look stark, untidy and uninviting in the cold, grey light. At this time of year, in the short, wet grass and leafless trees, the bare earth of new graves, the memorial plaques and cut flowers are at their most visible. In the absence of a living and thriving 'nature' the natural

Figure 8.8 *Reading from left to right and top to bottom, the images are a record of each passing month in 2012, starting in January. They are taken at the entrance to the burial ground and reveal changes in colour, texture, light and the extent to which it feels increasingly open or enclosed.*

burial ground feels somehow less natural and the presence of the dead more prominent. As Christmas approaches there is increased evidence of activity in the burial ground as friends and families reunite and visit their dead. In 2007, the first Christmas I visited the burial ground, a dozen or more trees were decorated with brightly coloured baubles and tinsel and on many of the graves there were wreaths and festive greeting cards addressed to the dead. Their appearance, also not uncommon in a municipal cemetery, to me felt somehow out of place here in the natural burial ground; too bright, too visible an intrusion on the rural landscape. More recently I have noticed a change in how people choose to decorate their tree at Christmas. This is partly in response to Peace Funerals taking a more proactive role in removing 'unnatural' decorations from graves and trees and in some cases reminding visitors, by attaching a note to the tree, of the regulations and that only 'natural' items are permitted. Baubles have been replaced by home-made decorations fashioned

Figure 8.9 *A display of Christmas decorations was once a familiar feature at Ulley (Ulley, December 2007).*

from items that have been gathered from the garden, hedges or local woods, including: fir cones, holly, ivy and nuts and fruit for wildlife to feed on. These decorations reveal a creative response to the regulations, and, while the suspended oranges and nuts are as visible as the baubles they have replaced, to me they appear more appropriate and in keeping with the ethos of the burial ground. Some are discreet enough to be unnoticeable, and it was not until the following summer that I discovered the fir cones that had been carefully tied with thin wire to a horse chestnut tree.

During these winter months the sudden arrival of snow transforms the burial ground, hiding each grave in a thick blanket that traces the movements of visitors and wildlife. In snow, the burial ground, like many landscapes, takes on a very different character; from my perspective it feels clean and uncluttered, the graves are no longer visible, and the dark silhouettes of the trees gain more prominence against this white backcloth. In February, the trees are now clear of their Christmas decorations and are used once again by some bereaved people to declare their love on Valentine's Day. Towards the end of winter there is the first glimpse of spring as clusters of snowdrops appear on quite a number of graves. Their emergence each year, especially on the older graves that no longer appear to be visited, reminds me of the care that somebody once took in tending the grave of a partner and who may now also be buried at Ulley.

Figure 8.10 *In recent years burial ground users have adopted a more creative approach to decorating the trees, attaching handcrafted decorations made from fruit and found items, some of which will provide food for wildlife and decay over time (Ulley, December 2009).*

Figure 8.11 *Thick snow transforms the burial ground, hiding away each grave and the memorials that are placed there, giving more prominence to the trees (Ulley, February 2009).*

Figure 8.12 *Heart-shaped decorations suspended from the branches of a tree on Valentine's Day (Ulley, February 2013).*

Figure 8.13 *The first sign of spring, a cluster of snowdrops emerges beneath a mature tree that displays no other memorials (Ulley, February 2009).*

Spring

The months of spring bring with them the most dramatic changes within the burial ground as new growth breaks through. The season also includes Easter and Mothering Sunday, annual events that move within the calendar, marked in the form of decorated eggs suspended from trees and Mother's Day cards. This year, 2013, there has been a cold spring and I am aware, looking back

Figure 8.14 *Painted Easter eggs suspended from a tree (Ulley, April 2009).*

through the photographs of previous years, just how late many of the trees are in coming into leaf. In March there is often a flourish of colour as daffodils, a popular choice, emerge from many of the graves. Beneath the hedge at the top of the burial ground there is a row of daffodils that forms a border of 20 metres or more. From one of our interviews we discovered they have been planted by an elderly man, whose intention is to enclose the entire burial ground and in doing so the grave of his wife, who is buried next to the hedge. As spring progresses more bulbs and annuals appear, including: cowslips, bluebells,

Figure 8.15 *The row of daffodils planted by a bereaved husband, near to the grave of his wife and whose intention, over a number of years, is to enclose the entire burial ground (Ulley, March 2012).*

forget-me-nots, red campion and on one grave a cluster of snakes head fritillary. In April, when the grass is still short, there is a carpet of yellow dandelions, which are followed in May by the large white flower heads of cow parsley. Some of these plants will continue to thrive as the woodland habitat becomes more dense, while others will struggle to survive in this increasingly competitive and shady environment.

Figure 8.16 *A circle of bluebells enclosed the grave in May 2008 but has now been lost after new burials disrupted this arrangement (Ulley, May 2008).*

Throughout spring the trees are also gradually coming into leaf. Some of the larger willows, with their bright lime-green leaves, are the first to appear and are accompanied by cherry blossom and later the small white flowers of hawthorn in the surrounding hedgerows.

Summer

Towards the end of spring and early summer the appearance of the burial ground changes rapidly from one week to the next. If it is warm and wet, the grasses and herbaceous vegetation can have grown to over a metre tall between my visits. Like the snowfall of winter, this herbaceous layer hides any evidence of the graves apart from the occasional cluster of flowers growing on a grave. Popular flowers include honesty, lupins and ornamental poppies. It is at this time of year that I find the burial ground to be at its most intriguing and inviting, when nature feels most present. I am struck by how different the burial ground now appears from the formal local authority cemetery at the end of the road where I live, where the grass is kept short and the individual graves remain prominent. At Ulley the dense vegetation creates a landscape that feels more private, protected and sheltered. I have on a number of occasions shown the burial ground to visitors who have been interested in our research. Their reaction is clearly influenced by the degree to which graves are either visible or invisible. In winter I sometimes feel their disappointment when the burial ground fails to meet their expectations of what it means to bury naturally. In summer, when the grass is green, there is always a more positive reaction to how different and alternative this landscape is.

Off the main pathway I trace the tracks that have been left in the broken and folded grass; like footprints in the snow, they often lead to an enclosed space, a grave with an improvised seat or bench where someone could tuck themselves away. Throughout the burial ground there is evidence of recent visits such as the clearing of encroaching vegetation and the planting of summer bedding. There are a number of graves that continue to evidence much greater

Figure 8.17 *In late spring and early summer, the burial ground is transformed by the emerging tall grasses and herbs which conceal the graves (Ulley, June 2013).*

Figure 8.18 *In summer the tall grass creates a haven of privacy and intimacy into which visitors can retreat (Ulley, June 2013).*

resistance to the advances of nature. The tall grass surrounding the grave is cut back with shears or a strimmer and removed. The natural world is now not only present in what I see but also what I touch, smell and hear, for the burial ground is now very much alive with the sound of insects and birdsong. On fine days I have seen people spending time here and on occasions sitting on the grass, relaxing with a book and a flask of tea or coffee at the graveside.

Figure 8.19 *Some of the graves display a resistance to the encroaching nature and the grass is cut back and removed (Ulley, June 2013).*

In late June or sometimes early July, depending on the weather and after the herbaceous plants and grasses have set their seeds, the grass is cut. It marks a dramatic change to both the appearance and feel of the burial ground. Individual memorials and the bare earth of new graves once again come into view and the private spaces that had been enclosed by the tall grasses and low branches are now lost. The wild, messy natural environment is replaced with a more managed landscape that for a short time resembles the appearance of a suburban park. When the burial ground was less populated, this annual cut was done with a large mower, but there are too many obstacles to negotiate including the trees, memorial stones and benches. It now takes three people two full days using strimmers to cut the grass.

Autumn

As autumn approaches, the cherries and *Rhus* are the first to reveal their autumn colour. Hallowe'en, or All Souls Day, a festival which is believed to have its origins in Pagan ritual, leaves its mark on the burial ground at the end of October in carved pumpkins and offerings of fruit. November often brings with it the first heavy frost that quickly returns the burial ground to its winter state, and strong winds strip the oak trees of their few remaining leaves.

During my visits I have also observed how the community of bereaved people and those who work in the burial ground continue to shape the landscape beyond the grave. They each leave their own marks that are not necessarily immediately apparent but, nevertheless, are an important part of the changing identity of the burial ground. The author Robert McFarlane, in *The Old Ways*, retraces ancient pathways and records how 'footpaths are the habit of a landscape'.[7] Equally at Ulley, in the worn grass and indented earth, the burial ground captures the habits of those bereaved people who visit regularly. Over the years I have witnessed how their journeys emerge and then fade as they retrace their steps over a period of weeks, months and years. Typically the paths are visible for just a short time and are only noticeable in the long summer grass. There are, however, footpaths that for the moment have become a more permanent feature of this landscape. These footpaths, which wind through the burial ground between unmarked graves, record a sensitive reading of the landscape that avoids trampling on the graves of others. During one of my early visits I followed a path that led through the tall grass, expecting it to lead to a grave; but instead it led to a small gap in the hedge. Here, a set of makeshift stone steps had been cut into the earth bank leading down to the stream. Visitors had therefore responded to the absence of a tap, finding their way to the stream and thus shaping the landscape to meet their needs.

The grave diggers, Mark and Charlie, are a family firm who have worked in the burial ground since it opened. As the numbers of burials have increased, they now work most weeks, and occasionally I will see them during my visits, preparing a new grave. The red earth is piled up next to a grave and on the day of the funeral, dressed in artificial grass. On one occasion I chatted with Mark after a funeral as he backfilled the grave. Standing in the grave, he pulled the soil in with a long-handled shovel. After he had filled the grave there was a small pile of earth left over which he shovelled into a wheelbarrow and then pushed to the edge of the burial ground and tipped into the base of the hedge.

Figure 8.20 *At Hallowe'en some of the graves display carved pumpkins and offerings of fruit (Ulley, November 2013).*

It was only then that I understood the low earth bank that he and Charlie had created over the past 16 years and which now encloses the burial ground. It has become a permanent feature of this landscape, reminiscent of an ancient defensive earthwork and symbolic of the space that is inhabited below-ground by the dead. While its construction may not have been intentional and only began to form after burial started at Ulley, like a cemetery or church wall it too contains the dead and will over time become a more prominent feature of this landscape.

Figure 8.21 *In autumn the graves can be temporarily carpeted in leaves, briefly hiding the memorials that lie beneath them (Ulley, November 2011).*

The grave

Here my attention turns from the overall burial ground landscape to focus on the individual grave and the many ways in which bereaved people memorialise their dead in the natural burial landscape. There is an expectation from providers that nature is the memorial and that it will replace the need to erect a permanent headstone or to enclose the grave. In Chapters 3 and 5 we discussed

Figure 8.22 *Footpaths materialise in the burial ground at different times of year and reveal how frequently some graves are visited, although there may be little indication of this on the grave they lead to (Ulley, February 2012 and June 2013).*

the ongoing challenges that many burial ground owners face in trying to discourage bereaved people from memorialising in ways that do not comply with their vision of natural burial. While Ulley permits the use of a small stone plaque and a tree or shrub, I was aware from my early visits in 2002 that a significant number of the graves included memorials that did not comply with the regulations and included: ornaments, solar lights and concrete benches. My regular visits were an opportunity to record the different ways bereaved people were marking the grave and, more importantly, to capture how this might change over time. I wanted to find out if, through inhabiting the landscape, the need of bereaved people to memorialise would lessen. Would they become more accepting of the grave losing its individual identity and merging with a shared memorial landscape? Olwig refers to this difference in understanding as the contrast between a 'binocular vision, movement and knowledge gained from a coordinated use of the senses in carrying out various tasks', in this case tending the grave, and 'a monocular perspective that is fixed and distant from the body' and begins to take in the wider landscape.[8]

To explore these questions, we identified seven graves that exhibited different degrees of memorialisation that I would record at each of my visits. The following information provides a short summary of each grave at the time they were chosen in December 2007.

Figure 8.23 *Makeshift stone steps have been cut into the earth bank providing access to the stream that flows beside the burial ground (Ulley, May 2011).*

Grave A: a recent burial of an elderly woman. The grave has been raised and contained by a timber curtilage and is covered with various objects that include a small artificial Christmas tree, cards, a plastic dog with his head buried in the soil, an angel, a mermaid, solar lights and, next to the grave, an imitation stone bench, cast in concrete. A worn path leads to and from the grave.

Grave B: a recent burial of an elderly man. On the bare soil there is a single bouquet of flowers wrapped in green cellophane.

Figure 8.24 *Mark back-filling the grave (Ulley, June 2009).*

Grave C: an established grave of a middle-aged man. On the grave there is a small tree with a bird feeder, shrubs and a raised stone plaque. The grass is cut short. The burial register records that his mother and wife have reserved the plots on either side. On the wife's plot there are three rustic carved wooden seats that resemble toadstools and on the mother's, two cut logs and a Christmas wreath.

Grave D: an established grave of an elderly couple. The area around the grave has been neatly mown into a rectangular square. In the middle of the grave there is a semi-mature silver birch tree. On one of the branches a Christmas card in a clear plastic envelope has been attached. The turf around the tree has been removed to form a neat circle. The stone plaque is propped up against the tree, against which rests a Christmas wreath.

Grave E: a new grave for an elderly woman that is next to the grave of her husband who died in 1998. On his grave there is an established oak tree, a stone plaque and a small earthenware pot. The lower branches of the tree have been

Figure 8.25 *The earth bank surrounding the burial ground has been formed from the spoil of each new grave (Ulley, August 2011).*

cut back to make space for the new grave, which is completely covered with flowers from the funeral.

Grave F: a cluster of three established graves of which two have the same family name recorded on the stone plaques. They are each planted with a cherry tree and attached to two of the trees there is a Sheffield United football team flag. On each grave there is a Christmas wreath.

Grave G: an established grave for an elderly woman. The grass around the grave has been cut short. Attached to a small cherry tree is a woven vase that contains freshly cut flowers. The stone plaque is large and has an irregular edge and has been supported so that it faces towards the main path.

There were two new graves in the sample, B and E. On grave B there was a single bouquet that remained throughout the winter months. After this was removed, or had simply blown away, I struggled to find the grave and would look for an area of soil that was slightly indented, for this grave has never had a plaque or tree placed upon it. At the end of the first summer a cluster of thistles that had grown tall above the grass revealed its location. By the end of the second summer (2009), a month or two after the grass had been cut, it was possible, if you knew approximately where to look, to see a rectangular patch where the grass grew less vigorously. Today the grave is not visible and even the familiar markers that I once used to help find it have been consumed in a landscape that has been reconfigured by the addition of new burials and memorial trees.

We might reasonably assume from the number of floral tributes that the funeral for grave E was well attended. In December 2008, a year after the burial, a stone plaque appeared on the grave and a wreath was placed on the grave of the husband and the more recently deceased wife. There has, however, been no evidence of visiting in recent years. Each spring snowdrops and daffodils appear on the husband's grave, and the branches of the oak tree now extend over both graves.

The Sheffield United flags that had made grave F initially so visible in the burial ground were removed before the end of the first year of my visits; and there has been little evidence of grave marking since, apart from a single Christmas decoration, suspended from the tree in December 2009 and again in 2011 when each of the three trees had a small wreath placed at their base. Graves D and G continue to be visited frequently; there are occasionally cards, cut flowers and each year a Christmas wreath. While there is still some evidence of tending the grave, removing weeds and clearing back the encroaching grass, their appearance has also softened. No longer does grave D sit within a neatly mown rectangular lawn but instead the grass is allowed to grow tall and wild.

Graves A and C also show evidence of being frequently visited, but there is also something different about each of these graves and the activities of the people who tend them that offer a different insight into the workings of the natural burial ground. The wife and mother of the man who is buried in grave C have each reserved a plot on either side of the grave. As I have already noted, their space has been marked by an arrangement of logs and carved stools where wreaths and flowers are displayed at Christmas and other times of the year. Beyond this there is very little grave marking, but what has been noticeable is how the wife, through the regular cutting of the grass, continues to attach her pre-purchased grave to that of her dead husband. This act of containment, of bounding the space, has been most noticeable following the annual cut when the tall grass that had defined this space is removed. Each year, the cut grass is gathered and neatly arranged around the edge of his and her grave. An opening is left at the entrance, accessible from the main path. What we observe here is a creative approach to preserving the grave without contravening the site regulations by constructing more permanent borders.

I have left grave A until last for, in many respects, the changes that I have observed here and which are recorded in Figure 8.27 reveal that while grave marking can appear inappropriate, it is rarely permanent. In the first six months I observed how the plastic ornaments and flowers were arranged and rearranged within the wooden border that contained the grave. Christmas decorations, Mother's Day cards, plastic and cut flowers came and went and the concrete bench that appeared in February of that first year was frequently moved to occupy new positions beside the grave. Throughout this period a mown pathway was also maintained leading to and from the grave.

In late September 2008, there was a dramatic change; the ornaments, bench and plastic flowers were removed altogether and the surface of the grave was set flush with the surrounding earth. Concerned about the increase in personal memorialisation in the burial ground, Peace Funerals had left a note on each grave where this was a concern, reminding users that only 'natural' items were acceptable and that if they were not removed they would be cleared and stored for collection. It is not clear whether Peace Funerals or the family made this initial change, but from this point on there has been a very different approach

Figure 8.26 *The pre-purchased grave of the wife and her deceased husband are contained within a temporary border that has been made from the gathered cuttings (Ulley, August 2011).*

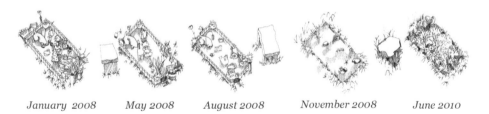

| January 2008 | May 2008 | August 2008 | November 2008 | June 2010 |

Figure 8.27 *Sequence of drawings showing the changing conditions of the grave.*

to memorialisation. The stone bench was replaced by a boulder reclaimed from the gravediggers' spoil and the ornaments exchanged for bedding plants. More recently a large stone has also been placed on the grave into which the name of the deceased has been engraved and the regular cutting of the grass around the grave has stopped.

The seven graves therefore reveal different approaches to memorialisation at Ulley. On three of the graves (B, E and F) there has been no marking since the funeral or beyond the first year of our study. The remaining four graves (A, C, D and G) are all still visited regularly, as evidenced by the display of Christmas, Mother's and Father's Day cards, cut flowers and displays of annual bedding plants. For each of these bereaved families there is clearly a need to access the grave and to preserve its location within the burial ground. While the grass around grave D has been left to grow long, graves A, C and G continue to be

Figure 8.28 *Grave covered in rose petals at the anniversaries of birth and death (May 2011).*

maintained through regular cutting or weeding, preserving not only the location but also the orientation of the body within the grave. Finally, beyond these seven graves I have also observed other strategies that bring the grave back into focus at the key times of year. One notable example includes the grave of a young woman. Each year, on the anniversaries of her birth and death the grave is carefully covered in rose petals, which lie there for a short time. After this they blow away or just gradually fade into the landscape.

9
Conclusion

As the preceding chapters show, the landscape of the natural burial ground and its associated practices have had a profound impact upon many aspects of the UK's mortuary culture. Moreover, in burying bodies and interring ashes into a whole range of British landscapes, those environments have undergone a series of important developments. These changes have unfolded in parallel with those going on in other countries, and mutual exchange between them has had consequent impacts. As described in Chapter 1, the project represented in this book is the work of a team drawn from three disciplines: landscape architecture, social anthropology and sociology. The methods used encompassed a large-scale geographical information system (GIS) survey, the creation of a database of core information about a large proportion of UK natural burial grounds, visits to 20 sites chosen to reflect the diversity of interpretations of 'natural burial' evident in the large-scale survey, and in-depth ethnographic work at four sites that exemplified this diversity.

What we emphasised in Chapter 1 is the capacity of our particular mix of disciplines to address all aspects of this major initiative in the way in which the disposal of the dead and their memorialisation are managed in the UK. Rather than a study of mourning and grief, which pays scant attention to the physical settings within which these practices and emotions take place, or an analysis of shifts in landscape design and planning for the disposal of bodies that stops short of the individuals who populate them, both above and below ground, what we offer in this book is a layering up of the insights of different disciplines, a dialogue between different perspectives and voices.

This is important for two main reasons. First, while landscape architecture provides key insights into the making of particular environments, the social life of a setting such as a burial ground is not always central to its remit. The project represented here has therefore set anthropological and sociological data alongside the insights offered by landscape architecture. Moreover, while place, space and embodiment have come to be recognised as important elements within the work on death and dying undertaken by anthropologists and sociologists,[1] this trend is relatively recent and, in the main, does not draw upon the expertise accumulated within landscape architecture.

Second, the project has one of its starting points in the question of public awareness of natural burial. While the number of sites grew rapidly during the 20 years that followed Ken West's initiative, with 242 either in existence or planned by 2010, uptake of this facility still constitutes a small proportion of overall disposals in the UK. National figures have not been recorded, but we estimate that by 2007 the practice accounted for approximately 1 per cent of the total number of burials and cremations. As we noted as well, what we refer to as 'natural burial' is also known as 'green burial' and 'woodland burial', a potentially confusing mix of terminology. We therefore began work by taking people into one particular natural burial ground – individuals without previous experience of such a site – and recording their interpretations of it.[2] One of this book's objectives is therefore not only to make available core data about particular sites local to individuals and their families, but also to give an account that conveys the experience of burying naturally, its diversity, scope and limitations, and, importantly, its longer-term impact – on memorialisation, grief and mourning, on the practices of celebrants and funeral directors and on landscapes themselves into which the dead are passing.

From landscape to loss

As noted, the project which underpins this book combines anthropological and sociological questions about religion, death ritual, landscape and nature with landscape architecture's perspectives on the management and usage of the natural environment. Through a focus on the trend towards natural burial, the project has generated data about broader-ranging belief systems and practices around death in the UK. As Chapter 1 identified, the questions addressed include: Do the ecological implications of natural burial make it a focus for more collective responses to death? Or is natural burial an indicator of a postmodern trend towards individualised lifestyle options, another item of consumption used to sustain particular identities? Do the values which natural burial represent have positively perceived yet vague meanings which unite individuals within an apparently cohesive 'Movement' – for example, ethical concerns for the environment, ecology, nature as a site for emotional solace, personal control over the body?

To address these questions, the book has offered an overview of the project itself, its rationale and its methods, as well as a history of the changing practices through which the bodies of the dead have been disposed of, their lives recorded and their subsequent status recognised. Values, beliefs and practices were central to this discussion and constitute a key focus throughout the book, making it an account not just of a particular way of disposing of the corpse and remembering the dead, but one that speaks more broadly to contemporary orientations towards identity, the environment, spirituality, memory and landscape. Chapter 2 develops the historical approach offered in Chapter 1, going on to explain how natural burial came into being in the early 1990s. This is, quite literally, groundwork. Through the perspectives offered by landscape architecture we have been able to explain how a whole variety of natural burial landscapes came into being and identify what led different providers to enter into an arena which, for many, was entirely new. Freed from the traditions and conventions of local authorities and the Church, these new providers were able to engage with the affordances[3] of a whole variety of landscapes and a complex range of environmental and mortuary agendas. Chapter 2 therefore sets out in detail the trajectories natural burial has followed, including their below-ground practices which, depending upon the site, have been informed by a concern with ecology and environmental impact. What follows in Chapters 3, 4 and 5 is therefore very much a materially grounded account, one that is mapped through

GIS survey data and illustrated in the images provided by Andy Clayden and Mark Powell. The reader who, in Chapters 6, 7 and 8, enters into the *social* life of the natural burial ground, does so with an informed sense of its appearance, scale, accessibility and maintenance strategy, as well as an understanding of what lies beneath its surface. In addition, the insights of landscape architecture allow the reader to engage with anthropological and sociological data, knowing that there is no one-size-fits-all to natural burial. Each site, we argue, constitutes a particular 'creative entanglement';[4] its geography, ownership and management strategy, as well as its usage as a landscape for burial and memorialisation, mesh to produce the dynamic, lived environment of the natural burial ground.

As a whole, the book explains how these settings come into being and begins to explore the implications of a key concept drawn upon in this work, one that derives from both landscape architecture and social anthropology: the nature of design. As we explain, design needs to be viewed not as an entity or thing, but a *practice*. Moreover, as a practice, it is not simply the imposition of an 'expert' model upon an external materiality. Instead, design is a process that evolves; in the case of natural burial, it is an interaction between the existing knowledge and practice of an individual or group who has access to land, their motivations and aspirations for that land, and their experience of 'inhabiting' that land.[5] Design is thus inextricably grounded in the past, embedded in the present and oriented towards the future. This aspect of 'design' is a major focus within Chapters 3 and 4, explaining the motivations of natural burial providers and the processes through which the diversity of UK sites came into being, but also in Chapter 5, which uses participant observation to investigate the approaches adopted by those who staff a natural burial ground, administer its policies and bury the dead in its woodland. In other words, it is through dwelling or inhabiting[6] landscapes that their design comes into being. As we have argued, drawing upon Ingold's work,[7] if we think of design as a template or cognitive map according to which something is made, we reinforce a culturally specific separation between human beings' internal worlds and their external environments, one which erroneously attributes individuals with an independence of that environment. When tsunami or tornadoes wreck human lives and habitations – environmental phenomena increasingly being traced to human-induced climate change – the inseparability of human beings and the world which surrounds them becomes self-evident. As the ethnographies of many non-Western societies make apparent, in many other cultures the 'non-human' environment is understood and experienced as one that has agency, whether through the actions of spirits, ancestors or totemic creatures.[8] In such settings, human beings' relationship with their environment is likely to be far more reciprocal than that between westerners and their urban or rural landscapes and the associated resources they consume.

Regulation, enchantment, ecology and identity

In sum, then, this volume has addressed four theoretical questions about the status of natural burial, questions that require an appraisal of contemporary cultural values and social mores and, in turn, promise answers that illuminate these spheres of everyday life. What we wanted to know, therefore, as Chapter 1 indicated, is whether natural burial constitutes (1) creative resistance to modernist death care, (2) part of a re-enchantment of death, (3) a form of collective environmental regeneration or (4) a site for individual identity-making.

What our data show is that many natural burial providers see themselves reclaiming control of death and disposal from traditional funeral directors, clergy and celebrants (see Chapter 7). In turn, many seek to empower users, enabling them to participate to whatever extent they are capable in the preparation of a relative/friend's body, its disposal and subsequent memorialisation (see Chapter 5). Users themselves welcome this, coupled with the lack of spatial and temporal boundaries at a natural burial ground. In this environment, then, many are able to generate forms of death ritual that reflect the identity of both the deceased and the mourners (see Chapters 6 and 8). Freed from the traditional temporal and spatial constraints of the church or crematorium, bereaved people often combined elements of mainstream, alternative and innovative ritual practice, a trend which confirms Walter's[9] argument that contemporary deathways are 'neo-modern', a fusion or bricolage[10] of traditional and modern approaches to the end of life and what comes afterwards. The snow angel in Chapter 8 is one example of how a familiar figure in a traditional churchyard or cemetery may enter the natural burial ground in reconfigured form, here a child's ephemeral marking, there the permanent product of a memorial mason's labour. The regulatory processes characteristic of modernist death care were not, however, entirely absent since many owner/managers actively discouraged choice in gravesite memorialisation, removing items as they saw fit.

As we showed in Chapters 5 and 6, the implementation of site policies was often a matter of negotiation, not only between owners and managers and users, but also between users themselves and their different orientations towards their shared mortuary landscape. Overall, a marked degree of willingness to be flexible was evident on the part of owners and managers, along with a readiness to modify memorialising practices on the part of bereaved people. What we suggest is that this tendency towards a reciprocal exchange of goodwill stems from an absence of the bureaucratisation and depersonalisation of death care provision which deterred many users from disposal at municipal crematoria and cemeteries. In its place, many owners and managers offered accessible, ongoing one-to-one guidance and support. While local authority sites represented the majority and this was a form of provision that militated against sustained personal contact with bereaved people, most farmers, landowners and the staff of charitable trusts had a relationship with the land available for burial that made them integral to the natural burial ground's design, as did their ongoing maintenance work. Indeed, many of them lived at or nearby the burial ground, a spatial relationship which contrasts markedly with that to be found in a municipal cemetery managed by the local authority's Bereavement Services department. As such, many independent providers were known personally to users, something users experienced as a very positive resource; for example, Catherine Hunt at Great Bradley Cottage offers natural burial in the orchard near her house and said she knew 79 of the 80 people buried there and is aware of the ongoing patterns of visiting at their graves (see Chapter 4). This geographical, social and emotional proximity could, however, bring new challenges for some providers: Al Blake, for example, at the East Meon site, would on occasions wear something more formal under his work clothes and effect a shift between manager and mourner where a family were known to him as friends. Given the personal, sometimes long-term nature of the care he provides for bereaved people, he had found it important to affirm his place as a manager in order to avoid emotional over-involvement. As he said to us, he buries 'boxes' or coffins, rather than the bodies they contain.[11] In addition, bereaved people themselves were potentially vulnerable if they became dependent on the support of a site owner or manager who subsequently became unavailable, perhaps moving to another job or retiring. This raises a question about the future of natural burial where current trends suggest the growth of larger, company-owned sites. In these settings, is the 'human' dimension likely to suffer as increased numbers demand a less personal approach and also potentially begin to place restrictions on the amount of time and space that is currently afforded at many funerals? If this is lost, natural burial potentially loses some of its distance from the concerns and frustrations that were expressed by providers, users and wider public about their experience of attending a funeral at the crematorium.

These findings can be understood in relation to the notion of a boundary between life and death,[12] in this context one framed through modernist control and management techniques. Thus, while natural burial enables many of the dividing lines between life and death to be transcended, making it a strategy for resisting regulated modernist death care, it remains the case that those who stand at a graveside are members of different social categories and, as such, occupy different relationships with death. As our data from among funeral directors and clergy show, formal dress remains important as a way of differentiating themselves from mourners. Mourners in turn, however, may wear distinctive dress, clothing that makes and marks the sacred, or set-apart, nature of the funeral. Yet the absence or minimal presence of a traditional material culture of death in the natural burial ground helps close the distance between deathly and everyday environments. A celebrant we interviewed pointed out that in this setting there are no headstones 'looking at you' around the grave. However, as Walter says of neo-modern death, while choice and autonomy may be among its core values, it is a passage that is not being made alone: 'Who accompanies the dying and the bereaved on this road?' he asks.[13] For some funeral directors, clergy and burial ground managers, then, a more regulated set of distinctions remains in place as a way of distinguishing between those 'on this road' and those who are accompanying them. For others, however, as Chapter 7 described, the temporal and spatial fluidity of a field or woodland militated against the mapping of distinctions and hierarchies in seating arrangements, lecterns and rostrums, or a rigid patterning of speeches and silences according to a traditional liturgy. Instead, people were likely to walk in an informal procession some distance through the natural burial ground environment, following, wheeling or carrying the coffin to the grave where they would then assemble more organically, a grouping into which a celebrant might integrate themselves. As such they were less in charge and more involved; pressure to perform and manage diminished and the more dynamic environment of a windswept wood, birdsong and uneven grass drew the company on in the process of burying a body and engaging with the memory of the deceased.

While the mortuary landscape of the natural burial ground did not operate to shore up a boundary between life and death, and indeed some sites did not have a physical boundary in any conventional sense, many of the bereaved people we interviewed attributed the 'natural' setting of their loved one's grave with special values and described a sense of well-being whenever they spent time at the site. Arguably, then, affective ties with the dead are being sustained through bereaved people's experience of the pastoral landscape, somewhere they inhabit on the day of the funeral and also when visiting, somewhere also inhabited on a more permanent basis by the deceased. This emotional orientation can be seen as characteristic of a re-enchantment of death; even when bereaved people lived 'in the country', the embodied experience of standing in wind, rain or sunshine, under trees and in long grass, for a potentially extended period might represent an altered perception of that countryside, might set it apart from everyday 'life'. And for many people who live in towns and cities or their suburbs, the countryside is effectively a place apart, somewhere associated with weekends and holidays, a distinction which parallels a separation made between the worlds of life and death.

This raises the question of whether the special or set-apart nature of the rural landscape informed collective environmental agendas and if these constituted a primary motivation among users. What Chapters 6 and 8 make clear is that bereaved people's conceptions of 'nature' were eclectic, encompassing 'natural human emotion', 'any biodegradable material', 'non-native species of vegetation', 'a managed environment'. Instead, users saw woodland, pastureland and wildflower meadows as sites of 'natural' beauty, appreciating qualities of peace, tranquillity and spiritual uplift. Rather than a concern with environmental sustainability, they espoused a surface-oriented perspective towards the natural burial ground. That is to say, they betrayed a monocular vision,[14] one that derives from a distanced, perspectival view of landscape as panorama. This 'view' of landscape not only has a history, but reflects a recognisable landscape language, one that responds to cues of care.[15] These are signals of a human intention to care for the landscape and form part of a shared cultural orientation within which a mown path, for example, is experienced as an indicator that nearby grasses which are not mown or trees and shrubs that are not pruned are intended to be in that condition. They are not evidence of neglect.

Importantly, however, while the panorama of a 'beautiful place' may initially represent a site's main attraction, participating in the funeral rather than being cast in the role of spectator can effect a shift from a monocular to a binocular view of natural burial. Thus, once individuals have taken a hand in dressing, transporting and indeed burying the body of someone close to them, a more engaged binocular perspective might then develop, one that encompasses 'movement and knowledge gained from a coordinated use of the senses in carrying out various tasks'.[16] As owners and managers found, the minimal memorialising that represents their view of natural burial might be experienced as a constraint by bereaved people wishing to sustain a more task-based, sensory engagement with the body in the ground. Effectively, at this point what had initially been viewed as a landscape becomes a taskscape,[17] an environment of movement and action. While owners and managers experimented with either negotiated removal of such memorialisation, as noted above, or the establishment of a collective form of remembrance separate from the grave itself, many users had little sense of collectivity, apart perhaps from those who became actively involved with the East Meon landscape as volunteers (see Chapter 5). Indeed, as Chapter 6 described, the relative invisibility of other graves allowed some bereaved families to treat the entire site as their loved one's memorial. In effect, then, bereaved people who tended a grave were introducing their own cues of care,[18] small, local acts of clearing, planting and adding memorialising objects, all of which lent a cared-for appearance to the broader and less fettered environment within which their friend's or relative's body was decomposing.

Rather than the compressed time of a cremation service, what happens in the natural burial ground therefore constitutes a more extended process of ritualisation,[19] one where the end point is less externally imposed – and indeed some owners or managers find it necessary to appropriate practice from more traditional burial practice, the casting of earth on the coffin, to bring the funeral to a recognisable conclusion and remind people when they should leave. During the period when we carried out the study, a natural burial ground would typically only accept one burial per day. As a result the connection or flow between the funeral as stand-alone 'ritual' and bereaved people's subsequent memorialising and grave-tending practices tends to be more marked, a connection that may indeed extend into the voluntary work undertaken by bereaved people for the sustainability centre within which East Meon is located. Seremetakis'[20] term 'ritualisation' thus more adequately encompasses this sustained trajectory. While individual identity is not inscribed in a slab set up above the place where a body is buried, the processes of ritualisation described here can be seen to resonate with notions of identity as unfolding, embodied and multiple.[21] Thus the dynamic nature of the natural burial ground, as a site which affords considerable embodied engagement as a funeral cortège or individual visitor makes their way through untamed vegetation and across uneven terrain where wildlife proliferates, can be seen as conducive to the ongoing integration of the dead into the lives of the living, a site where social life may extend beyond the limits of physical embodiment.[22] It is, however, important to recognise that the experience of a funeral where spatial and temporal constraints are less evident than in a crematorium, an experience which may initiate the social life-after-death of the deceased,[23] may be vulnerable to change if natural burial becomes a more popular disposal option, one catered for by companies who set up a chain of larger sites.

These data underscore the implications of a particular landscape for mortuary practice, the ways in which it is shaped within this physical and social environment. As Chapter 8 described, our development of a longitudinal photographic survey of one natural burial ground is a methodological innovation which has helped us understand the entanglement of owners, managers and users with the materialities of a site. By repeatedly visiting and visually recording one particular site, we became aware of the interlinking of linear and cyclical time as patterns of weather and vegetation returned and returned, while the site itself underwent dynamic change of a linear nature, the density of trees increasing as more burials took place and growth proceeded unfettered. Within this 'natural' setting, personal and calendrical time would be marked out in memorial items, Christmas, Easter and Hallowe'en decorations, and the emergence of plantings that resonated with key points in the annual cycle of the deceased's life.

Unlike other burial sites, then, a natural burial ground constitutes both a recent, untested model and a far more dynamic environment. While visitors and mourners have developed visual literacy within established cemeteries and churchyards, natural burial grounds bear few markers of a sacred site. Similarly, the environmentally damaging spraying, clipping and manicuring of vegetation in traditional burial grounds is absent. In the new natural burial ground environment, our coupling of longitudinal visual methods with more established survey and interview methods has made dynamic cycles of natural growth available for scrutiny. Only through repeated recordings, however, do the many subtle indicators of familial, affective and calendrical imperatives become evident.[24]

The future

As we have intimated, the data we present in this book reflect a particular period during the life of the Natural Burial Movement and, as such, the insights we have drawn from them may not pertain if this disposal option becomes more popular and the nature of natural burial provision changes accordingly. So, for example, the personal service offered by independent providers may not be feasible if larger companies with a chain of sites increase their market share. As the macro-level data presented in Chapter 2 reveal, it is larger companies that are on the increase, smaller-scale providers possibly being deterred by the rise in investment costs following the introduction of new planning regulations.

Are the values embodied within natural burial likely to be sustained if both the demand for natural burial and the scale of provision increase? Here we are thinking of: personal service and a sustained relationship between provider and user; a landscape free of non-organic memorials; and a relatively unconstrained time and space for a funeral procession, service and burial. In other words, has our study documented what will subsequently come to be seen as a 'golden age' of natural burial provision?

Taking a longer view, our data lead us to suggest that natural burial provision is likely to influence currently mainstream deathways, the approach to cemetery maintenance and the personal nature of bereavement care. Indeed, a more pervading commitment to preserving ecologically valuable environments is likely to support a context where the natural burial ground is one among a range of settings where vegetation is free from chemical interventions, over-mowing and rigid pruning regimes. Similarly, the practice of minimal, ephemeral grave marking in the natural burial ground already supports more creative approaches to remembering the dead; for example, through matched plantings in the burial ground and the domestic garden. This development is one which may increase, so eroding the relegation of all visible reminders of the dead to the sequestered environment of the cemetery. Death, thereby, becomes a more overt dimension of everyday life. Finally, the temporal and spatial flexibility afforded to the natural burial ground funeral has implications for the workload of professionals who are involved in supporting bereaved people. Funeral directors inevitably accrue more income from busy days at the crematorium – and fewer cleaning bills. It may therefore be the case that for natural burial to routinely become one among the list of options offered by a funeral director, the cost of their extra time will need to be factored in. Alternatively, their role as primary guardian of the body of the deceased and as ultimate events manager at the funeral may need reconfiguring. A more collaborative approach where other practitioners and indeed bereaved families themselves provide time and labour may make funeral directors' roles less demanding and time-consuming.

Natural burial can therefore be seen as a practice which has challenged the ways in which death is managed. As an alternative it nonetheless speaks to the mainstream; and, as much as it is likely to move closer to that kind of provision, our data suggest that its resonance with broader social, cultural and economic trends and indeed its increasing popularity mean that we cannot overlook the significance of its influence upon more mainstream sites and practices.

Notes

Chapter 1

1 Clayden (2003; 2004; 2011); Clayden and Woudstra (2003); Clayden and Dixon (2007); Clayden *et al.* (2009).
2 West (2010)
3 HC91-1 (2000–01)
4 www.naturalburialresearchproject.group.shef.ac.uk/sites.html (retrieved 15 August 2013)
5 Clayden *et al.* (2010a)
6 Clayden *et al.* (2010b)
7 www.naturalburialresearchproject.group.shef.ac.uk/sites.html (retrieved 15 August 2013)
8 HC91-1 (2001)
9 Gorer (1965); Elias (1985); Giddens (1991); Bauman (1992); Mellor and Shilling (1993); Seale (1998)
10 Weinrich and Speyer (2003)
11 Bradfield (1994)
12 Payne *et al.* (2008)
13 Weinrich and Speyer (2003).
14 Santino (2006)
15 Francis *et al.* (2005)
16 Roberts and Vidal (2000)
17 Hockey *et al.* (2007a; 2007b); Kellaher *et al.* (2005)
18 Hallam and Hockey (2001)
19 Klass *et al.* (1996)
20 Rugg (1999)
21 Davies (2005: 87)
22 Walter (1994)
23 Horrox (1999)
24 Davies (2005)
25 Walter (1994)
26 Walter (1994: 40–44)
27 Kellaher *et al.* (2005: 237)
28 Arber (2000)
29 Hallam *et al.* (1999: 96)
30 Howarth (1996: 204)
31 Gore (2001)
32 Davies and Mates (2005)
33 Hockey (2001)
34 Parsons (2003: 67)
35 Parsons (2003: 67)
36 Rugg (2003)
37 Garattini (2007)
38 Morley (1971: 41)
39 Francis *et al.* (2005: 30)
40 Curl (1975: 15)

41   Morley (1971: 35)
42   Francis *et al.* (2005: 31)
43   Francis *et al.* (2005)
44   Cited in Morley (1971: 41)
45   Morley (1971)
46   Cited in Grainger (2005: 17)
47   Curl (1975: 13)
48   Curl (1975: 21)
49   Bourke (1996)
50   Winter (1995: 223)
51   Cited in Bourke (1996: 226)
52   Bourke (1996: 226)
53   Francis *et al.* (2005)
54   Loudon ([1843] 1981)
55   Cited in Francis *et al.* (2005: 39)
56   Cited in Curl (1975: 25)
57   Francis *et al.* (2005)
58   Cited in Curl (1975: 15)
59   Francis *et al.* (2005: 41)
60   Davies and Mates (2005)
61   Francis *et al.* (2005: 43)
62   Rugg (2006: 230)
63   Rugg (2006)
64   Rugg (2006)
65   Francis *et al.* (2005)
66   Klass *et al.* (1996)
67   West (2010)
68   Rugg (2006: 223)
69   Francis *et al.* (2005: 45)
70   Francis *et al.* (2005: 46)
71   Rugg (2006)
72   Curl (1975: 13)
73   Curl (1975: 40)
74   Grainger (2005: 22)
75   Grainger (2005)
76   Curl (1975: 40)
77   Geertz (1973: 5)
78   Geertz (1973: 46)
79   Ingold (2000; 2010; 2011)
80   Ingold (2011: 12)
81   Ingold (2000: 42)
82   Ingold (2007)
83   Ingold (2011)
84   Davies and Rumble (2012)
85   Rugg (2000: 259)
86   Rugg (2000)
87   Bille *et al.* (2011: 4)
88   Jenkins (2004)
89   Davies and Rumble (2012: 14)
90   Ingold (2011)
91   Leach (1961)
92   Rapport and Overing (2007)
93   Dilley (2005: 236)

94 Adam (1990)
95 www.olneygreenburial.co.uk (accessed 20 November 2013)
96 Van Gennep ([1909] 1960)
97 Turner (1969)
98 Seremetakis (1991)
99 Rugg (2000: 264)
100 Seremetakis (1991)
101 Davies and Rumble (2012)
102 Clayden and Dixon (2007)
103 Hockey (2001)
104 Durkheim ([1915] 1965)
105 Klass *et al.* (1996)
106 Walter (1996)
107 Worden (1991)
108 Kellaher *et al.* (2005)
109 Prendergast *et al.* (2006)
110 Olwig (2008: 81)

Chapter 2

1 West (2010)
2 Ken West changed the name from Cemeteries and Crematorium to Bereavement Services, which was felt to be less prescriptive and better reflected the breadth of services provided.
3 Dunk and Rugg (1994)
4 Bereavement Services manage the local authority cemeteries and crematorium and included in their other services arrangement of funerals and cremations.
5 West (1992)
6 Olwig (2008: 81)
7 Constant (1994)
8 Clayden and Woudstra (2003); Johansson (1996)
9 Brookes (1989: 55–60)
10 Grainger (2005: 426)
11 www.camlins.com/index.php?section=projects&id=5 (retrieved 29 August 2013)
12 Parsons (2010)
13 Walter (1994)
14 Weinrich and Speyer (2003: 5)
15 Ibid: 7.
16 West (2010: 41)
17 Bradfield (1994)
18 West (1994)
19 IBCA (1996: 5)
20 West (2010: 43–45)
21 Ibid.: 47
22 Ibid.: 52
23 Ministry of Justice (2009)
24 Callender *et al.* (2012: 167–170)
25 West (2010: 1)
26 Natural Burial Research project website and Google Maps showing the location of all UK natural burial grounds at the time our research, concluded in September 2010. www.naturalburialresearchproject.group.shef.ac.uk/sites.html (retrieved 15 August 2013)
27 UK Natural Burial Conference, University of Sheffield (September 2010)

28 Gibson (1979)
29 Native Woodlands: www.nativewoodland.co.uk (retrieved 2 September 2013)
30 For a more detailed account of the issues regarding the submission of a planning application for a natural burial ground, see West (2010).
31 Environment Agency (2004)
32 Young *et al.* (2002)
33 Association of Natural Burial Grounds (2012)
34 Quance (2013: 23)
35 Eggener (2010), Thomspon (2002)
36 http://memorialecosystems.com/ConservationBurial/tabid/110/Default.aspx (retrieved 2 September 2013)
37 Kendle and Rose (2000)
38 Green Burial Council: www.greenburialcouncil.org (retrieved 2 September 2013)
39 See guidance on burial law in Germany, Friedwald website: www.friedwald.de/bestattung/bestattungsrecht (retrieved 2 September 2013)
40 Ruheforst burial sites: www.ruheforst.de (retrieved 2 September 2013)
41 Klaassens (2011) www.dissertations.ub.rug.nl/FILES/faculties/rw/2011/m.klaassens/05c5.pdf (retrieved 20 August 2013)
42 A summary of the report produced by Vollmer and Partners can be accessed from the company website.
43 www.srgw.demon.co.uk/CremSoc4/Stats/National/ProgressF.html (retrieved 15 August 2013)
44 Annual mortality figures for England and Wales are collated by the Office for National Statistics, the Office of the General Register of Scotland and the Northern Ireland Statistics and Research Agency.
45 www.srgw.demon.co.uk/CremSoc4/Stats/National/ProgressF.html (retrieved 15 August 2013)
46 These data only take account of burial. If the figures for the interment of ashes are also included there is an increase from 1 per cent to 1.4 per cent for all interments at natural burial sites in 2007–2008.
47 Quance (2012: 22–23)
48 Ibid.
49 Ibid.
50 West (2010: 1–2)

Chapter 3

1 Clayden (2011)
2 Clayden *et al.* (2010a)
3 The Institute of Burial and Cremation Administration later became the Institute of Cemetery and Crematorium Managers (ICCM).
4 IBCA (1996)
5 West (2010: 5)
6 Bradfield (1994)
7 *Countryfile*, which is focused at the agricultural community, was mentioned by several of our research participants as their motivation to provide natural burial.
8 Beeson and Hanson (2010)
9 Telephone conversation with Nigel Lowthrop, co-founder of Hill Holt Wood, 21 August 2012.
10 GreenAcres (2012: 26)

Chapter 4

1 Ingold (2011: 12)
2 Clayden *et al.* (2010a)
3 Ingold (2011)
4 Ingold (2011: 12)
5 Gibson (1979)
6 Rugg (2000)
7 Ingold (2007: 167)
8 Scott (2003)
9 www.forestry.gov.uk/website/forstats2011.nsf/0/4D22A57508CE3090802573670
   038F557 (accessed 10 March 2013)
10 www.memorialwoodlands.com/pdfs/WOODLANDS-NEWS-SPRING-2012.pdf
   (accessed 10 October 2013)
11 Olwig (2008)
12 Ingold (2010)
13 Ingold (2011)

Chapter 5

1 Pocock (1998)
2 Francis *et al.* (2005), Woodthorpe (2007)
3 Howarth (1996)
4 Blake (2013: 12–14)
5 Walter (1994: 186)
6 'Each grave is dug especially by hand to minimise any impact on the flora, fauna and
   tranquility of the site' (Extract from the Sustainability Centre website (accessed 23
   August 2013)).
7 Blake (2013: 12–14)
8 Powell *et al.* (2011)
9 Powell *et al.* (2011)
10 Ingold (2010: 9–13)
11 Olwig (1993)
12 Putlocks, also referred to as putlogs, are wooden posts that support the coffin when
   placed above the grave.
13 Bourdieu (1977)
14 Walter (1994)
15 Davies (2005: 87)
16 Blake (2013: 12–14)
17 Klass *et al.* (1996)
18 Olwig (1993)

Chapter 6

1 Hockey *et al.* (2010)
2 Hockey (2001)
3 See NDC handbook, Callender et al (2012)
4 Rugg (2000)
5 Davies and Rumble (2012)
6 Clayden *et al.* (2009)

Chapter 7

1 Clayden *et al.* (2010a); see also Ingold (2007, 2011); Olwig (1993); Rapport (1997)
2 Foucault (1986)
3 Bradfield (1994); Weinrich and Speyer (2003); West (1992)
4 Howarth (1993, 1996); Parsons (1999)
5 Adams (1993); Howarth (1993; 1996); Parsons (1999)
6 Parsons (1999); Howarth (1993, 1996)
7 Personal communication, Al Blake, East Meon
8 Howarth (1993; 1996)
9 Howarth (1993; 1996)
10 Howarth (1993; 1996)
11 Green *et al.* (2010)
12 Olwig (1993)
13 Powell *et al.* (2011)
14 Howarth (1996)
15 Howarth (1996)
16 Howarth (1996)
17 See www.naturalwayburial.org.uk/page6.htm (accessed 14 November 2013).
18 Gore (2001); Hockey (2001)
19 Jones (2008: 156)
20 Howarth (1996); Parsons (1999); Walter (1994)
21 Walter (1994)
22 'Funeral parties occasionally camped at the site over a weekend'; personal communication, Al Blake, East Meon

Chapter 8

1 There had been four burials in 1995 but these are not included here as it was not a full year of burial.
2 Olwig (2008)
3 Ingold (2010)
4 Olwig (2008)
5 Clayden and Dixon (2007)
6 Clayden and Dixon (2007)
7 McFarlane (2012: 17)
8 Olwig (2008: 81)

Chapter 9

1 Hockey *et al.* (2010); Maddrell and Sidaway (2010)
2 Clayden *et al.* (2010b)
3 Gibson (1979)
4 Ingold (2010)
5 Ingold (2011)
6 Ingold (2011)
7 Ingold (2011)
8 See, for example, Levi-Strauss (1966)
9 Walter (1994)
10 Levi-Strauss (1966)
11 Powell *et al.* (2011)
12 Hockey (1990); Howarth (2000)
13 Walter (1994: 190)

14 Olwig (2008)
15 Nassauer (1995)
16 Nassauer (1995: 81)
17 Ingold (2000)
18 Nassauer (1995)
19 Seremetakis (1991)
20 Seremetakis (1991)
21 Jenkins (2004)
22 Hallam *et al.* (1999); Richardson (2014)
23 Hallam *et al.* (1999)
24 Clayden *et al.* (2009)

References

Adam, B. (1990) *Time and Social Theory*, Cambridge, MA: Polity Press.

Adams, S. (1993) A gendered history of the social management of death in Foleshill, Coventry, during the interwar years, in D. Clark (ed.) *The Sociology of Death*, Oxford: Blackwell, 149–168.

Arber, R. (2000) Disposal of cremated remains: a European perspective. Unpublished report to the International Cremation Federation from the Secretary-General.

Association of Natural Burial Grounds (ANBG) (2012) List of natural burial grounds in the British Isles, *The ICCM Journal*, 80(1): 24–29.

Bauman, Z. (1992) *Mortality, Immortality and Other Life Strategies*, Cambridge: Cambridge University Press.

Beeson, I. and Hanson, K. (2010) Eco-burials at Norton Big Wood, *The ICCM Journal*, 78(3): 24–29.

Bille, M., Hastrup, F. and Sorensen, T.F. (2011) *An Anthropology of Absence: Materializations of Transcendence and Loss*, New York: Springer.

Blake, A. (2013) Woodland burial: earth to earth, *Funeral Service Times*, July: 12–14.

Bourdieu, P. (1977) *Outline of a Theory of Practice*, Cambridge: Cambridge University Press.

Bourke, J. (1996) *Dismembering the Male: Men's Bodies, Britain and the Great War*, London: Reaktion Books.

Bradfield, J. (1994) *Green Burial: The D-I-Y Guide to Law and Practice*, London: The Natural Death Centre.

Brookes, C. (1989) *Mortal Remains: The History and the Present State of Victorian and Edwardian Cemetery*, Exeter: Wheaton Publishers Ltd.

Callander, R., Dinus-Inman, L., Inman-Cook, R., Jarvis, M., Mallatratt, J., Morris, S., Pidgeon, J. and Walwyn, B. (2012) *The Natural Death Handbook*, London: Strange Attractor Press.

Clayden, A. (2011) Reclaiming and reinterpreting ritual in the woodland burial ground, in P. Post and J. Krosen (eds) *Sacred Places in Modern Western Culture*, Leuven: Peeters Publishing House, 289–294.

——(2004) Natural burial British style, *Landscape Architecture*, 94(5): 68–77.

——(2003) Woodland burial, *Landscape Design*, 322: 22–25.

Clayden, A. and Dixon, K. (2007) Woodland burial: memorial arboretum versus natural native woodland?, *Mortality*, 12(3): 240–260.

Clayden, A. and Woudstra, J. (2003) Twentieth-century European cemetery design: continental solutions for British Dilemmas, *Mortality*, 8(2): 189–208.

Clayden, A., Green, T., Hockey, J. and Powell, M. (2010a) From cabbages to cadavers: natural burial down on the farm, in A. Maddrell and J. Sidaway (eds) *Deathscapes*, Aldershot: Ashgate, 119–138.

Clayden, A., Hockey, J. and Powell, M. (2010b) Natural burial: the de-materialising of death, in J. Hockey, C. Komaromy and K. Woodthorpe (eds) *The Matter of Death: Space, Place and Materiality*, Basingstoke: Palgrave Macmillan, 148–164.

Clayden, A., Hockey, J., Green, T. and Powell, M. (2009) Living with the dead, *Thinking Eye: Journal of Landscape Architecture*, Autumn: 48–55.

Constant, C. (1994) *The Woodland Cemetery: Toward a Spiritual Landscape*, Stockholm: Byggföflagert.

Curl, J.S. (1975) The architecture and planning of the nineteenth century cemetery, *Garden History*, 4(3): 13–41.

Davies, D.J. (2005) *A Brief History of Death*, Oxford: Blackwell Publishing.

Davies, D.J. and Mates, L.H. (2005) *Encyclopaedia of Cremation*, Aldershot: Ashgate.

Davies, D.J. and Rumble, H. (2012) *Natural Burial: Traditional Secular Spiritualities and Funeral Innovation*, London: Continuum.

Dilley, R. (2005) Time-shapes and cultural agency among West African craft specialists, in W. James and D. Mills (eds) *The Qualities of Time: Anthropological Approaches*, Oxford: Berg, 235–250.

Dunk, J. and Rugg, J. (1994) *The Management of Old Cemetery Land*, Crayford: Shaw and Sons.

Durkheim, E. ([1915] 1965) *The Elementary Forms of the Religious Life*, New York: Free Press.

Eggener, K. (2010) *Cemeteries*, New York: W.W. Norton & Company.

Elias, N. (1985) *The Loneliness of the Dying*, New York: Continuum.

Environment Agency (2004) *Assessing the Groundwater Pollution Potential of Cemetery Developments*, Bristol: Environment Agency.

Foucault, M. (1986) Of other spaces, *Diacritics*, 16(1): 22–27.

Francis, D., Kellaher, L. and Neophytou, G. (2005) *The Secret Cemetery*, Oxford: Berg.

Garattini, C. (2007) Creating memories: material culture and infantile death in contemporary Ireland, *Mortality* 12(2): 193–206.

Geertz, C. (1973) *The Interpretation of Cultures*, New York: Basic Books.

Gibson, J. (1979) *The Ecological Approach to Visual Perception*, Boston, MA: Houghton Mifflin.

Giddens, A. (1991) *Modernity and Self Identity*, Cambridge, MA: Polity Press.

Gore, P. (2001) Funeral ritual past and present, in J. Hockey, J. Katz and N. Small (eds) *Grief, Mourning and Death Ritual*, Buckingham: Open University Press, 212–217.

Gorer, G. (1965) *Death, Grief and Mourning in Contemporary Britain*, London: Cresset.

Grainger, H.J. (2005) *Death Redesigned: British Crematoria: History, Architecture and Landscape*. Reading: Spire Books.

Green, T., Clayden, A. and Hockey, J. (2010) 'I just think all the water and the rain is washing through him': postmortem imaginings and the practice of natural burial. Unpublished paper, Vital Signs Conference, September, University of Manchester.

GreenAcres (2012) GreenAcres: change of name and representing the UK, *The ICCM Journal*, 80(3): 26.

Hallam, E. and Hockey, J. (2001) *Death, Memory and Material Culture*, Oxford: Berg.

Hallam, E., Hockey, J. and Howarth, G. (1999) *Beyond the Body: Death and Social Identity*, London: Routledge.

HC91-1 (2000–01) *Cemeteries: Environment, Transport and Regional Affairs Committee*, London: The Stationery Office.

Hockey, J. (2001) Changing death rituals, in J. Hockey, J. Katz and N. Small (eds) *Grief, Mourning and Death Ritual*, Buckingham: Open University Press.

——(1990) *Experiences of Death: An Anthropological Account*, Edinburgh: Edinburgh University Press, 185–211.

Hockey, J., Green, T. and Clayden, A. (2010) Natural burial: its local interpretations and implications for a good send-off. Unpublished paper, Centre for Death and Society, University of Bath.

Hockey, J., Kellaher, L. and Prendergast, D. (2007a) Of grief and well-being: competing conceptions of restorative ritualization, *Anthropology and Medicine*, 14(1): 1–14.

——(2007b) Sustaining kinship: ritualisation and the disposal of human ashes in the United Kingdom, in M. Mitchell (ed.) *Remember Me: Constructing Immortality*, New York: Routledge, 35–50.

Horrox, R. (1999) Purgatory, prayer and plague: 1150–1660, in P.C. Jupp and C. Gittings (eds) *Death in England: An Illustrated History*, Manchester: Manchester University Press, 90–118.

Howarth, G. (2000) Australian funerals, in A. Kellehear (ed.) *Death and Dying in Australia: Interdisciplinary Perspectives*, Melbourne: Oxford University Press, 80–92.

——(1996) *Last Rites: The Work of the Modern Funeral Director*, Amityville, NY: Baywood Publishing Company Inc.

——(1993) Investigating deathwork: a personal account, in D. Clark (ed.) *The Sociology of Death*, Oxford: Blackwell.

Ingold, T. (2011) *Being Alive: Essays on Movement, Knowledge and Description*, Abingdon: Routledge.

——(2010) *Bringing Things to Life: Creative Entanglements in a World of Materials*, Working Paper No. 15, Realities.

——(2007) *Lines: A Brief History*, London: Routledge.

——(2000) *The Perception of the Environment: Essays in Livelihood, Dwelling and Skill*, London: Routledge.

Institute of Burial and Cremation Administration (IBCA) (1996) *Charter for the Bereaved*, Carlisle: IBCA.

Jenkins, R. (2004) *Social Identity*, London: Routledge.

Johansson, B.O.H. (1996) *Tallum: Gunnar Asplind's and Siguard Leweretz's Woodland Cemetery in Stockholm*, Stockholm: Byggföflagert.

Jones, P.O. (2008) The challenge of green burial, in P.C. Jupp (ed.) *Death Our Future: Christian Theology and Pastoral Practice in Funeral Ministry*, London: Epworth, 148–157.

Kellaher, L., Prendergast, D. and Hockey, J. (2005) In the shadow of the traditional grave, *Mortality*, 10(4): 237–250.

Kendle, A.D. and Rose, J.E. (2000) The aliens have landed! What are the justifications for 'native only' policies in landscape plantings?, *Landscape and Urban Planning*, 47: 19–31.

Klaassens, M. (2011) Bergerbos natural burial ground: an innovative burial place in the Netherlands, www.dissertations.ub.rug.nl/FILES/faculties/rw/2011/m.klaassens/05c5.pdf (retrieved 20 August 2013).

Klass, D., Silverman, P.R. and Nickman, S.L. (eds) (1996) *Continuing Bonds: New Understandings of Grief*, Washington, DC: Taylor & Francis.

Leach, E. (1961) *Rethinking Anthropology*, London: Athlone.

Levi-Strauss, C. (1966) *The Savage Mind*, London: Weidenfield and Nicholson.

Loudon, J.C. ([1843] 1981) *On the Laying Out, Planting, and Managing of Cemeteries and on the Improvement of Churchyards*, Redhill: Ivelet Books Ltd.

McFarlane, R. (2012) *The Old Ways*, London: Penguin Books Ltd.

Maddrell, A. and Sidaway, J. (eds) (2010) *Deathscapes: Spaces for Death, Dying, Mourning and Remembrance*, Aldershot: Ashgate.

Mellor, P. and Shilling, C. (1993) Modernity, self-identity and the sequestration of death, *Sociology*, 27(3): 411–431.

Ministry of Justice (2009) Natural burial grounds: guidance for operators, www.justice.gov.uk (retrieved 5 September 2013).

Morley, J. (1971) *Death, Heaven and the Victorians*, London: Studio Vista.

Nassauer, J.I. (1995) Messy ecosystems, orderly frames, *Landscape Journal*, 14(2): 161–170.

Olwig, K.R. (2008) Performing on the landscape vs. doing landscape: perambulatory practice, sight and the sense of belonging, in T. Ingold and J.L. Vergunst (eds) *Ways of Walking: Ethnography and Practice on Foot*, Aldershot: Ashgate, 81–91.

——(1993) 'Views' on nature, in L.J. Lundgren (ed.) *Views of Nature: Report from Two Seminars*, Lund: Swedish Council for Planning and Coordination of Research.

Parsons, B. (2010) New or rediscovered?, *Funeral Service Journal*, 78(3): 22–24.

——(2003) Conflict in the context of care: an examination of the role of conflict between the bereaved and the funeral director in the UK, *Mortality*, 8(1): 67–87.

——(1999) Yesterday, today and tomorrow: the lifecycle of the UK funeral industry, *Mortality*, 4(2): 127–145.

Payne, S., Seymour, J. and Ingleton, C. (2008) *Palliative Care Nursing: Principles and Evidence for Practice*, Maidenhead: Open University Press.

Pocock, D. (1998) *Understanding Social Anthropology*, London: The Athlone Press.

Powell, M., Hockey, J., Green, T. and Clayden, A. (2011) 'I bury boxes, not bodies': identity, emotionality and natural burial, *Association of Social Anthropologists (ASA) Online Journal*, 1(3): 1–18.

Prendergast, D., Hockey, J. and Kellaher, L. (2006) Blowing in the wind? Identity, materiality and the destinations of human ashes, *Journal of the Royal Anthropology Institute*, 12(4): 881–898.

Quance, I. (2013) Progressing the ICCM natural burial charter, *The ICCM Journal*, 81(2): 22–24.

——(2012) The ICCM natural burial charter, *The ICCM Journal*, 80(1): 22–23.

Rapport, N. (1997) Edifying anthropology: culture as conversation; representation as conversation, in A. Dawson, J. Hockey and A. James (eds) *After Writing Culture: Epistemology and Practice in Contemporary Anthropology*, London: Routledge, 177–193.

Rapport, N. and Overing, J. (2007) *Social and Cultural Anthropology: The Key Concepts*, London: Routledge.

Richardson, T. (2014) Spousal bereavement in later life: a material culture perspective, *Mortality* (forthcoming).

Roberts, P. and Vidal, L.A. (2000) Perpetual care in cyberspace: a portrait of memorials on the web, *Omega*, 40(4): 521–545.

Rugg, J. (2006) Lawn cemeteries: the emergence of a new landscape of death, *Urban History*, 33(2): 213–233.

——(2003) Introduction, *Mortality* (special issue: Cemeteries), 8(2): 107–112.

——(2000) Defining the place of burial: what makes a cemetery a cemetery?, *Mortality*, 5(3): 259–276.

——(1999) From reason to regulation: 1760–1850, in P.C. Jupp and C. Gittings (eds) *Death in England: An Illustrated History*, Manchester: Manchester University Press.

Santino, J. (ed.) (2006) *Spontaneous Shrines and the Public Memorialization of Death*, New York: Palgrave Macmillan.

Scott, S. (2003) Woodland Burial grounds: a case study, *Quarterly Journal of Forestry*, 97(1): 35–43.

Seale, C. (1998) *Constructing Death: The Sociology of Dying and Bereavement*, Cambridge: Cambridge University Press.

Seremetakis, C.N. (1991) *The Last Word: Women, Death and Divination in Inner Mani*, Chicago, IL: University of Chicago Press.

Thompson, W.J. (2002) A natural death: is the industrial-strength American funeral the right way to bury our loved ones?, *Landscape Architecture*, 92(10): 74–79.

Turner, V. (1969) *The Ritual Process*, Harmondsworth: Penguin.

van Gennep, A. ([1909] 1960) *The Rites of Passage*, Chicago, IL: University of Chicago Press.

Walter, T. (1996) A new model of grief: bereavement and biography, *Mortality*, 1(1): 7–25.

——(1994) *The Revival of Death*, London: Routledge.

Weinrich, S. and Speyer, J. (2003) *The Natural Death Handbook*, London: Rider.

West, K. (2010) *A Guide to Natural Burial*, London: Shaw and Sons.

——(1994) Presidential Address, Joint Conference of Burial and Cremation Authorities Report, 32–38.

——(1992) Woodland burial: a return to nature?, Joint Conference of Burial and Cremation Authorities Report, 52–58.

Winter, J. (1995) *Sites of Memory, Sites of Mourning: The Great War in European Cultural History*, Cambridge: Cambridge University Press.

Woodthorpe, K. (2007) Negotiating ambiguity and uncertainty in the contemporary cemetery landscape. Unpublished PhD thesis, University of Sheffield.

Worden, W. (1991) *Grief Counselling and Grief Therapy: A Handbook for the Mental Health Practitioner*, London: Routledge.

Young, C.P., Blackmore, K.M., Reynolds, P. and Leavens, A. (2002) *R&D Technical Report P223: Pollution Potential of Cemeteries*, Bristol: Environment Agency.

Index

T - #0039 - 280521 - C234 - 246/189/14 - PB - 9780415631693 - Gloss Lamination